Books P 123

P. 41 China Public

P. 1

P 110 Structural Disarmament

The Next Major War

Structural Inequality

Figure 9 P. 127

The Next Major War

Can the US and its Allies Win Against China?

Ross Babbage

Rapid Communications in Conflict and Security Series
General Editor: Geoffrey R.H. Burn

CAMBRIA PRESS

Amherst, New York

Library of Congress Cataloging-in-Publication Data
Names: Babbage, Ross, 1949- author.
Title: The next major war : can the US and its allies win against China? / Ross Babbage.
Other titles: Can the US and its allies win against China
Description: Amherst, New York : Cambria Press, [2023] |
Series: Cambria rapid communications in conflict and security |
Includes bibliographical references and index. |
Summary: "The risk of major war between China and the United States and its allies has risen substantially in recent years. Several books have been written about the growing risks of war and how such a conflict might start. Nearly all of these contributions have focused on the foreign and defense policy challenges prior to, and in the early stages of, such a war. This book takes a more wide-ranging and in-depth look at the demands such a war would make on the US alliance. Drawing on several years of research on Chinese and American planning, it describes the rather different types of war the two sides are planning to fight. One side is focusing primarily on military preparations. The other is preparing not only its military but also much of its economy, its society, and its political system to endure and ultimately prevail in such a war. This book explains the strengths and weaknesses of each side, the key phases that would likely characterize such a struggle, the probable economic and business impacts, and the factors that would determine its duration and outcome. It discusses the military aspects of such a conflict and goes much further to also address the economic, industrial, social, political, and other dimensions. The Next Major War will be important reading for the US and allied defense and national security communities. It will also appeal to many corporate and business leaders, researchers, students, and members of allied publics who are concerned about the growing international security challenges"-- Provided by publisher.

Identifiers: LCCN 2022058778 (print) | LCCN 2022058779 (ebook) |
ISBN 9781621966531 (library binding) | ISBN 9781621966708 (paperback) |
ISBN 9781621966807 (pdf) | ISBN 9781621966814 (epub)

Subjects: LCSH: United States--Military relations--China. | China--Military relations--United States. | Indo-Pacific Region--Strategic aspects. | United States--Foreign relations--21st century. | China--Foreign relations--21st century.

Classification: LCC E183.8.C5 B214 2023 (print) | LCC E183.8.C5 (ebook) |
DDC 327.73051--dc23/eng/20230104
LC record available at https://lccn.loc.gov/2022058778
LC ebook record available at https://lccn.loc.gov/2022058779

Table of Contents

List of Figures

Preface

The need for this book became clear in 2019. Tensions between Beijing and Washington were rising, trust was fading, policy stances were hardening, and senior officials on both sides were talking openly about preparing for an era of greater competition. Some strategic thinkers debated how a major power clash might occur, when it could happen, and how it might be avoided. Others discussed options for boosting military deterrence and defense. A major conflict in the Indo-Pacific, while still only a possibility, no longer seemed remote.

Despite the deteriorating international security environment, there appeared to be no serious analysis of what a major war in the Indo-Pacific would look like. What shape would a major US-China conflict take? How would it evolve? How long would it last? What would be the driving goals and game plans of each side? What would be each side's strengths and weaknesses? What would be the economic and business costs? And how could America and its allies prevail in such a calamitous contingency?

Initially it was assumed that someone must have produced the type of complex multidimensional analysis needed somewhere in the allied community. However, private discussions with several senior officials and other leading experts revealed that nothing quite like this was known to exist at any level of security classification. Nevertheless, there was universal appreciation of the need for such work and considerable enthusiasm for something to be done. It was time to make a start.

In order to focus expert discussions on the key issues, research papers were prepared on war planning by the Chinese and the Americans and the probable dimensions of a major Indo-Pacific conflict. Private conversations followed with relevant officials, senior business executives, and trusted strategic analysts. Three high-level closed workshops debated draft judgements in Canberra. In addition, a leading Indo-Pacific economist participated strongly, making many significant contributions and injecting far-sighted wisdom.

While most of those involved cannot be named because of their official positions, their contributions were substantial. I owe them a great debt. Four people who provided particularly important advice can be identified. They were Aaron Friedberg from Princeton University, Andrew Krepinevich from Solarium Consulting, and Jan Van Tol and Thomas Mahnken from the Center for Strategic and Budgetary Assessments. They all made very helpful suggestions. Greg Hewitson and Elise Knotek did a quality job with the figures. Exceptional research, sharp-eyed editing, administrative assistance, and never-ending encouragement were provided by my wife, Lynne. She made many difficult things possible.

It is hoped that this book makes a useful contribution to planning and preparations for the security challenges now confronting the United States and its security partners. But this analysis is not meant to be the last word. It will hopefully prompt new thinking and encourage some readers to make additional points or contribute alternative perspectives. I hope that they head to their keyboards and join the debate.

There is much to consider, many decisions to take, and a great deal of practical work to be done. And the faster that progress is made, the better.

Ross Babbage
January 2023

The Next Major War

Chapter 1

The Risk of War Is Rising —It's Time to Prepare

A major war in the Indo-Pacific is probably more likely now than at any time since the Second World War. China is at loggerheads with the United States and its security partners over the future of Taiwan, the Senkaku Islands, the South China Sea, and India's and Bhutan's northern border territories. Both sides hold their positions firmly, and neither is prepared to budge.

The most likely trigger point is Taiwan, largely because the Chinese president, Xi Jinping, has repeatedly expressed his determination to incorporate the territory into China. In October 2017 he stated that "we will never allow anyone, any organization, or any political party, at any time or in any form, to separate any part of Chinese territory from China!"[1] Then in a speech in October 2021 Xi underlined his commitment by stating, "The historical task of the complete reunification of the motherland must be fulfilled and will definitely be fulfilled."[2] A month later the Central Committee of the Chinese Communist Party released a resolution stating that "resolving the Taiwan question and realizing China's complete reunification is a historic mission and an unshakable commitment of the Party. It is also a shared aspiration of all the sons and daughters of the Chinese nation, and it is essential to realizing national rejuvenation."[3] Then in a speech delivered in Singapore on June 11, 2022, China's defense minister, Wei Fenghe, stated that "if anyone dares to secede Taiwan from China, we will not hesitate to fight...We will fight at all costs. And we will fight to the very end. This is the only choice for China."[4] The Chinese leadership's repeated promise to the 97 million members of the Chinese Communist Party and to the broader Chinese public is now a core element of the regime's legitimacy.

In his major speech to the 20th National Congress of the Party on October 15, 2022, Xi Jinping declared:

> We will continue to strive for peaceful reunification with the greatest sincerity and the utmost effort, but we will never promise to renounce the use of force, and we reserve the option of taking all measures necessary. The wheels of history are rolling on towards China's reunification and the rejuvenation of the Chinese nation. The complete reunification of our country must be realized, and it can without a doubt be realized.[5]

Then on October 23, 2022, General Zhang Youxia, one of the few remaining PLA generals with combat experience, was appointed first vice chairman (immediately under Xi Jinping) of the Central Military Commission (the body that directs and oversees all Chinese military decisions). At the same time General He Weidong, a relatively young general who previously served as commander of the PLA's Eastern Theater Command and had been heavily involved in Taiwan contingency planning, was dramatically elevated to be the second-ranked vice chairman of the Central Military Commission.[6] This suggests that Xi Jinping has appointed the two PLA generals who are best placed to advise on Taiwan options to be his most senior military advisors.

On the US side, successive administrations have made it clear that if China uses force to seize control of Taiwan, America has the capabilities to intervene and will do so. The foundation of this commitment is the Taiwan Relations Act of 1979 that states, in part:

> ...that any effort to determine the future of Taiwan by other than peaceful means, including by boycotts or embargoes is considered a threat to the peace and security of the Western Pacific area and is of grave concern to the United States....the United States shall provide Taiwan with arms of a defensive character and shall maintain the capacity of the United States to resist any resort to force or other forms of coercion that would jeopardize the security, or social or economic system of the people of Taiwan.[7]

Taiwan is receiving strong American support because it is a vibrant democracy of 24 million people, it is centrally located in a strategically vital part of the Western Pacific, and it has developed world-leading electronic industries. In recent decades the US and its allies have developed wide-ranging economic, security, and people-to-people ties with Taiwan.

In August 2021, American president Joe Biden took American declaratory policy to a new level by comparing the US commitment to defend Taiwan to the NATO Treaty's Article 5, stating that "we made a sacred commitment to Article Five that if in fact anyone were to invade or take action against our NATO allies, we would respond. Same with Japan, same with South Korea, same with Taiwan."[8]

In October 2021 during a CNN townhall meeting, Biden was asked twice whether the United States would come to the defense of Taiwan were it to be attacked and he said: "Yes, we have a commitment to do that."[9]

Then in Tokyo on May 23, 2022, when Biden was asked by a reporter whether the United States would defend Taiwan militarily if it were attacked by China, the president again said: "Yes, that's the commitment we made."[10]

Later on September 18, 2022, when asked whether US forces would defend "the island [Taiwan]" during a *60 Minutes* television interview, President Biden said: "Yes, if in fact there was an unprecedented attack."[11]

The CBS interviewer (Scott Pelley) followed up with a further question: "So unlike Ukraine, to be clear, sir, US Forces, US men and women would defend Taiwan in the event of a Chinese invasion? President Biden responded: "Yes."

Reinforcing these presidential remarks, the US Department of State has repeatedly described the American commitment to Taiwan as "rock solid."[12] Following each presidential statement, American officials hastened to "clarify" the situation and emphasize that US policy on Taiwan had not changed. But the effect of the president's comments has been to dilute much of the deliberate ambiguity that has been at the core of American policy towards Taiwan since the late 1970s. It is remarkable that at a time when there are deep political divisions in Washington on many areas of policy, both sides of Congress now believe that the US must resist China's international assertiveness and territorial expansionism, including with military force if required.

In testimony before the US Senate Armed Services Committee in February 2022, the Director of National Intelligence, Avril Haines, underlined the seriousness of the situation by stating: "It's our view that (the Chinese are) working hard to effectively put themselves into a position in which the military is capable of taking Taiwan over our intervention" and that the threat to Taiwan between now and 2030 is "acute."[13]

Then in October 2022, US Secretary of State, Antony Blinken, stated that China was accelerating its preparations to act:

> There has been a change in the approach from Beijing toward Taiwan in recent years...a fundamental decision that the status quo was no longer acceptable and that Beijing was determined to pursue reunification on a much faster timeline.[14]

Although Beijing knows that if it moves to seize Taiwan, it would probably find itself fighting not only the Taiwanese but also an alert United States and many of its allies, the Chinese leadership appears confident and determined.

Xi Jinping repeatedly asserts China's supremacy with statements that "...there is a vivid contrast between the order of China and the chaos of the West ... the East is rising and the West is declining."[15] Underpinning this assertive posture is not only the rapid rise of China's economy but also the numerical dominance of China's People's Liberation Army (PLA) in the Western Pacific. China operates what is now by far the biggest army, the largest number of naval vessels, and the highest number of combat aircraft in the theater. It also has a rapidly expanding strategic nuclear force.[16] Many of these capabilities are modern and some, such as hypersonic missiles, are more advanced than anything currently operated by the West.

When Xi Jinping and his colleagues view the United States they see a country growing at a modest rate, losing its technological lead in several sectors, and becoming handicapped by high levels of domestic tension and polarization. They also believe that during the last two decades the American military has "lost" two long, drawn-out wars. And, in contrast to their own confident and assertive behavior, Chinese leaders have noted the American leadership's deep risk aversion, reactive behavior, periodic incoherence, and occasional fumbling. Xi and his colleagues believe that they have every reason to be confident. They perceive no real obstacle to continuing their active programs to undermine the United States, push it out of the Western Pacific, and complete the reunification of the "motherland" and the rejuvenation of the Chinese nation.

The potential for a major war in the Indo-Pacific is therefore real. Such a war is certainly not inevitable, but there is a serious risk that it might break out quickly.

Moreover, Xi Jinping has strong incentives to move sooner rather than later. This is because China's strategic power may have peaked and his window of opportunity may be starting to close. China's economy is now close to the size of America's and its manufacturing output is nearly double that of the United States. But China's growth has been slowing in recent years, its productivity has stalled, it is losing its competitiveness in many sectors, its population is aging rapidly, and its workforce is shrinking. Moreover, the regime's assertive international behavior, its quasi-alliance with Russia, and its support for Vladimir Putin's invasion of Ukraine have seriously damaged China's international reputation. Indeed, when combined with the regime's human rights abuses at home and aggressive industrial and trade policies, much of the international community has come to see China as a serious geopolitical problem.

A further complication for Xi is that the Western allies across the globe and many formerly nonaligned states have moved to cooperate more closely to reinforce their security against Chinese coercion and intrusions.

So while Xi Jinping continues to exude great confidence, he is fast approaching a critical decision point. He knows that the national and international winds are shifting and that if he is to achieve his primary goals and enshrine his place in the Chinese Communist pantheon, he needs to accelerate the country's coercive pressure and seize his strategic opportunity, even if it risks major war.

The implications are profound. A major war in the Indo-Pacific would have huge consequences not only for security planners and defense forces but also for the management of economies, for corporations, for nearly all parts of regional societies, and for many more distant communities. There is an urgent need to understand what a major Indo-Pacific war would be like and what can be done to avoid, deter, or defer open hostilities. And there is a pressing need for the allies to advance priority preparations.

These are complex questions that are difficult to address. For starters, a major war between China and the United States and its allies would probably not resemble anything we have seen in the past. Such a war would most likely be undertaken on a very large scale, involving numerous new operational concepts and weapons, several of which have global reach. Homelands on both sides would be subjected to at least some types of direct attack. There would be few, if any, sanctuaries. All relevant states would be seriously impacted, and many would embark on emergency industrial mobilization and civil defence programs.

Neither side can be confident about the effectiveness of their campaign plans and many of their systems in advance. China and the United States have not fought a war with a peer competitor for many decades, and their performance in such a conflict is shrouded in doubt. They are like two football teams displaying different levels of preparation and match fitness. They have been able to practice a few combat moves on their home grounds and occasionally somewhere else, but neither has played a real-life, full-length match against a strong opponent for over 70 years. So while they can model and game some contingencies, the actual course of a high-end conflict and its length remain uncertain.

A further complication is that the two sides have different visions of such a war. They have very different approaches to strategy and theater campaigning. They also have markedly dissimilar programs of planning, doctrine, and capability development. Hence it is unclear which vision of war will dominate. Nevertheless, the side that seizes the initiative in the first hours and days is likely to have the greatest influence on the initial phases of such a war, and possibly on its entire course.

The primary purpose of this book is to address the multidisciplinary challenges a major war would pose to both sides. This book not only discusses the political and military dimensions of such a war but also assesses the probable economic, social, and other impacts. It considers the likely phases of such a war, the differing demands each major phase is likely to make, and the strengths and weaknesses of the two sides. It asks whether the US and its allies are adequately prepared to fight and win a major Indo-Pacific war. Are they fighting fit? And finally, the book highlights a number of initiatives that deserve priority allied attention.

The book traverses this complex strategic terrain in the following sequence: Chapter 2 considers the primary features of China's war planning. Chapter 3 then discusses the key elements of United States and allied war planning. Drawing together the conclusions from the first three chapters, chapter 4 addresses the likely shape, form, and duration of a major war that breaks out between China and the United States and their respective allies and partners in the period till the late 2030s. Each side's strengths and weaknesses are examined, together with their stark asymmetries. Establishing the primary features of such a conflict sets the scene for assessing the probable economic, supply chain and business impacts in chapters 5 and 6. Then finally, key lessons for the United States and its allies are highlighted and priorities for allied action are detailed in chapter 7.

The bottom line is that the United States along with its allies and their security partners now need to take the risk of major war in the Indo-Pacific very seriously. They need to accelerate their planning and urgently prepare themselves to deter and, if necessary, to fight and win what threatens to be a very demanding struggle.

Notes

1. "Full text of Xi Jinping's report at 19th CPC National Congress," Xinhua, October 18, 2017, http://www.chinadaily.com.cn/china/19thcpcnationalcongress/2017-11/04/content_34115212.htm.
2. Carlos Garcia and Yew Lun Tian, "China's Xi Vows 'Reunification' with Taiwan," Reuters, October 10, 2021, https://www.reuters.com/world/china/chinas-xi-says-reunification-with-taiwan-must-will-be-realised-2021-10-09/.
3. "Full Text: Resolution of the Central Committee of the Communist Party of China on the Major Achievements and Historical Experience of the Party Over the Past Century," Xinhua, November 16, 2021, https://english.www.gov.cn/policies/latestreleases/202111/16/content_WS6193a935c6d0df57f98e50b0.html.
4. See this reported by Peter Martin, "China Alarms US with Private Warnings to Avoid Taiwan Strait," Bloomberg, June 12, 2022, https://www.bloomberg.com/news/articles/2022-06-12/china-alarms-us-with-new-private-warnings-to-avoid-taiwan-strait#xj4y7vzkg.
5. "Key Takeaways From Xi Jinping's Two-Hour Speech," Bloomberg, October 16, 2022, https://www.bloomberg.com/news/articles/2022-10-16/key-takeaways-from-xi-jinping-s-speech-at-china-s-20th-party-congress-2022.
6. Benjamin Kang Lim and Danson Cheong, "New Military Leadership Appointments Show China is Bracing Itself for Conflict," *The Straits Times,* October 23, 2022, https://www.straitstimes.com/asia/east-asia/new-military-leadership-appointments-show-china-is-bracing-itself-for-conflict.
7. "Summary: H.R.2479 - 96th Congress (1979-1980)," US Congress, March 24, 1979, https://www.congress.gov/bill/96th-congress/house-bill/2479.
8. Gerrit van der Wees, "Did Biden's Taiwan Remarks Represent a US Policy Change?," *The Diplomat,* August 24, 2021, https://thediplomat.com/2021/08/did-bidens-taiwan-remarks-represent-a-us-policy-change/.
9. The White House, *Remarks by President Biden in a CNN Town Hall with Andrew Cooper* (Baltimore: October 22, 2021), https://www.whitehouse.gov/briefing-room/speeches-remarks/2021/10/22/remarks-by-president-biden-in-a-cnn-town-hall-with-anderson-cooper-2/.

10. Seung Min Kim, et al, "Biden Takes Aggressive Posture Towards China on Asian Trip," *Washington Post*, May 23, 2022, https://www.washingtonpost.com/politics/2022/05/23/biden-japan-taiwan-china/.
11. Scott Pelley, "President Joe Biden: The 2022 60 Minutes Interview," *60 Minutes – Newsmakers* (September 18, 2022).
12. See this discussed in Elbridge Colby, "America Must Prepare for a War Over Taiwan," *Foreign Affairs*, August 10, 2022, https://www.foreignaffairs.com/united-states/america-must-prepare-war-over-taiwan.
13. Director of National Intelligence Avril Haines, *Annual Threat Assessment of the U.S. Intelligence Community* (Washington, DC, Office of the Director of National Intelligence, February 2022).
14. Remarks by Antony J Blinken, US Secretary of State during "A Conversation on the Evolution and Importance of Technology, Diplomacy, and National Security with 66th Secretary of State Condoleezza Rice" Hoover Institution, Stanford University, Stanford, CA, October 17, 2022, https://www.state.gov/secretary-antony-j-blinken-at-a-conversation-on-the-evolution-and-importance-of-technology-diplomacy-and-national-security-with-66th-secretary-of-state-condoleezza-rice/.
15. Quoted by Shi Jiangtao, "China Says 'East is Rising and West is Declining' but has it been misunderstood?," *South China Morning Post*, October 22, 2021, https://www.scmp.com/news/china/diplomacy/article/3153379/china-says-east-rising-and-west-declining-has-it-been.
16. Office of the Secretary of Defense, *Annual Report to Congress: Military and Security Developments Involving the People's Republic of China 2021* (Washington, DC: Department of Defense, 2021), V1, 82–86. See also The International Institute for Strategic Studies, *The Military Balance 2022* (London: Routledge, 2022), 255–261.

Chapter 2

China's Concepts and Planning for War in the Indo-Pacific

How the Chinese Would Fight a War

Some might assume that little is known about the Chinese Communist Party (CCP) regime's planning for a major war with the United States and its partners. The detailed campaign plans are not known beyond China's borders, at least at an unclassified level. Nevertheless, a careful assessment of the strategic culture, doctrine, debates, and actions of the Chinese leadership, the People's Liberation Army, and other agencies does provide clear insights into the type of war Beijing would wage if such a conflict broke out. This chapter highlights nine of the key indicators of Chinese planning for war and then lists eleven key characteristics that would likely feature prominently in the way the Chinese would fight such a war.

Nine Indicators of China's War Plans

Indicator #1: Deep History of Building Strength to Thwart Foreign Intrusions

China's concept of major conflict draws on the regime's civilizational roots, its status as a major continental power, and its unique strategic culture. For thousands of years, Chinese regimes have been forced to fight for their survival against powerful invaders that either swept across the Eurasian plains or assaulted over the eastern seaboard. The few geographical barriers on this continental land mass have provided only limited protection, and the resulting security challenges have fostered compelling historical narratives, a strong civilizational identity, and deep nationalism. These historical and cultural strengths have been mobilized by Chinese regimes for hundreds of years to reinforce their legitimacy, unite the country, and oftentimes generate xenophobia.

Since the Chinese Communist Party's seizure of power in 1949, China's leaders have built on this historical legacy by drawing on the party's deeply entrenched Marxist-Leninist-Maoist ideological roots. A core goal has been to overcome the shame of the "century of humiliation" in which foreign powers "invaded and exploited" the Chinese nation from the middle of the nineteenth century till the end of the Chinese Civil War in 1949.[1] The CCP has committed itself to rebuilding China's political, economic, and military power, winning back all contested territories, and restoring the Chinese civilization to its "rightful place" of regional and global preeminence.

To achieve these goals, the Chinese leadership sees itself as being engaged in an epic struggle against the United States and its partners. When looking abroad, the regime's biggest fear is that the rest of the world will seek to surround China, contain its development, block it from strengthening its international power, undermine its domestic legitimacy, and threaten the party's survival. Party leaders have studied the gradual weakening and collapse of the Soviet Union in great detail and are determined to avoid a similar fate. To these ends, the regime has fostered powerful nationalist themes and worked hard to unite the population behind the party leadership.

This strong sense of striving to restore China's rightful international place has underpinned the nation's sustained economic growth, its drive for technological leadership, its greatly expanded military capabilities, and its launching of the Belt and Road Initiative. The same thinking energizes the regime's determination to win control over key international institutions and move from being an international rule taker to becoming the dominant rule maker. Many Chinese have a sense of predestined superiority: of driving to fully restore the country as the "middle kingdom" in world affairs.

Indicator #2: A Strong Tradition of Conducting Very Early Operations to Undermine, Weaken, and Divide Enemies

It is not just the Chinese leadership's goals and geostrategic mindset that differ from the United States and other Western powers but also the means and modes that the regime employs to progress them. A key part of China's approach involves seizing the initiative early, mobilizing a very wide range of instruments in multiple domains, and striving to undermine, cripple, and divide opponents and win a superior position before launching any kinetic operations. Indeed, skillful use of non-kinetic combined arms operations can sometimes secure Beijing's primary goals on their own and obviate the need for escalation to kinetic fighting.

The origins of this unconventional strategic thinking can be traced back to Sun Tzu who served at least one Chinese warlord around 500BC. He argued that China's rulers should use political, psychological, subversive, and other noncombat operations to weaken, divide, and subdue enemies prior to committing armies to combat. Sun Tzu summarized his logic by stating that "attaining a hundred victories in one hundred battles is not the pinnacle of excellence. Subjugating the enemy's army without fighting is the true pinnacle of excellence."[2]

Early in the twentieth century, Mao Zedong combined this tradition of unconventional, intelligence- and subversion-heavy strategic culture with insights from Carl von Clausewitz, Vladimir Lenin, Leon Trotsky, and others. One of the core ideas was that if war was politics by other means, then politics, or political action, could also be fashioned to be war by other means.[3]

Mao drew extensively on this thinking as he developed, tested, and refined his own concept of revolutionary war to undermine, corrupt, divide, and overthrow the technologically more advanced forces of the nationalist government of Chiang Kai-shek and then Japan's Imperial Army.[4] The importance of early and sustained political and subversive operations throughout the theater of operations, including in enemy strongholds, was powerfully reinforced as a foundation of Chinese military doctrine, not only for revolutionary war but also for a wide range of other campaigns.[5]

Once the Chinese Communist Party seized power in 1949, it immediately set about consolidating its position by subverting and then invading Tibet, actively supporting revolutionary movements in neighboring countries, and undermining the regional operations of the technologically superior United States, Japan, and other "enemy" states. During its first 30 years the regime achieved some notable successes, especially in Vietnam, Cambodia, and Laos.

Consequently, offensive political warfare[6] and the many subversive instruments for its use are now even more deeply etched into China's strategic culture and security structures. Indeed, from the perspective of a Chinese strategic planner, it is difficult to conceive of large-scale operations against foreign powers that do not involve intrusive political and psychological operations from an early stage that can be sustained indefinitely during the course of a major crisis or war.[7]

These are the sorts of operations that Chinese government agencies and associated entities have been conducting in recent years against the leaderships and populations of Taiwan, the United States, Japan, South Korea, Australia, and most of those countries close to China's borders.[8]

One important consequence is that while the Western allies currently believe that they are in a state of "peace," Chinese security planners have quite a different perception. They believe that China is already engaged in an intense struggle that they often describe as a form of warfare—political warfare. The primary instruments used have been activist diplomacy, propaganda, media manipulation, information campaigns, intense cyber operations, subversion, political corruption, economic coercion, facilitated trade in fentanyl and other opioids to the US and the West, and the preemptive occupation and militarization of contested territories. Some Chinese officials and others have described these operations as "new generation war"[9] and "non-war warfare"[10].

PLA writings emphasize the importance of the cognitive domain and achieving mental dominance.

> In an era of informatized warfare, conflict in the cognitive domain attempts to undermine the adversary's will and resolve, undermine perception and command capabilities to weaken fighting spirit, and manipulate decision-making...PLA thinkers are...exploring the potential employment of intelligent agents to enable "guidance" of public opinion. In particular, the prominence of social media and advances in artificial intelligence, including such techniques as deep fakes, have created new options for subversion and manipulation.[11]

Kerry Gershaneck emphasizes the key role of such operations in Chinese military education, training, and operations:

> PLA officers become acquainted with employing the Three Warfares [Public Opinion/Media Warfare, Psychological Warfare, and Legal Warfare or Lawfare] early in their careers, and as they rise in rank they study the concept in depth in various texts on military strategy....Through study of history and war games, senior CCP officials and PLA commanders learn to employ

> Media Warfare in conjunction with Psychological Operations and Lawfare to manipulate an adversary's cognitive process both prior to and during a conflict by targeting national and theater command structures and forward deployed units.[12]

Indicator #3: National Unity Enforced Through Unquestioned Party Authority, Mass Surveillance, and Strict Discipline

Another key feature of China's planning of major war is that the Chinese Communist Party—not the state—decides everything of importance. The party has unchallenged authority over the domestic and international operations of all Chinese agencies. State and privately owned organizations of any size must have at least one party branch, and in corporations party committees carry equal authority to company boards.[13] Chinese law requires local- and foreign-owned companies operating in China to cooperate with the country's security services. Moreover, when the party or government agencies move to counter foreign economic sanctions, Chinese law authorizes security agencies to seize the assets of foreign corporations and even those of foreign individuals.[14]

The Marxist-Leninist-Maoist culture of the regime builds on a long-standing theme in Chinese history of strong centralization, cohesion, and national unity. There is no encouragement of deviation, debates, or disagreements. Rather, the party's instinct and habit are to suppress internal dissent, humiliate opponents and doubters, and instill unquestioning loyalty.

Since Xi Jinping's election as General Secretary of the Communist Party in November 2012 and then President of the People's Republic of China in March 2013, he has worked to further concentrate power into his hands. As General Secretary of the Chinese Communist Party, he not only chairs the Politburo and the Politburo Standing Committee but also personally oversees all of the important agencies of the party and the state. When reviewing the regime's extreme concentration of power, some analysts have described Xi as the "Chairman of everything" and others have labeled him "the Emperor."[15]

One of Xi Jinping's most important roles is Chairman of the Central Military Commission, which oversees all issues relating to China's military and paramilitary forces. He has frequently emphasized that the PLA is the party's military force. The military does not report to the state or any other element of Chinese society but rather to the party and effectively to Xi himself. The military is hence available to defend Xi's regime and pursue the party's interests with few constraints.

Emphasizing the leading role of the party effectively means that Xi Jinping has undisputed authority over every area of importance to China's security—including the country's "main strategic direction," its strategy, its planning for war, its major force deployments, and decisions on the initiation of conflict. These authorities and responsibilities were codified in the revision of the Chinese Communist Party's charter in October 2017, which explicitly grants the Chairman of the Central Military Commission the power to "direct the work of the commission, command the armed forces and make decisions on all major issues regarding national defence and the military."[16]

A related theme in the Chinese Communist Party's strategic doctrine is that the PLA and associated agencies are not only required to conduct military operations to a very high standard but also to organize ideological education and propagate the party's values, culture, and priorities. This includes a requirement to actively counter the encroachment of modern revisionism, capitalist ideology, and deviant beliefs. An important consequence is that the military and related security agencies view a future war as not only a violent and deadly physical struggle but also as a fight for the international victory of the party's Marxist-Leninist-Maoist ideology.

The party has built numerous enforcement mechanisms to ensure that its approach to these matters cannot be seriously questioned. The party is effectively above the law, not only because it writes all legislation but also because it approves major prosecutions and determines all important sentences. The Political-Legal Commission manages the operational details of this activity.

Xi Jinping's anti-corruption campaign provides a further, very powerful layer of discipline. All members of the party, and indeed all citizens, are aware that there is an ever-present potential for them to be subjected to investigation and prosecution for either real or manufactured indiscretions or corrupt practices. They know that they will be especially vulnerable if they pose a threat to Xi Jinping's authority or seriously question his judgment. In recent years, a succession of potential rivals and indiscreet senior officials has been investigated, charged, and given long prison sentences. Some who have been charged with "corruption" have been executed. The incentives are exceptionally strong for all members of Chinese society, whether in the party, the military, business, the media, or elsewhere to toe the party line.

Xi Jinping has also established an organization called the National Supervision Commission which stands above the court and criminal justice system to review personnel performance, investigate breaches of discipline by party officials and government employees, and administer relevant punishments under the direction of the party leadership. Xi has been ruthless in his enforcement of party loyalty and ideological conformity.

Another powerful layer of regime security has been the rollout of highly sophisticated public surveillance and control systems. These programs have been designed primarily to ensure that there are strict controls on unwelcome foreign influences, terrorism, crime, and any activity that could undermine the nation's progress and "the leading role of the party." In order to operate these systems, the People's Armed Police and associated militia forces have been allocated a higher level of funding in recent years than the People's Liberation Army.[17] In consequence, the number of police personnel and the quality of most of the internal security systems and equipment are relatively high.

The Great Firewall of China that censors internet traffic within and beyond China has been greatly strengthened. Domestic internet providers that are fully compliant with party directives and surveillance requirements have been encouraged to dominate domestic online markets. These arrangements are being continuously updated to facilitate party propaganda and thwart undesirable messaging.

The deployment of advanced surveillance systems has become far more pervasive during the last decade. These systems have sprung partly from the almost universal application of computerized systems to everything—banking, health, transport, employment, criminal justice, and other domains. Closed-circuit television coverage is now very extensive, with over 540 million cameras networked across the nation, using sophisticated coordination and tracking software.[18] Additional surveillance capabilities have been added with vehicle-number-plate and facial recognition scanning, DNA-sampling technologies, and sophisticated telephone and internet surveillance technologies. These systems can be used to combat crime, but they are also being used to detect, monitor, and control politically sensitive behavior.

The result is a vast searchable database that is now formally called the Integrated Joint Operations Platform (IJOP). Within minutes, it can produce detailed profiles of individuals, including their education and employment histories, their shopping preferences, their financial circumstances, their social media status, their networks of personal relationships, and even their political and religious views.[19] This system has scores of uses, but one of the most important is to detect and monitor the earliest signs of dissent from the party and trigger prompt police and security service intervention. The system is greatly valued by the regime not only to monitor and control current circumstances but also to ensure tight party control in the event of future crises and conflicts.

Meng Jianzhu, the Politburo member in charge of internal security, has championed these systems, describing them as a "multidimensional, all-weather and foolproof prevention and control grid." Xi Jinping described the concept as providing "mega national security."[20] Indeed, there are strong indications that Xi follows many of the ruthless approaches to party discipline that characterized Joseph Stalin's rule of the Soviet Union.[21]

The result is that China is now ruled by a communist dictator who wields extraordinary personal power. Xi's political thoughts are now enshrined in the Chinese constitution, legal constraints on his continuing to rule for the rest of his life have been removed, and his acolytes have fostered a growing cult of personality, including by periodically calling him "Great Leader," a title hitherto reserved for Mao Zedong. When these security measures are considered as a whole, the regime has hardened the country physically, politically, and psychologically so that the party and the nation can better ride through the extreme pressures and privations that the leadership anticipates in a major war.

Indicator #4: Regime Plans a Coordinated Struggle on an Unusually Large Number of Fronts

The Chinese Communist Party perceives the range of factors at play in a major war in a much more expansive manner than is normally done in the West. Instead of just considering the standard factors of diplomacy, information, military, and economic (DIME) strength, the Chinese go much deeper into each of these factors and then extend the list to include 20–30, and sometimes more, additional variables.

The Chinese pay particularly close attention to many political, ideological, and psychological factors, along with other dimensions such as morale, resilience, social cohesion, and logistics. They have not forgotten that during the wars in Korea and Vietnam as well as in a number of more recent conflicts, leadership strength, national unity, ideological commitment, propaganda leverage, capacity to conduct rapidly paced political warfare operations, human resilience, and related capabilities were at least as important as the diplomatic, economic, military, and other assets traditionally given prominence by the West.

Xi Jinping gave this multidisciplinary, multi-domain thinking a new face when he introduced what he called the Overall National Security Outlook in April 2014.[22] This concept encompasses just about every conceivable type of domestic and international risk to his regime. His intent is to anticipate all potential threats very early, proactively organize counters in advance, and ensure that relevant agencies of the party and the state are geared to respond effectively at short notice. In order to conduct operations in this very large number of domains, the regime has built a set of formidable organizations tailored for the purpose. All of these agencies would be very active in a major crisis or war.

The central positioning of these organizations within the Chinese regime can be readily seen in figure 1. This figure shows that most of the functions that are central to China's diverse security, defense, and political warfare operations are at the core of the Chinese Communist Party's structure. The Propaganda Department, the Political-Legal Commission with its Ministry of State Security, the People's Liberation Army, and the United Front Work Department, are all central players. A key role of the United Front Work Department is to foster many mass organizations that have branches working to advance CCP interests not only within China but also in key foreign countries, especially in the United States and its close allies. All of these activities are planned, directed, and overseen by the Politburo Standing Committee that Xi Jinping chairs.

A key consequence is that in the run-up to and at the commencement of a major war the Chinese will already be active in a large number of domains using a very wide range of instruments to weaken, confuse, corrupt, and divide targeted states. During a major conflict, China plans to intensify these operations in a whole-of-nation effort to corrode, divide, outflank, and outlast its enemies.

Figure 1. Core Structures of the Chinese Communist Party.

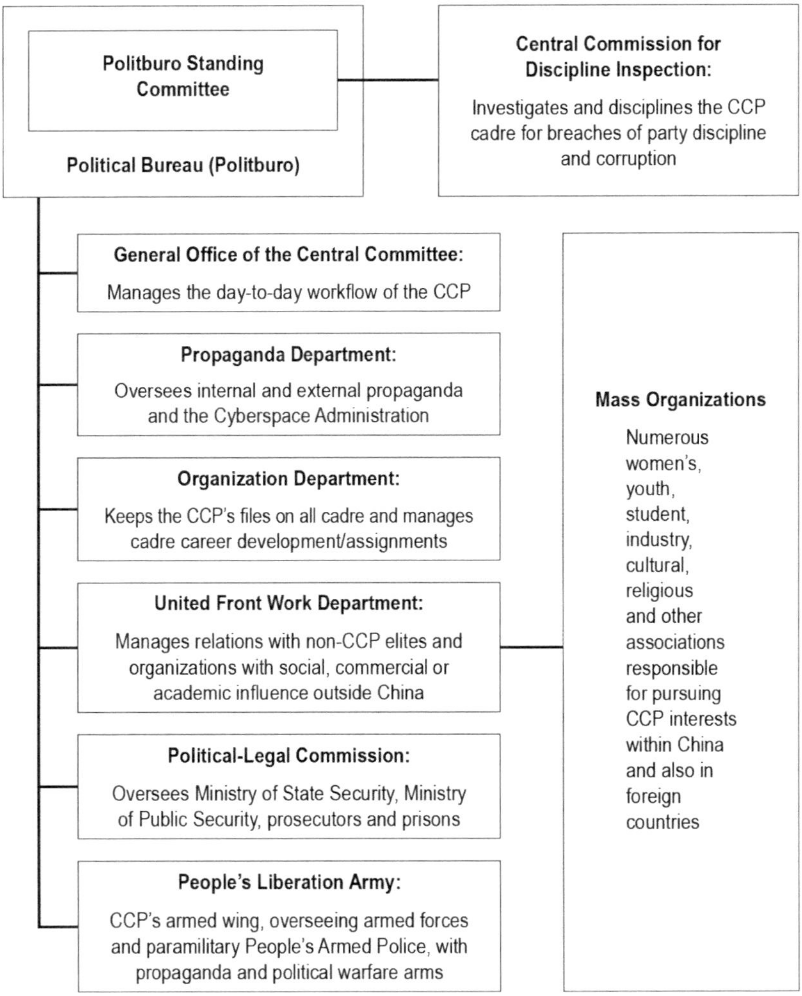
Politburo Standing Committee
Political Bureau (Politburo)
Central Commission for Discipline Inspection:
Investigates and disciplines the CCP cadre for breaches of party discipline and corruption
General Office of the Central Committee:
Manages the day-to-day workflow of the CCP
Propaganda Department:
Oversees internal and external propaganda and the Cyberspace Administration
Organization Department:
Keeps the CCP's files on all cadre and manages cadre career development/assignments
United Front Work Department:
Manages relations with non-CCP elites and organizations with social, commercial or academic influence outside China
Political-Legal Commission:
Oversees Ministry of State Security, Ministry of Public Security, prosecutors and prisons
People's Liberation Army:
CCP's armed wing, overseeing armed forces and paramilitary People's Armed Police, with propaganda and political warfare arms
Mass Organizations
Numerous women's, youth, student, industry, cultural, religious and other associations responsible for pursuing CCP interests within China and also in foreign countries

Note. This figure was adapted from a diagram by Peter Mattis, "Form and Function of the Chinese Communist Party," September 28, 2017, https://www.linkedin.com/pulse/form-function-chinese-communist-party-peter-mattis.

In a sense, the Chinese strategy for major war involves very extensive horizontal escalation. While China plans to be very competitive in the standard military, diplomatic, information, and economic domains, it also plans to be exceptionally strong in many other fields which are usually weakly contested or ignored by the United States and its allies. China plans to fight on a much larger canvas for a prolonged period and eventually outflank and overwhelm the West's more standard strategic thinking and conventional military forces.

Indicator #5: The Chinese People are Being Prepared for an Epic Fight Against the Democratic World and its Partners

Further insights on the Chinese regime's views about the nature of a future major war can be gained from the speeches and other remarks of Xi Jinping and his colleagues. Xi often asserts that China is in the ascendancy and its destiny is assured. When Xi made a congratulatory call to President Biden on election night in November 2020, he stated that:

> Democracies cannot be sustained in the 21st century. Autocracies will run the world. Why? Things are changing so rapidly. Democracies require a consensus, and it takes time, and you don't have the time.[23]

Xi believes that "the East is rising and the West is declining."[24] He emphasizes that "there is a vivid contrast between the order of China and the chaos of the West." In January 2021, Xi told a group of high-ranking CCP officials that:

> The world is in a turbulent time that is unprecedented in the past century. But time and momentum are on our side. This is where we show our conviction and resilience, as well as our determination and confidence.[25]

Xi and his colleagues view the current era as a time of great opportunity in which the rejuvenation of the Chinese nation can be accelerated and the "China Dream" achieved. As Jude Blanchette observes, "Xi is impatient with the status quo, possesses a high tolerance for risk, and seems to feel a pronounced sense of urgency in challenging the international order."[26]

There is little doubt about which country the Chinese leadership sees as its primary rival. Xi and his colleagues often refer to the United States[27] as "the strong enemy" or the "powerful adversary,"[28] although these terms are also occasionally used to describe Japan and India.

Xi often draws on China's campaign history to emphasise the importance of military and broader national strength, toughness, and resilience. For instance, in commemorating the 70th anniversary of China's intervention in the Korean War in 1950 he said:

> The forces of China and North Korea defeated their armed-to-teeth rival and shattered the myth of invincibility of the US military. We Chinese know well we must speak to invaders with the language they understand: So we use war to stop war, we use military might to stop hostility, we win peace and respect with victory.[29]

This type of language has become common in recent years and is sometimes accompanied by a degree of swagger. Articles in the PLA Daily referring to the "strong enemy" are now ten times more frequent than in 2009.[30]

Xi Jinping has also been forthright in asserting that the PLA must be a force that can "fight and win." In the 19th Party Congress Work Report he stated: "A military is built to fight. Our military must regard combat capability as the criterion to meet in all its work and focus on how to win when it is called on."[31]

But Xi has not hidden the fact that fighting the "strong enemy" will be demanding and dangerous. When visiting a bomber base in 2015, he said:

> We must have strong combat skills and strengthen actual combat training to ensure that we can go up, fight and win at critical moments. Our fighting style must be strong, carrying forward the spirit of not being afraid of hardship, and not being afraid of

> death. We must dare to charge into battle, and we must dare to face the strong enemy.[32]

In January 2021, Xi stressed the need for "full-time combat readiness" and the importance of being ready to "act at any second."[33] Xi said:

> No matter the country, no matter the military, no matter how powerful, if they are standing in opposition to the world's trends, bullying the world's weak, trying to turn back history, engage in aggression and expansion, this will inevitably lead to bloodshed...Once provoked, things will get ugly.[34]

In referring to the PLA's experience during the Korean War, Xi Jinping highlighted the differing characteristics of the two sides. He argued that "China won with less steel, more spirit against an enemy equipped with more steel, less spirit."[35] He implies strongly that this experience of what he called "extremely asymmetric war"[36] may need to be repeated in a future conflict.

Drawing on this thinking, the Chinese leadership's approach to a future war is to encourage a toughening of the entire population. The Chinese people are frequently exhorted to strengthen their resilience and take active steps to prepare for a future conflict that is likely to be very demanding.

In encouraging this toughening and reinforcement of national resilience, Xi and his colleagues have urged the Chinese people to prepare for "a new long march" against the West. For the Chinese people, this is a dramatic allusion to the tortuous trek of Mao Zedong's Red Army from the south to the northwest of the country in 1934–1935 in which fewer than a tenth of those who commenced the march survived the ordeal. These warnings about the extreme challenges that may lie ahead are not lost on the Chinese people.

In April 2021 Xi urged citizens, when facing the formidable challenges of the future, to demonstrate the revolutionary zeal of the Red Army during the Chinese Civil War:

> The lofty spirit of the Red Army soldiers, who did not fear death, lived for death, went forward and dared to overcome all difficulties without being overwhelmed by any difficulties, is always worth remembering and carrying forward. On the new Long March to achieve the second centenary goal, we must hold the belief of the certainty of our victory, bravely overcome all kinds of major risks and challenges from home and abroad, and march forward bravely towards the goal of realizing the great rejuvenation of the Chinese nation.[37]

Indicator #6: The CCP Regime's Perceived Security Needs are Expanding

Since the Chinese Communist Party seized power in 1949, the nation's security goals have mostly been expressed in general terms. The emphasis has been on "resolutely safeguarding"[38] China's sovereignty, security, and development interests. These have focused on maintaining domestic security, deterrence, and defense against external attacks, and strengthening the PLA's capabilities to protect China's interests in its immediate regional approaches. However, in China's 2019 Defense White Paper, these long-standing themes were expanded and substantially extended. They were listed as:

1. To deter and resist aggression;
2. To safeguard national political security, the people's security and social stability;
3. To oppose and contain "Taiwan independence";
4. To crack down on proponents of separatist movements such as "Tibet independence" and the creation of "East Turkistan";
5. To safeguard national sovereignty, unity, territorial integrity and security;
6. To safeguard China's maritime rights and interests;
7. To safeguard China's security interests in outer space, electromagnetic space and cyberspace;

8.To safeguard China's overseas interests; and,

9.To support the sustainable development of the country.[39]

Particularly notable is the prominence given to operations beyond China's immediate approaches to secure China's maritime and overseas interests and the priority accorded the nation's interests in space, electronic domains, and cyberspace.

An important part of this more expansive international vision is Xi Jinping's announcement of the Global Security Initiative in April 2022. Using this concept, Xi encourages other countries to work with China to build "common security" and stronger cooperative frameworks for joint purposes. He is driving especially hard to sign up countries in the developing world to reinforce national (and regime) resilience and build partnerships that can resist security, economic, and other pressures from the United States and its allies. Over time, he may plan to develop the network of Global Security Initiative members into a form of quasi-alliance.

Xi Jinping's extension of China's international goals coincided with a rise in PLA operations in distant theaters, the commissioning of China's first foreign base in Djibouti, and sustained indications of Chinese interest in establishing further military bases and operating facilities in Southeast Asia, the Indian Ocean, Africa, Central Asia, the Persian Gulf, and the South Pacific. Commander of the People's Liberation Army Navy (PLAN) Wu Shengli explained this new emphasis:

> China must "give full play to the Navy's mobile and offensive force employment characteristics and operational strengths." in part by "actively expanding the maritime strategic defense depth, implementing offshore mobile operations along the strategic internal lines, and flexibly carrying out long-sea attack operations along the strategic external lines."[40]

The PLA clearly intends to move early to influence, deter, and—where required—intervene militarily to secure the nation's interests in distant regions, and it is building and training forces for those purposes. These developments have implications for the ways the Chinese regime addresses international developments in many parts of the world during periods of relative peace. But they also signal that in a major conflict the PLA plans to have some capabilities that can reach into far distant theaters and threaten opposing forces in depth.

That thinking is further underlined by the newly explicit priority given to the space, cyberspace, and electronic domains. Some of these capabilities have the potential to disrupt and destroy systems in many parts of the world, including within enemy homelands. In the event of war, the Chinese are likely to conduct some offensive operations of these types for extended periods.

Indicator #7: China's Pattern and Pace of Military and Security Investments

The pattern of China's military force structure and the pace of its development also tell us a great deal about how China is preparing to fight any future war. China's rapidly growing military capabilities are not directly comparable to those of the United States and its allies. The PLA is being developed with different priorities, strategies, structures, and operational practices. They are focused primarily on dominating operations on the Chinese homeland and in its regional approaches, while simultaneously being able to threaten enemy forces in depth. The Pentagon's assessment states that:

> the PLA is developing capabilities ... to dissuade, deter, or, if ordered, defeat third-party intervention during a large-scale, theater campaign such as a Taiwan contingency... The PLA's anti-access/area-denial (A2/AD) capabilities are currently the most robust within the First Island Chain [in the Western Pacific], although the PRC aims to strengthen its capabilities to reach farther into the Pacific Ocean. The PLA is [also] developing the capabilities and operational concepts to conduct offensive operations within

> the Second Island Chain, in the Pacific and Indian Oceans, and in some cases, globally.[41]

China's strategic view of the Western Pacific is portrayed in figure 2.

The PLA now operates the world's largest regular army, military aviation forces, and navy. All parts of this force are modernizing at a rapid rate, training standards are rising, and capabilities for integrated joint operations—while not at Western standards—are improving.

The PLA's "core operational concept" is "Multi-Domain Precision Warfare".[42] This might appear at first sight to be a Western operational concept. However, the PLA's extensive surveillance and targeting systems and its large force of ballistic and cruise missiles, its strong cyber capabilities, its growing range of space and counter-space systems, and its exceptionally strong supporting militia and paramilitary forces underline China's dissimilar and asymmetric combat power.

China operates a sophisticated array of skywave and over-the-horizon radars, a strong network of land-, sea-, and space-based electronic surveillance systems, and several optical and other airborne and satellite systems that can provide real-time targeting data to PLA units. The data streams from these systems can be fused to provide precise guidance to Chinese strike aircraft, submarines, ships, and special force raiding parties. But this target data can also be used to guide China's powerful People's Liberation Army Rocket Force (PLARF).

The PLA has now deployed over 1,300 short-, medium-, and intermediate-range ballistic and cruise missiles. As seen in figure 3, these are capable of striking all major allied military bases and many operational units up to 4,000 miles from the Chinese coast. The target area includes Japan, Taiwan, Southeast Asia, vast areas of the Pacific beyond Guam, and all of India. This missile force is capable of doing serious damage to allied bases and some deployed forces in the theater in the first hours of a major war. The United States and its allies will not possess a theater missile strike capability that is comparable until the late 2020s at the earliest.

Figure 2. China's View of the First and Second Island Chains in the Western Pacific.

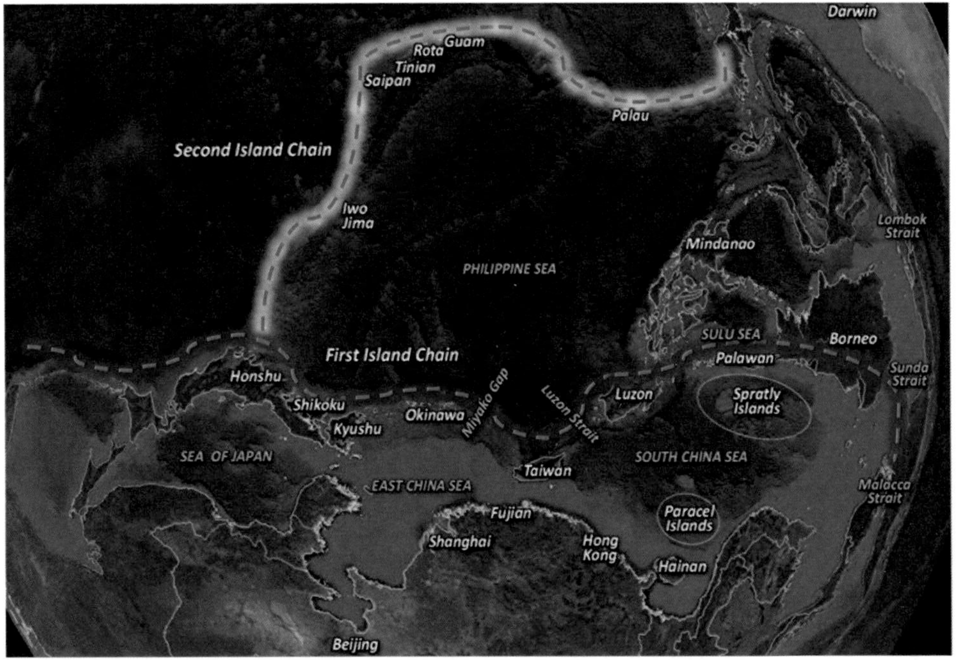

Source: Ross Babbage, "Which Way the Dragon? Sharpening Allied Perceptions of China's Strategic Trajectory," Center for Strategic and Budgetary Assessments, 2020, https://csbaonline.org/research/publications/which-way-the-dragon-sharpening-allied-perceptions-of-chinas-strategic-trajectory.

Figure 3. Approximate Maximum Range of China's Land-Based Conventionally Armed Strike Capabilities.

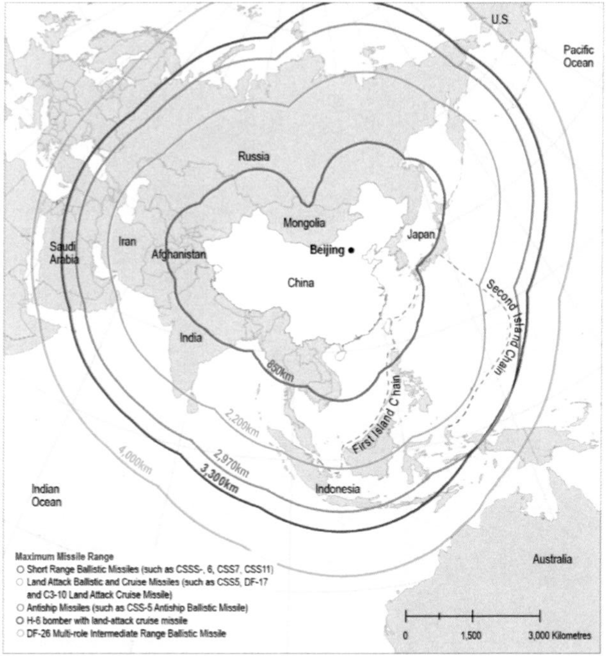

Note. This figure is a slightly modified version of a map published in US Department of Defense, *Military and Security Developments Involving the People's Republic of China 2020 – Annual Report to Congress*, Washington DC, 2020. p.57. It also draws on a similar map published in the 2019 edition of the same report. Some of the range estimates appear to bunch unevenly because the range lines have been drawn from different baselines in China so as to reflect credible launch locations for each system. Representations of locations, points of origin, and ranges are approximate.

In recent years the PLA has also made rapid progress in fielding sophisticated cyber, electronic warfare, and counter-space capabilities.[43] These assets have the potential to penetrate, mislead, incapacitate, and destroy many allied military and civilian systems not only within the Indo-Pacific but also in allied and partner countries across the globe.

A further unusual feature of the PLA is its close partnership with, and effective operational control of, very large land-based People's Armed Police, the China Coast Guard (CCG), and People's Armed Forces Maritime Militia (PAFMM) forces at sea. During the last decade the CCG's fleet of patrol vessels has more than doubled, and other paramilitary forces have also been greatly strengthened.

The CCP regime views rapid expansion and modernization of the PLA to be an essential part of the nation's "national rejuvenation." The 2019 Defense White Paper highlighted the regime's milestones for the PLA's progressive development as follows:

> **By 2020**: "To generally achieve mechanization...with significantly enhanced informationization and greatly improved strategic capabilities;"
>
> **By 2035**: "To comprehensively advance the modernization of military theory, organizational structure, military personnel, and weaponry and equipment in step with the modernization of the country and basically complete the modernization of national defense and the military ..."; and,
>
> **In 2049**: "To fully transform the people's armed forces into world-class forces."[44]

The precise meaning of these commitments remains the subject of debate but these statements, together with the priorities revealed in China's military and paramilitary budgets, underline the leadership's commitment to the development of not only dominant theater forces but also, in time, of very strong forces for global operations.

This pattern of military and security force development suggests that the Chinese leadership is giving priority to the following types of operation in the event of a major conflict.

First, priority is maintaining tight control of China's own population in any future crisis or conflict.

Second, the regime has developed large, highly sophisticated organizations to conduct a wide range of influence, coercion, and dis-integration operations. These political warfare operations are designed primarily to strengthen China's strategic position and undermine, corrupt, and divide potential enemy states.

Third, China has deployed an unmatched force of short- and intermediate-range ballistic and cruise missiles and other theater-strike capabilities that have the potential to damage or destroy most of the operating bases of US and its allies in the Western Pacific within hours.

Fourth, China has developed a select range of forces that can operate within and adjacent to the continental United States and to other distant enemy states. Special force raids, maritime strikes, and sea-mine attacks should be anticipated.

And fifth, China has developed very large forces that are widely dispersed. Many of these capabilities are likely to survive the type of intense military exchanges that might be anticipated during the kinetic phases of a major war. They are well structured and prepared to fight for an extended period.

Indicator #8: Preparations to Fight a Protracted War

Chinese leaders talk not only about a long-term "struggle" with the United States and the need to prepare for a "protracted war," but they have also taken many steps to prepare the country for an extended war and to be able to prevail in one.

In addition to primary combat units, the PLA also maintains scores of military reserve and paramilitary formations. The Chinese have moved many strategically important military assets underground. They have hardened strategic communications and command-and-control systems, and they have built large reserves of munitions, spare parts, fuel, and food. And, as discussed earlier, they have also propagated a powerful nationalist narrative, built formidable information-control mechanisms, and taken many steps to prepare the Chinese population psychologically for the possibility of a long war.

Driven partly by a perceived need to strengthen security, Xi Jinping has accelerated a process of decoupling the Chinese economy from significant reliance on the US and its allies. At the cost of reduced growth, he has championed increased self-reliance and refocused production and investment on meeting domestic rather than international demands. Xi's "Made in China 2025," "dual circulation," and "New Development Phase" initiatives are all designed to vertically integrate the Chinese economy and reduce China's exposure to external pressures[45]. Were a major conflict to erupt, the CCP leadership would obviously welcome a quick and easy victory. But some informed commentators have noted that Xi's initiatives are aimed, at least in part, at ensuring that China is prepared for a long, drawn-out, protracted war in a manner that would be very familiar to Mao Zedong.[46]

China's concept of protracted war has been inherited from Mao Zedong's campaigns against the Kuomintang and the Japanese Imperial Army in the first half of the twentieth century. During those struggles, Mao delivered a series of speeches that were subsequently published as an influential book entitled *On Protracted War*.[47]

Xi Jinping's appointment to party and national leadership coincided with a growing sense in the PLA and elsewhere that Mao's strategy of protracted war had renewed relevance. Xi and his colleagues started to make public references not only to "protracted war" but also to the associated Maoist concepts of "people's war" and "active defence." Indeed, when China's Ministry of National Defense published the first edition of *China's Military Strategy* in 2015, it announced that: "The strategic concept of active defence is the essence of the (CCP's) military strategic thought."[48]

Hence, the Maoist concepts of fighting revolutionary wars that have long been taught in Chinese military colleges and many high schools have now returned to center stage in an updated twenty-first-century form.

When Mao's strategic and operational concepts received renewed attention, *On Protracted War* was returned to the printing presses at the People's Publishing House in Beijing. A modest run of the reprinted book sold out almost immediately, and a succession of much larger print runs followed. There are many indicators that the general strategy and principles in this book now play a central role in China's planning for major war.

What then are the primary concepts that Mao Zedong emphasized in *On Protracted War*? The first is the logic, need, and desirability of defeating a strong enemy by fighting a long, draining war. When comparing China's war-fighting capabilities to those of the more advanced military systems of the relatively wealthy Japan, Mao said that China needed to exploit its continental size, vast population, and rich resources to draw out the conflict, undermine enemy resolve, and eventually exhaust the enemy state. He wrote:

> China must unavoidably travel a hard stretch of road, and that the War of Resistance will be a protracted war and not a war of quick decision...... Not that we would not like a quick victory; everybody would be in favour of driving the "devils" out overnight. But we point out that, in the absence of certain definite conditions, quick victory is something that exists only in one's mind and not in objective reality, and that it is a mere illusion, a false theory. Accordingly, having made an objective and comprehensive appraisal of all the circumstances concerning both the enemy and ourselves, we point out that the only way to final victory is the strategy of protracted war..... our conclusion is derived from the interrelations of all the factors at work on both sides. The enemy is strong and we are weak, and the danger of subjugation is there.

> But in other respects the enemy has shortcomings aggravated by our efforts. On the other hand, our advantages can be enhanced and our shortcomings remedied by our efforts. Hence, we can win a final victory and avert subjugation, while the enemy will ultimately be defeated and will be unable to avert the collapse of his whole imperialist system.[49]

Having emphasized the necessity of fighting a protracted war, Mao describes three phases of the war, the shifting "correlation of forces" at each stage, and the changing nature of the tactical and theater operations of Chinese forces.

> The first phase covers the period of the enemy's strategic offensive and our strategic defensive. The second stage will be the period of the enemy's strategic consolidation and our preparation for the counter-offensive. The third stage will be the period of our strategic counter-offensive and the enemy's strategic retreat.[50]

In elaborating on the first phase Mao says:

> On the enemy side, there are already signs of flagging morale, and his army's momentum of attack is less in the middle phase of this stage than it was in the initial phase, and it will diminish still further in the concluding phase. Signs of exhaustion are beginning to appear in his finances and economy, war-weariness is beginning to set in among his people and troops and within the clique at the helm of the war, "war frustrations" are beginning to manifest themselves and pessimism about the prospects of the war is growing....
>
> In the first stage, changes of two kinds are also occurring on the enemy's side. The first kind is a change for the worse and manifest itself in hundreds and thousands of casualties, the drain on arms and ammunition, deterioration of troop morale, popular discontent at home, shrinkage of trade, condemnation by world opinion, etc.[51]

Mao sees the primary tasks for the first phase being to draw the enemy into a war of attrition in which space is traded for time, the enemy suffers serious losses, frustrations increase, and the seeds are sown for a climate of collapse in the enemy's homeland.

Mao emphasises that the second stage requires a significant change of China's gears. Nevertheless, it is also likely be long and gruelling.

> The second stage may be termed one of strategic stalemate....we should be prepared to see this stage last a comparatively long time and to weather its hardships. It will be a very painful period for China; the two big problems will be economic difficulties and the disruptive activities of the traitors.... Widespread guerrilla warfare and the people's anti-Japanese movement will wear down this big Japanese force, greatly reducing it and also disintegrating its morale by stimulating the growth of homesickness, war weariness and even anti-war sentiment.[52]

In the third phase, Mao foresaw that there would be an even more marked shift in the nature of the struggle:

> In the third stage, our war will no longer be one of strategic defensive, but will turn into a strategic counter-offensive manifesting itself in strategic offensives; and it will no longer be fought on strategically interior lines but will shift gradually to strategically exterior lines.[53]

Mao then describes some of the critical factors in winning such a prolonged war. Weapons are an important factor in war but not the decisive factor; it is people not things, that are decisive. The contest of strength is not only a contest of military and economic power, but also a contest of human power and morale. Military and economic power is necessarily wielded by people.

> In order to achieve victory we must as far as possible make the enemy blind and deaf by sealing his eyes and ears and drive his commanders to distraction by creating confusion in their minds. ... When mass support is sufficiently good to block the leakage of news, it is often possible by various ruses to succeed in leading the enemy into a morass of wrong judgements and actions so that

> he loses his superiority and the initiative. The saying, "There can never be too much deception in war", means precisely this...
>
> Only by persevering in the united front can we persevere in the war; and only by persevering in the united front and the war can we win final victory.[54]

The concept of the united front is central to both Mao Zedong's and Xi Jinping's conceptions of war. Mao-era United Front cadres recruited and trained agents to conduct intelligence gathering, espionage, sabotage, and other operations behind enemy lines, including within enemy bases. The primary goals of these operations were to inform Chinese decision-making and use enemy territory to spread disinformation, encourage division and confusion, and induce war weariness and exhaustion.

Modest extensions of these United Front activities were also undertaken in the Japanese homeland and within other major countries of relevance. These international operations were designed primarily to undermine Japanese morale, foster international sympathy for the communist cause, damage Japan's reputation, and increase the pressure on Tokyo to withdraw.

Mao's concept of United Front operations remains very relevant to China's current "struggles" with the outside world and to its preparations for major war. Xi Jinping periodically describes United Front activities as one of his "magic weapons."[55] In the current era, these operations parallel those of Mao both in reinforcing the loyalty of the population at home and also penetrating, undermining, dividing, and weakening those countries that stand in the regime's way.

In *On Protracted War* Mao also addresses some key aspects of how to fight and win an extended war at the operational and tactical levels. He emphasizes that while the strategy requires a very extended conflict, the theater and tactical campaigns need to be mainly short and sharp offensives. He argues that these operations require well-chosen "quick-decision" or "active-defence" offensive operations:

> ...the enemy forces, though small, are strong (in arms and training) while our forces, though large, are weak (in arms and training but not in morale), and in campaigns and battles, therefore, we should not only employ large forces against small and operate from exterior against interior lines, but also follow the policy of seeking quick decisions...... If in each month we could win one sizeable victory .... It would greatly demoralise the enemy, stimulate the morale of our own forces and evoke international support. Thus our strategically protracted war is translated in the field into battles of quick decision...
>
> In a word, the *operational* principle for fighting campaigns and battles is one of "quick-decision offensive warfare on exterior lines". It is the opposite of our *strategic* principle of "protracted defensive warfare on interior lines", and yet it is the indispensable principle for carrying out this strategy.... On the basis of this ingenuity, we can win more victories in quick-decision offensive warfare on exterior lines, change the balance of forces in our favour, gain the initiative over the enemy, and overwhelm and crush him so that the final victory will be ours.[56]

This Maoist strategic and operational approach is echoed directly in the 2015 official publication of *China's Military Strategy*, which states that "...the people's armed forces have developed a complete set of strategic concepts of active defense, which boils down to adherence to the unity of strategic defense and operational and tactical offense..."[57]

In summary, Mao's concept of protracted war required strong advancement on two strategic arms. The first was the political struggle to win the overwhelming support of the Chinese people as well as to undermine and ultimately induce the collapse of the enemy's willpower. The second was the military struggle on the battlefield. Mao appreciated that in order to defeat the advanced technology and well-trained Imperial Japanese Army, his forces needed to achieve clear ascendancy in both the political and the military arms of strategy. However, he also realized that winning in both strategic arenas would take time; hence his unwavering commitment to fighting a protracted war.

Indicator #9: Reshaping China's Economy to Build Resilience and Reduce Vulnerability

Xi Jinping is deeply concerned about the medium- and long-term trajectory of China's economy and the consequential vulnerability of the country and his regime in a crisis. These worries have spurred a series of actions to strengthen China's economic future while simultaneously reducing the country's vulnerability to foreign coercion and to the extreme pressures it would face in a major war.

Xi Jinping has given high priority to reducing China's dependence on foreign supply chains while simultaneously strengthening China's advanced-technology manufacturing and other high-technology capabilities. His driving motivations are to ensure not only that China is an industrial leader in coming decades but also that the country and the regime can survive and ultimately prevail in a protracted war.

Xi has good reason to be concerned because China faces serious economic challenges. Although the economy is very large and produces about 18% of the global GDP, its official rate of growth in 2022 was a fifth of that of 2007[58]. Indeed, largely because of declining economic efficiency and the regime's drawn-out battle with COVID-19, China's real rate of growth in 2022 was probably around 2–3%, possibly even lower.[59] The 2021–2025 Five-Year Plan announced in November 2020 assumes an average annual growth rate of only about 3.5 % to 2035.[60] These figures are comparable to the growth rates projected for the United States in coming years. Indeed, despite many predictions that China's GDP will surpass that of the United States during the 2020s, there are now doubts that this will ever occur.[61]

When the economy has faced strong headwinds in recent years, Xi has pumped more money into the society mostly by launching major programs of infrastructure development or directing the banks and financial institutions to loosen flows of commercial and private credit, or both. This has helped maintain short-term economic stability, but it has also distorted the structure of the economy and produced many unproductive and wasteful projects. Very fast train systems and highways have been built to sparsely inhabited regions.[62] More than 50 "ghost cities" containing empty apartment blocks, offices, shopping malls, and airports have been constructed.[63] An artificially stimulated property market has resulted in 20% of homes (or some 50 million) in China being vacant and contributed to the serious reversal of the sector in 2021–2022.[64] About a third of China's production capacity is reportedly surplus to requirements.[65]

The scope for further "pump priming" of the economy to maintain economic and political stability is now substantially reduced. This is not only because the returns on further infrastructure and property investments are minimal but also because China's public debt now exceeds 300% of GDP and the debt-to-GDP ratio continues to grow by about 11% each year.[66]

A closely related problem for Xi Jinping is that China's economic productivity is still only half that of the United States and in recent years little progress has been made in closing the gap. Chinese productivity growth provided around half of China's rapid economic expansion in the 1990s, but now it only generates about 1% of China's growth, or even less.[67] A key consequence is that China is becoming uncompetitive in many sectors, and this is placing increased pressure on some manufacturing and other industries.

In order for productivity growth to return and GDP to rise at a faster rate, Xi would need to embrace serious market reforms. The regime's current preference for state-owned enterprises over the more efficient private corporations would need to change. Major land and property reforms would be required. Labor mobility would need to be improved by abolishing the *hukou* system that ties workers to their place of birth. Barriers to foreign participation in the economy would also need to be reduced, and the regime's habit of arbitrarily intervening in the operations of fast-moving sectors of the economy would need to be curtailed.

The reality is that few, if any, of these reforms are likely to be introduced so long as Xi Jinping remains in power. The primary reason is that Xi places a higher priority on maintaining the regime's authority and legitimacy than on fostering rapid economic growth.[68] In his view, most of the economic reforms that have been proposed could generate competing centers of power, increase China's vulnerability to foreign forces, and threaten the personal interests of key members of his regime.

Xi Jinping now also faces three other long-term challenges that are placing increasing strains on the economy, the society, and on the party's legitimacy. The first of these is the declining size and rapid aging of China's workforce. Largely as a consequence of the 30 years of the CCP's one-child policy, Xi knows that China's labor pool will decline by 45 million people by 2030 and by around 200 million by 2050. China's fertility rate is now less than half the rate required to maintain the current workforce. This means that in contrast to 2016 when there were seven workers for every retired person, by 2030 there will be four, and by 2050 only about two workers for every retired person.[69] The consequences for China's tax base and its budget priorities, especially for health, social welfare, national security, and defense will be profound.

A second longer-term challenge for Xi Jinping is to maintain national unity in the face of increasing wealth disparities across the country. While several of the coastal cities are thriving with average incomes approaching those of some Western countries, the average disposable incomes of residents in the central, western, and northeastern regions are only 60–70% of those in the southeastern cities. In 2020 Premier Li Keqiang reminded his party colleagues that over 600 million Chinese citizens still lived on less than 1,000 yuan (US$154) per month, a sum that wouldn't pay the rent for a single room in a city.[70]

A third rising challenge for Xi Jinping is the increasingly difficult international environment. In marked contrast to the 1980–2016 period when the major Western powers largely welcomed China's rise, Beijing's domestic and international behaviour during the last decade has generated stiffening international resistance. These headwinds are now blowing in almost all areas of previous cooperation and may increase to gale force in the period ahead.

In response to China's heavy subsidization of exports, its tightening regulatory controls on foreign participation in China's economy, and the regime's coercive behaviour internationally, Washington imposed a range of economic sanctions in 2018. In the period since, a growing number of countries have reviewed their relations with Beijing and many have moved to constrain Chinese access to their economies in general and to their telecommunications and other sensitive sectors in particular. These processes of distancing from China have been further accelerated by Beijing's sustained support for Russia's invasion of Ukraine and its intensified intimidation of Taiwan and other regional states. Many more countries are now looking to reduce or diversify their links with China, not only in the Indo-Pacific but also in Europe and elsewhere.

Xi realizes that he now faces the evaporation of trust in large parts of the international community and growing detachment from much of the world. Worse still, he now has to worry about the development of security networks and alliances that are forming to thwart many of China's international goals and, potentially, to prevent a Chinese victory in any future conflict.

It is this combination of serious domestic and international challenges that has brought Xi Jinping to take far-reaching steps in recent years to secure the country's and the party's future. He is rallying the country to resist foreign interference, to build a much stronger domestic economy, develop next-generation technologies to dominate international markets, and to maintain his drive for regional and global leadership. He aims to markedly reduce the country's dependence on imports and simultaneously work to build the dependence of other countries on China.

Xi Jinping described his vision for the way forward in a landmark speech he delivered to the Central Committee of the party on April 10, 2020.

> In order to protect China's industrial security and national security, we should focus on building an independent and controllable, safe and reliable industrial chain and supply chain, and strive to have at least one alternative source for important products and supply channels to form the necessary industrial backup system. Now that the whole country is resuming production [following COVID], we should not and can no longer simply repeat the past model but should strive to reshape the new industrial chain and comprehensively increase scientific and technological innovation and import substitution, which is the focus of deepening supply-side structural reform and the key to achieving high-quality development.
>
> First, we should expand our strengths, consolidate and enhance the international position of advantaged industries, forge some "killer" technologies, continuously enhance the advantages of the whole industrial chain in such fields as high-speed rail, electric power equipment, new energy, communication equipment etc., improve industrial quality, tighten the dependence of the international industrial chain on China, and form a strong counter-measure and deterrent ability for outsiders to artificially cut off supply.
>
> Secondly, we need to make up for the shortcomings, that is, we need to build an independent and controllable, safe and reliable domestic production and supply system in areas and points of national security, so that we can achieve self-circulation at critical moments and ensure normal economic functioning in extreme situations...[71]

The first steps in reducing China's international exposure commenced several years before Xi Jinping assumed leadership of the Chinese Communist Party. China's trade as a percentage of GDP started to fall in 2007. It is now less than half the level of that year.

Xi describes this reduced involvement in the international economy as being required as part of his "dual circulation" theory. He envisages a much stronger domestic economy that is the primary driver of growth and prosperity with connections to the international economy being reduced to supplementary status that would be nonessential in a crisis.

This renewed domestic economy post-COVID is not to be just an updated version of China's pre-COVID economy. In 2015 Xi launched the "Made in China 2025" policy that foreshadowed vast investments in ten fields of advanced technology including artificial intelligence, quantum computing, high-end semiconductors, and integrated circuits, genetic and biological research, neuroscience, aerospace, advanced robotics, next-generation telecommunications, and electric vehicles. Although the title of this program is now rarely heard, it continues to accelerate strongly. Xi is investing vast sums in order to build corporate champions in these and related fields as he strives to win global leadership in key high-technology sectors.[72] Progress, however, has been slower than anticipated with numerous state-owned initiatives being handicapped by uncompetitive practices and some large high-technology start-ups failing.[73] In order to achieve a degree of financial stability, many of the new technology enterprises have abandoned the most advanced and demanding markets and focused instead on medium-technology components suitable for applications in mass consumer goods.[74]

Xi's determined investments in advanced-technology industries are motivated not only by a determination to gain market share and dominate international markets. He is also driving the concept of civil-military fusion, in which technological advances and related investment funds can be used simultaneously to build world-leading civilian *and* military systems. To those ends, Chinese military and security personnel are now actively involved in many advanced-technology programs that appear to many foreign observers to be developing commercial products. The reality is somewhat different.

It is in the context of these major changes in economic direction that flows of Chinese investment overseas contracted sharply from 2016 onwards.[75] Not only did the total outflow of funds fall but the regime directed that the bulk of the remaining funds flow away from advanced Western economies. Priority was given instead to opportunities in developing countries, especially where they promised strategic advantages, such as providing alternative sources of supply for critical raw materials and opening potential locations for Chinese military facilities.[76]

Xi Jinping is insistent that his strong shift towards domestic resilience must be accelerated, despite a high price being paid in economic efficiency and national growth. When pressed on the primary motivation for these restructuring efforts, one independent Chinese economist summed up the logic by saying: "It's a kind of preparation for the worst-case scenario, including the decoupling with the United States and even the whole Western world."[77]

Xi Jinping spoke openly about the regime's revised economic priorities in July 2021. Bloomberg summarized the change as follows:

> China this year began a "new development phase," according to Xi. It puts three priorities ahead of unfettered growth:
>
> • National security, which includes control of data and greater self-reliance in technology
>
> • Common prosperity, which aims to curb inequalities that have soared in recent decades
>
> • Stability, which means tamping down discontent among China's middle class.[78]

Progress with this transformational agenda has so far been patchy. While strong advances appear to have been made in artificial intelligence and space systems, serious weaknesses remain in several of the core technologies, such as high-end semiconductors, the specialized manufacturing plants for advanced chip manufacture, sophisticated medical systems, and advanced jet engines. Moreover, when fast-moving private enterprises have emerged, Xi has not hesitated to intervene to bring them into line with party goals, insist on corporate compliance, and force access to vast private databases on the grounds of national security.[79] Some sectors of the economy such as for-profit private educational providers have been banned with little notice, and others have been confronted by unexpected waves of regulatory control.

Xi Jinping has made clear that although he wants world-leading advanced technologies, sustainable economic efficiency, and strengthened international competitiveness, these will not be allowed to compromise national or regime security.[80] He is driving a substantial strengthening of China's economic independence and resilience.[81] And he is determined to reinforce the party's and the nation's ability to fight and win a major war—a war that he believes he may need to fight during his lifetime.

Primary Features of the War China Plans to Fight

There are eleven elements that will be prominent in the way China fights any war with the United States and its allies in the Indo-Pacific in coming decades.

1. The Chinese regime will have clear goals. They will include an effective withdrawal of the United States from most of the first island chain in the Western Pacific, along with the seizure of Taiwan and probably some other territories in the theater. Beijing will also want international recognition that China is the predominant power in the Indo-Pacific and a leading rule-maker that possesses equal or superior global status to the United States.
2. China will have confident and determined political leadership. Xi Jinping and his close colleagues will likely make all important decisions in the lead up to, and during, any major war until at least the late 2020's.
3. The regime will be prepared to take high levels of risk in pursuit of its core goals.

4. The Chinese leadership will continue to proclaim a potent ideology and a strong nationalist narrative that will resonate strongly at home, with much of the Chinese diaspora abroad and with many foreign "fellow travellers." The Chinese leadership will view any major war as a struggle to establish the dominance of their Marxist-Leninist-Maoist ideology over the "weak and corrupt" values and practices of the West.
5. The regime will have unity of command as well as comprehensive surveillance and enforcement systems to ensure mass compliance across all Chinese national communities, and especially all military and paramilitary forces.
6. The Chinese people will be psychologically and physically prepared for an intense, prolonged, and demanding conflict. The regime will describe it as a true "People's War" that will engage all Chinese citizens, ethnic Chinese abroad, and many others to perform a diverse range of operational and support tasks.
7. The CCP's wartime campaigns will be supported by large government organizations structured and trained to conduct multi-domain integrated joint operations[82] employing asymmetric means during a protracted war.
8. China's economy and society will be mobilized to provide capabilities and conflict endurance that have only modest dependence on international resources. Civil-military fusion will be evident in nearly all domains—from information and political warfare to widely dispersed conventional military operations.
9. The regime will aim to fight a war with up to four conflict layers that are likely to be employed in various combinations at specific phases:
    - Intensified political and hybrid warfare and other non-kinetic operations designed to "dis-integrate" opposing societies and centres of resistance.

- Large-scale offensive strikes in multiple domains designed to incapacitate the enemy, impose demoralizing costs, and force enemy recalibration and withdrawal.
- Periodic short offensives designed to maximize the enemy's military, economic, and political costs during an extended struggle.
- Large-scale multi-domain offensive operations timed to accelerate the opponent's political divisions and ultimately trigger the enemy's collapse from exhaustion.

10. While the Chinese would be delighted to win a quick war, they will be increasingly structured and prepared for protracted asymmetric conflict. Key features of Chinese operations at the theater and tactical levels will probably include:
    - Intensified political warfare and hybrid operations to gain strategic advantages prior to and during kinetic operations.
    - Extensive subversion and sabotage in priority foreign countries.
    - Strategic and operational surprises in a range of domains—including in cyberspace, underwater, space, biological, and chemical operations and, potentially, in some completely new hybrid domains.
    - Multi-domain campaigns waged on an exceptionally large canvas that often involve horizontal escalation into new theaters and environments. These operations are likely to include offensives into new geographical regions; extensive use of cyber, electronic warfare, and space operations; and many types of unconventional operation, some of which would involve major acts of sabotage deep within allied homelands.
    - A succession of surprise offensives of short duration designed to catch allied forces off-guard and impose high human, resource, and political costs. This type of "active defense" will be commonplace.

- Selected strikes in depth to force the US and its allies to defend in depth, in order to drive home to allied publics the costs of continuing the struggle and to induce war weariness.
- While China could threaten its opponents with tactical nuclear weapons, their actual use to directly strike allied forces is much less likely and would probably only be considered seriously if the regime faced catastrophic defeat. Most of China's growing strategic nuclear forces are likely be held in remote continental and maritime locations in order to deter allied escalatory use of weapons of mass destruction.[83] However, there is a possibility that Beijing might be tempted in some circumstances to use nuclear weapons in unexpected ways—such as high-altitude detonations to incapacitate allied command and control systems across an entire theater or deep-sea detonations to generate tsunamis that cause extensive damage to targeted coastal regions.

11. Largely because of China's rising domestic and international challenges, Xi Jinping appears to be in a hurry.[84] There is a real possibility that he will be tempted to launch a lightning surprise war over Taiwan, the South China Sea, the Senkaku Islands, or some other dispute so as to force the United States and the rest of the developed world on to the defensive from the outset.

Xi is pushing hard for China to be prepared for a major war by the second half of the 2020s at the latest. He realizes that by 2030 the strategic tide will likely have turned against his regime—possibly very strongly. In that timeframe, the economic development challenges, the income disparities, the demographic burdens, and the pressures on party unity may have intensified.

When Xi Jinping looks internationally, he is concerned by the rapid development of anti-China sentiment in many parts of the world and the rising determination of the democratic world to thwart Beijing's international goals. An additional concern is the regime's appreciation that by the mid-2020s the United States and its allies will be deploying some formidable new military capabilities into the Indo-Pacific that will likely shift the military balance of power back in Washington's favor.

Xi Jinping's strategic calculations may have also been sharpened by the impact of the war in Ukraine. Xi and his colleagues have probably been surprised by the Russian military's poor operational performance, the strength and cohesion of Ukraine's defensive operations, and the immediate rallying of the NATO and other democratic allies to support Kyiv. Xi has probably also been surprised by the speed with which wide-ranging economic and other sanctions have been imposed on the Putin regime and the determination of the Americans, the Western Europeans, and others to maintain their pressure, even at substantial cost and inconvenience to their own societies and businesses.

Many allied commentators have concluded that the Ukraine experience should give Xi Jinping pause.[85] Russia's serious intelligence, operational planning, and execution failures were unexpected. After all, an invasion across a land border by Russia's well-equipped army should be a much simpler, quicker, and less risky operation than a combined-arms assault across a major sea gap against a well-armed defending force that would likely be supported by the United States, Japan, and other allies. Can Xi be certain that a major Chinese military operation against Taiwan would not also be flawed and suffer serious reverses?

Many PLA officers probably doubt the wisdom of risking such an operation. They would realize that it might fail and would inevitably result in the loss of hundreds, possibly thousands, of young people who are the offspring of single-child families. Moreover, it must be obvious to all members of the regime that such an assault—even a militarily successful one—would trigger intense economic and political sanctions that would cripple China and result in its long-term isolation from most of the developed world. Indeed, such an operation could produce a pyrrhic victory that was catastrophic for Xi Jinping and for the Chinese

Communist Party.[86] It would probably make China a pariah state. And so it is possible that Xi may be deterred.

However, Xi Jinping is not an American or allied strategic decision-maker. He comes to these issues with a very different ideological and cultural mindset, having learned hard lessons in his younger days, especially during Mao's Cultural Revolution.[87] Moreover, his sense of personal and regime destiny has already driven him to launch risky operations, especially in the South China Sea and across India's northern borders. Xi may conclude that a major reason for Putin's problems in Ukraine is that he failed to capitalize immediately on his seizure of Crimea in 2014. By only going partway and waiting eight years to resume his offensive, Putin gave the Ukrainians time to retrain, rearm, and prepare defenses that proved to be much more formidable. Xi may not want to wait and give the newly alert Taiwanese a similar opportunity to reinforce their defenses.

Xi will also be weighing the changing correlation of forces in the Indo-Pacific. He is well aware of the stiffening domestic and international headwinds. His bottom-line judgement may be that China is unlikely to have a better time to launch a strategic offensive, at least in his lifetime. And he might conclude that it is best to move sooner rather than later. So the risks for the coming decade are high.[88]

Notes

1. Office of the Secretary of Defense, *Military and Security Developments Involving the People's Republic of China 2021*, 1–5.
2. Sun Tzu and Sun Pin, *The Art of War*, trans. Ralph D. Sawyer (Boulder, Co.: Westview Press, 1996), 50,
3. See this discussed in Jacob W. Kipp, "Lenin and Clausewitz: The Militarization of Marxism, 1914–1921," *Military Affairs* (October 1985): 189.
4. See Robert Taber, *The War of the Flea: A Study of Guerrilla Warfare Theory and Practice* (London: Paladin, 1970), 26.
5. See Taber, *The War of the Flea: A Study of Guerrilla Warfare Theory and Practice*, 27, 32–33.
6. Political warfare is defined here to be: Diverse operations to influence, persuade, and coerce nation states, organizations, and individuals to operate in accord with one's strategic interests without employing kinetic force.
7. See this argued in some depth in Ross Babbage, *Winning Without Fighting: Chinese and Russian Political Warfare Campaigns and How the West Can Prevail* (Washington, DC: Center for Strategic and Budgetary Assessments, 2019), 49–54.
8. For details, see Thomas G. Mahnken, Ross Babbage, and Toshi Yoshihara, *Countering Comprehensive Coercion* (Washington, DC: Center for Strategic and Budgetary Assessments, 2018) and Babbage, *Winning Without Fighting* for a more detailed examination, including eight case studies.
9. Qiao Liang and Wang Xiangsui, *Unrestricted Warfare: China's Master Plan to Destroy America* (Dehradun, India: Natraj Publishers, 2007), 36–45, 107–110, 123–125.
10. Ibid.
11. Nathan Beauchamp-Mustafaga, "Cognitive Domain Operations: The PLA's New Holistic Concept for Influence Operations," Jamestown Foundation, *China Brief* 19, issue 16, (September 6, 2019), and Wang Zhaowen and Fu Minghua, "Analysis of Cognitive Domain Warfare in Informatized Warfare," *PLA Daily*, July 28, 2015.
12. Kerry K. Gershaneck, *Media Warfare: Taiwan's Battle for the Cognitive Domain* (Washington, DC: Center for Security Policy, 2021), 147–148.

13. Charles Parton, "China – A Look Ahead to 2021 and Beyond," *Sinocism*, February 5, 2021, https://sinocism.com/p/china-a-look-ahead-to-2021-and-beyond.
14. See the provisions of China's anti-sanction law at "China Passes the Anti-Foreign Sanctions Law to Counter US, EU Sanctions," *China Briefing*, June 11, 2012, https://www.china-briefing.com/news/chinas-anti-foreign-sanctions-law-approved-counter-us-eu-sanctions/.
15. Thomas G. Mahnken, Ross Babbage, and Toshi Yoshihara, *Countering Comprehensive Coercion,* 28.
16. Quoted by Minxin Pei in "Xi Jinping's Political Agenda and Leadership: What Do We Know From His Decade in Power," *China Leadership Monitor*, September 1, 2022, https://www.prcleader.org/pei-september-2022.
17. Elizabeth Economy, "China's Inconvenient Truth: Official Triumphalism Conceals Societal Fragmentation," *Foreign Affairs*, May 28, 2021, https://www.foreignaffairs.com/articles/china/2021-05-28/chinas-inconvenient-truth.
18. Paul Bischoft, "Surveillance Camera Statistics—Which Cities Have the Most CCTV Cameras?," *Comparitech*, July 11, 2022, https://www.comparitech.com/vpn-privacy/the-worlds-most-surveilled-cities/
19. Bethany Allen-Ebrahimian, "Exposed: China's Operating Manuals for Mass Internment and Arrest by Algorithm," *International Consortium of Investigative Journalists: China Cables*, November 24, 2019, https://www.icij.org/investigations/china-cables/exposed-chinas-operating-manuals-for-mass-internment-and-arrest-by-algorithm/.
20. Willy Wo-Lap Lam, "Beijing Harnesses Big Data & AI to Perfect the Police State," Jamestown Foundation, *China Brief* 17, no. 10, July 21, 2017, https://jamestown.org/program/beijing-harnesses-big-data-ai-to-perfect-the-police-state/.
21. See this argued convincingly in John Garnaut, "Engineers of the Soul: what Australia needs to know about ideology in Xi Jinping's China," *Sinocism*, January 17, 2019, https://sinocism.com/p/engineers-of-the-soul-ideology-in.
22. For a discussion of these and related issues, see Jude Blanchette, "The Edge of an Abyss: Xi Jinping's Overall National Security Outlook," *China Leadership Monitor*, September 1, 2022, https://www.prcleader.org/blanchette-september-2022.
23. Remarks by President Biden at the United States Naval Academy's Class of 2022 Graduation and Commissioning Ceremony, *The White House*, May 27, 2022, https://www.whitehouse.gov/briefing-room/statements-

releases/2022/05/27/remarks-by-president-biden-at-the-united-states-naval-academys-class-of-2022-graduation-and-com.

24. Shi Jiangtao, "China Says 'East is Rising and the West is Declining,' but has it been Misunderstood?," *South China Morning Post*, October 22, 2021, https://www.scmp.com/news/china/diplomacy/article/3153379/china-says-east-rising-and-west-declining-has-it-been.
25. SCMP Reporter, "As the Communist Party Turns 100, Xi Jinping has a Problem: Who will Take Over?," *South China Morning Post*, June 25, 2021, https://scmp.com/news/china/politics/article/3138653/communist-party-turns-100-xi-jinping-has-problem-who-will-take.
26. Jude Blanchette, "Xi's Gamble: The Race to Consolidate Power and Stave Off Disaster," *Foreign Affairs*, 100, No. 4(July/August 2021), https:www.foreignaffairs.com/articles/china/2021-06-22/xis-gamble.
27. See Xi Jinping quoted as stating this explicitly in Chris Buckley, "The East is Rising: Xi Maps Out China's Post-Covid Ascent," *New York Times*, March 3, 2022, https://nytimes.com/2021/03/03/world/asia/xi-china-congress.html.
28. Nathan Beauchamp-Mustafaga, "Dare to Face the 'Strong Enemy,' How Xi Jinping Has Made the PLA Talk About the United States," *Sinocism*, March 5, 2021, https://sinocism.com/p/dare-to-face-the-strong-enemy-how.
29. Ibid.
30. Ibid.
31. Ibid.
32. Ibid.
33. Liu Zhen, "Xi Jinping Orders China's Military to be Ready for War 'at any second,'" *South China Morning Post*, January 5, 2021, https://www.scmp.com/news/china/military/article/3116436/xi-jinping-orders-chinas-military-be-ready-war-any-second.
34. Joel Gehrke, "Once Provoked, Things Will Get Ugly: Xi Jinping Implies that US Rivalry could 'Lead to Bloodshed,'" *Washington Examiner*, October 23, 2020, https://www.washingtonexaminer.com/policy/defense-national-security/once-provoked-things-will-get-ugly-xi-jinping-implies-that-us-rivalry-could-lead-.
35. Quoted in Shannon Tiezzi, "In Korean War Commemoration, Xi Warns that China Will 'Use War to Prevent War,'" *The Diplomat*, October 24, 2020, https://thediplomat.com/tag/china-in-the-korean-war/.
36. Ibid.

37. "Xi Stresses Advancing High-quality Development in Border Ethnic Regions," Xinhua, April 28, 2021, http://www.china.org.cn/china/2021-04/28/content_77447140.htm.
38. The State Council Information Office of the People's Republic of China, *China's National Defense in the New Era* (Defense White Paper, Foreign Languages Press, July 2019), Part 2, https://english.www.gov.cn/archive/whitepaper/201907/24/content_WS5d3941ddc6d08408f502283d.html.
39. Ibid.
40. Nathan Beauchamp-Mustafaga, "Dare to Face the 'Strong Enemy': How Xi Jinping Has Made the PLA Talk About the United States."
41. Office of the Secretary of Defense, *Military and Security Developments Involving the People's Republic of China 2020: Annual Report to Congress* (Washington, DC: US Department of Defense, 2020), https://media.defense.gov/2020/Sep/01/2002488689/-1/-1/1/2020-DOD-CHINA-MILITARY-POWER-REPORT-FINAL.PDF.
42. U.S. Department of Defense, *Military and Security Developments Involving the People's Republic of China 2022: Annual Report to Congress* (Washington, DC, Department of Defense 2022), p. v, https://media.defense.gov/2022/Nov/29/2003122279/-1/-1/1/2022-MILITARY-AND-SECURITY-DEVELOPMENTS-INVOLVING-THE-PEOPLES-REPUBLIC-OF-CHINA.PDF
43. Anthony Capaccio, "Pentagon Sees China's Offensive Space Technology 'On the March,'" Bloomberg, July 10, 2021, https://www.bloomberg.com/news/articles/2021-07-10/pentagon-sees-china-s-offensive-space-technology-on-the-march.
44. The State Council Information Office of the People's Republic of China, *China's National Defense in the New Era*, Part II.
45. Allicia Garcia Herrero, "What is Behind China's Dual Circulation Strategy," *China Leadership Monitor*, September 1, 2021, https://www.prcleader.org/herrero.
46. See, for example, Wang Xiangwei, "Under US Pressure, China is Planning an Economy that Can Survive a Protracted War," *South China Morning Post*, August 15, 2020, https://www.scmp.com/week-asia/opinion/article/3097274/under-us-pressure-china-planning-economy-can-survive-protracted; and Katsuji Nakazawa, "Xi's US Strategy Recalls Mao's 'Protracted War,'" *Nikkei Asia*, January 10, 2019, https://asia.nikkei.com/Editor-s-Picks/China-up-close/Xi-s-US-strategy-recalls-Mao-s-protracted-war.

47. Mao Tse-tung, *On Protracted War* in *Selected Works of Mao Tse-tung* (Peking: Foreign Languages Press, 1967), vol. 11.
48. Information Office of the State Council of the People's Republic of China, *China's Military Strategy* (Beijing: Foreign Languages Press, May 2015): Part 3, http://english.www.gov.cn/archive/white_paper/2015/05/27/content_281475115610833.htm.
49. Mao Tse-tung, *On Protracted War* in *Selected Works of Mao Tse-tung*, 127, 133, 135, 136.
50. Ibid., 137.
51. Ibid., 137, 138, 142.
52. Ibid., 138–140.
53. Ibid., 140.
54. Ibid., 141, 143, 167,
55. Mao Tse-tung, *Introducing the Communist* in *Selected Works of Mao Tse-tung*, vol. II, 288, 289, http://www.marx2mao.com/PDFs/MaoSW2.pdf.
56. Mao Tse-tung, *On Protracted War* in *Selected Works of Mao Tse-tung*, vol. II, 159, 160.
57. Information Office of the State Council of the People's Republic of China, *China's Military Strategy*, Part III, http://en.people.cn/n/2015/0526/c90785-8897779.html.
58. In September 2022, the World Bank cut its estimate of China's growth for the year to 2.8%. Edward White and Mercedes Ruehl, "China Growth to Fall Behind Rest of Asia for First Time Since 1990," *Financial Times*, September 27, 2022, https://www.ft.com/content/ef425da7-0f94-484a-9f0c-40991be70ccc.
59. See Logan Wright, "Rethinking China's Economic Future," Rhodium Group, May 31, 2022, https://rhg.com/research/rethinking-chinas-economic-future/; and James Mayger, Tom Hancock, Yujing Liu, and Danny Lee, "China Data Show Economy Shrinking in Challenge to Xi's Target," Bloomberg, July 7, 2022, https://www.bloomberg.com/news/articles/2022-07-06/china-data-show-economy-shrinking-in-challenge-to-xi-s-target.
60. Wang Cong, Cao Siqi, and Chen Qingqing, "China Sets 'Pragmatic' Targets Through 2035," *Global Times*, October 29, 2020, http://www.globaltimes.cn/content/1205131.shtml.
61. See, for example, George Magnus, "From Economic Miracle to Mirage – Will China's GDP Ever Overtake the US?," *The Guardian*, December 29, 2021, https://www.theguardian.com/business/2021/dec/28/from-economic-miracle-to-mirage-will-chinas-gdp-ever-overtake-the-us.

62. Michael Beckley, "The United States Should Fear a Faltering China: Beijing's Assertiveness Betrays Its Desperation," *Foreign Affairs*, October 28, 2019, https://www.foreignaffairs.com/articles/china/2019-10-28/united-states-should-fear-faltering-china.
63. Ibid.
64. Ibid.
65. Ibid.
66. Antonio Graceffo, "Could China's Massive Public Debt Torpedo the Global Economy?," *War on the Rocks*, December 2, 2021, https://warontherocks.com/2021/12/could-chinas-massive-public-debt-torpedo-the-global-economy/.
67. Daniel H. Rosen, "China's Economic Reckoning: The Price of Failed Reforms," *Foreign Affairs*, July/August 2021, https://www.foreignaffairs.com/articles/china/2021-06-22/chinas-economic-reckoning; and David P. Goldman, "China is First Out of the Gate to Industry 4.0," *Asia Times*, June 26, 2021,, https://asiatimes.com/2021/06/china-is-first-out-of-the-gate-to-industry-4-0/.
68. Karen Yeung, "China's Economy Downshifts to Slower Growth Path as Focus Turns to Social Equality, National Safety," *South China Morning Post*, August 3, 2021, https://www.scmp.com/economy/china-economy/article/3143651/chinas-economy-downshifts-slower-growth-path-focus-turns?utm_medium=email&utm_source=cm&utm_campaign=enlz-chinaec.
69. Qiushi Feng, Wei-Jun Jean Yeung, Zhenglian Wang, and Yi Zeng, "Age of Retirement and Human Capital in an Aging China, 2015–2050," *European Journal of Population* 35, no. 1 (February 2019, 29–62, https://www.ncbi.nlm.nih.gov/pmc/articles/PMC6357252/.
70. Parton, "China – A Look Ahead to 2021 and Beyond."
71. Xi Jinping, "Some major issues of the national medium- and long-term economic and social development strategy," (A speech by Xi Jinping at the seventh meeting of the Central Committee on April 10, 2020, reported in detail in Bill Bishop, *Sinocism*, November 3, 2020).
72. For an excellent report that compares China's and America's progress in high-technology sectors, see Graham Allison, Kevin Klyman, Karina Barbesino, and Hugo Yen, *The Great Tech Rivalry: China vs the U.S.* (Cambridge, MA: Belfer Center, Harvard Kennedy School, December 2021).
73. Yoko Kubota, "Chips are Down for Chinese Tech Start-ups," *Wall Street Journal*, January 10, 2022, https://www.theaustralian.com.au/business/the-wall-street-journal/chips-are-down-for-chinese-tech-startups/news-story/f1747438217ded67be4d93d241f81781.

74. Semiconductor Industry Association, "China's Share of Global Chip Sales Now Surpasses Taiwan's, Closing in on Europe's and Japan's," January 10, 2022, https://www.semiconductors.org/chinas-share-of-global-chip-sales-now-surpasses-taiwan-closing-in-on-europe-and-japan/.
75. "Annual FDI Outflow From China 2010–2020," *Statista*, October 28, 2021, https://www.statista.com/statistics/865550/china-stock-of-direct-investments-abroad/.
76. Dirk Van Der Kley, "Do Belt and Road Projects Provide Local Benefits?," *The Interpreter*, The Lowy Institute, May 13, 2021, https://www.lowyinstitute.org/the-interpreter/bri-increasingly-focused-benefits-locals.
77. Frank Tang, "China's Economic Strategy Shift Shows Xi Jinping is Preparing for 'Worst Case Scenario,' Analysts Say," *South China Morning Post*, May 25, 2020, https://www.scmp.com/economy/china-economy/article/3085969/chinas-economic-strategy-shift-shows-xi-jinping-preparing.
78. Tom Hankok and Tom Orlic, "Xi Jinping's Capitalist Smackdown Sparks $1 Trillion Reckoning," Bloomberg, August 2, 2021, https://www.bloomberg.com/news/features/2021-08-01/china-tech-crackdown-communist-party-policy-changes-behind-1-trillion-selloff?sref=aLHq7grJ.
79. Lingling Wei, "Xi Jinping Aims to Rein in Chinese Capitalism, Hew to Mao's Socialist Vision," *Wall Street Journal*, September 20, 2021, https://www.wsj.com/articles/xi-jinping-aims-to-rein-in-chinese-capitalism-hew-to-maos-socialist-vision-11632150725.
80. See, for example, "Secretive Chinese Committee Draws Up List to Replace U.S. Tech," Bloomberg, November 17, 2021, https://www.bloomberg.com/news/articles/2021-11-16/secretive-chinese-committee-draws-up-list-to-replace-u-s-tech.
81. "Xi Doctrine Downplays GDP Growth as Yardstick for China Success," Bloomberg, November 17, 2021, https://www.bloomberg.com/news/articles/2021-11-17/xi-doctrine-downplays-gdp-growth-as-yardstick-for-china-success; and Derek Scissors, "China's Growth Spurt Ends. What's Next?," *American Enterprise Institute*, November 2021, https://www.aei.org/research-products/report/chinas-growth-spurt-ends-whats-next/.
82. See commentary in Marcus Clay and Roderick Lee, *Unmasking the Devil in the Chinese Details: A Study Note on the "Science of Military Strategy 2020"* (Alabama: China Aerospace Studies Institute, US Air University, January 2022), https://www.airuniversity.af.edu/Portals/10/

CASI/documents/Research/Other-Topics/2022-01-24%20SMS%202020%20in%20Perspective.pdf.
83. Steve Trimble, "Power Shift," *Aviation Week and Space Technology*, (September 13–26, 2021): 16–18, https://archive.aviationweek.com/issue/20210913#!&pid=16.
84. See this argued in Jude Blanchette, "Xi's Gamble: 'The Race to Consolidate Power and Stave off Disaster."
85. See, for example: Bonnie S. Glaser and Jude Blanchette, "Ukraine War Should Counsel Chinese Caution on Taiwan," *Wall Street Journal*, March 8, 2022, https://www.wsj.com/articles/ukraine-war-chinese-caution-taiwan-russia-china-putin-xi-jinping-invasion-sovereignty-11646769700 ; Keith Nobles and Jimmy Sengenberger, "The Chinese Communist Party is Rethinking its Taiwan Strategy," *Newsweek*, March 1, 2022, https://www.newsweek.com/chinese-communist-party-rethinking-its-taiwan-strategy-opinion-1683774; Bonny Lin and John Culver, "China's Taiwan Invasion Plans May Get Faster and Deadlier," *Foreign Policy*, April 19, 2022, https://foreignpolicy.com/2022/04/19/china-invasion-ukraine-taiwan/.
86. This case is made in Jude Blanchette, "'Reunification' with Taiwan Through Force Would be a Pyrrhic Victory for China," *CSIS Brief*, November 22, 2022, https://www.csis.org/analysis/reunification-taiwan-through-force-would-be-pyrrhic-victory-china
87. See Xi Jinping's decision-making culture discussed in John Garnaut, "Engineers of the Soul: What Australia needs to know about ideology in Xi Jinping's China," https://sinocism.com/p/engineers-of-the-soul-ideology-in.
88. There are many quality journals and books that address China's strategic development. Online journals that are particularly useful include Bill Bishop's *Sinocism* (a weekday catalogue of events in China) and the Jamestown Foundation *China Brief* and *The China Leadership Monitor* (a quarterly online journal discussing issues relevant to the Chinese leadership). Amongst the many books of relevance include Michael Pillsbury, *The Hundred Year Marathon* (New York: Henry Holt and Company, 2019); Rush Doshi, *The Long Game* (Oxford: Oxford University Press, 2021); Richard McGregor, *The Party* (London: Penguin Books, 2012); George Magnus, *Red Flags* (New Haven: Yale University Press, 2018); Aaron L. Friedberg, *Getting China Wrong* (Cambridge, Polity Press, 2022); Joe Reynolds, ed., *China's Evolving Military Strategy* (Washington, DC: The Jamestown Foundation, 2016); Robert D. Blackwill and Jennifer M. Harris, *War by Other Means* (Cambridge: Harvard University

Press, 2017); Col. Qiao Lian and Col. Wang Xiangsui, *Unrestricted Warfare* (New Delhi: Natraj Publishers, 2007); Roger Faligot, *Chinese Spies* (Brunswick, Australia: Scribe Publications, 2019); Clive Hamilton, *Silent Invasion: China's Influence in Australia* (Melbourne: Hardie Grant Books, 2018); Alex Joske, *Spies and Lies* (Melbourne: Hardie Grant Books, 2022); and Elizabeth C. Economy, *The Third Revolution* (New York: Oxford University Press, 2018).

Chapter 3

US Concepts and Planning for War in the Indo-Pacific

How the US Would Fight a War

Planning for war in the United States contrasts markedly with that in China. While details of specific American campaign strategies and operational plans are classified, many relevant issues are discussed in administration statements, reports to Congress, think tank and academic publications, and in open debates. This chapter draws on these public sources to highlight seventeen key indicators of the US planning for war and then lists fifteen key characteristics that would likely feature prominently in the way America would fight such a war.

The United States approaches the challenge of major war against China with its own strategic positioning, interests, culture, and set of assumptions. The US has many strengths but also some notable weaknesses. The implications for deterrence, how such a major war would be fought, the possible duration of such a war, and the prospects of victory are profound.

Seventeen Key Indicators of American War Plans

Indicator #1: Geography, History, and Strategic Culture

A key issue for the United States is that its continental landmass is located a long way from the most likely centers of combat in the Western Pacific, along India's northern borders and in Central Asia. While the United States has some important territories in the Western and Central Pacific and major military bases in the Indian Ocean and the Persian Gulf, the primary weight of American military power is located on the eastern side of the Pacific. This has many strategic implications.

The expanses of the Pacific and Indian Oceans are vast. Most American ships based on the US West Coast take about 21 days to reach Taiwan, and ships based in Alaska would take 17 days to arrive. Deploying to key parts of the Indian Ocean takes even longer. Some American aircraft can reach key operational areas in the Western Pacific within 10–20 hours from the continental United States, but nearly all aircraft need to refuel en route and the times they can remain on station are modest. Most of the priority areas of operation require transits of 4,000–8,000 miles.

This geographic separation accentuates the importance of American forward bases in and close to relevant theaters. In the Indo-Pacific the primary naval and air bases operated by the United States are in Japan, South Korea, Guam, the Philippines, Diego Garcia, and the Persian Gulf. However, as can be seen in figure 4, they are few in number, highly concentrated, and would be difficult to defend in a major war. There are also limits on the scale and types of forces that could be deployed sensibly to these facilities.

The American defense community appreciates the vulnerability of its forces and bases in the Indo-Pacific, and innovative work has been undertaken in recent years to disperse, protect, enhance mobility, and strengthen combat sustainability in the theater.

Figure 4. Primary United States Military Operational Bases in the Western Pacific and the Indian Ocean.

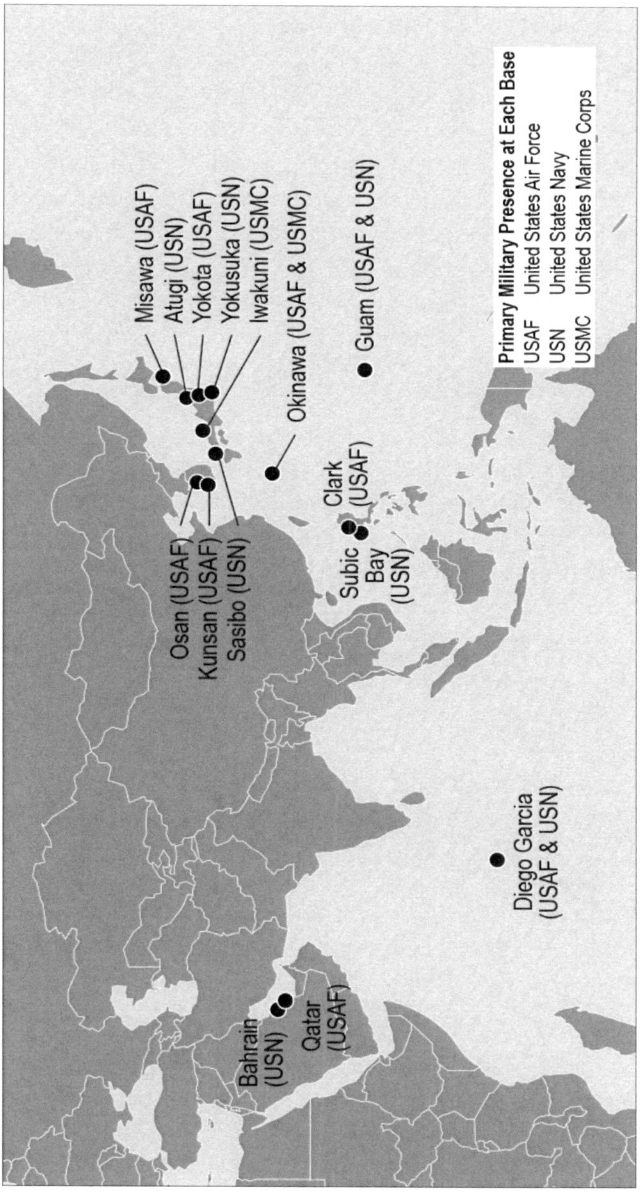

The US Navy can certainly conduct operations in forward locations, but units on the surface of the sea maneuvering between the first and second island chains and the Chinese coast would face high levels of risk, especially in the opening phases of a major war. The US Marines are gearing up to conduct widely dispersed, small-unit denial operations in the island chains and adjacent littoral areas. The US Air Force can launch some transoceanic strikes, but most of its aircraft have shorter ranges and would need to operate from or through operational facilities within the theater. The US Army is also capable of conducting operations in the Indo-Pacific, but it too lacks the logistics capability to sustain operations for extended periods in the theater unless supported by long supply chains from the US mainland or from local allied resources.

There are many implications. During the first days of a major war, the United States would have little choice but to fight with whatever forces were already in the theater and the few units based in continental US that could launch strikes across the breadth of the Pacific. In the face of surprise attacks, some in-theater forces could disperse and seek greater protection but they would likely be outnumbered and out-gunned, and those operating on the surface of the sea or on land may suffer heavy casualties. Most reinforcements coming from the continental United States would need to fight their way into the theater, fight to stay on station, and then probably fight their way out again. Operations of this type are likely to be very demanding and may need to be limited in scope and scale during the initial phases of a war.

These intense, highly dispersed, multi-domain operations would be markedly different from the types of operations the United States and its allies have conducted in Afghanistan, Iraq, and elsewhere in recent decades. Those were mostly low-intensity campaigns conducted against medium-technology, subnational groups, with the US and its allies being supported by large and relatively secure in-theater base and logistic systems. Fighting a high-technology peer opponent who is conducting intense multiple-domain operations supported by well-developed base and logistic facilities in their nearby homeland would be a far more demanding task.

Having most strategic assets and forces located in the continental United States at the beginning of a major war would, of course, provide relatively high levels of security for key assets and personnel during the processes of mobilization. However, these phases of activation would take many months, and the costs of recovering campaign momentum and territories lost in the interim could be very high.

These challenges are not dissimilar to those that faced American forces in both world wars. In each of those conflicts, it took more than a year for the United States to prepare, properly equip, and deploy substantial forces over transoceanic distances, and it took two years for the full weight of American military power to be brought to bear.

Gearing up now to fight and prevail in broadly similar circumstances in the Indo-Pacific would require strong and sustained administration and congressional support. Large parts of the US national security community and many parts of industry and the broader society would need to be reorientated, redirected, relocated, and retrained. Emergency measures would be required to fill many capability gaps. Even in a crisis, these initiatives could not be completed quickly.

One of the more obvious capability shortfalls is in transport and logistic ships that would be essential to support such transoceanic operations. American forces currently have ready access to only about 160 cargo and tanker vessels.[1] Beyond that, intra-theater transport would be heavily reliant on chartered vessels, most of which would need to be obtained from foreign companies.

A key conclusion is that in most respects, the American military would need to fight a major war with China at a geographic disadvantage. This handicap would probably be especially acute in the first few weeks and months when forward-deployed American and allied forces could expect to be heavily pressed. These dispersed, mobile, well-armed, and difficult-to-target marine and other forces operating in and around the first island chain are sometimes called the "inside forces."[2] They would operate in close partnership with forward-deployed submarines and long-range air force units. Some capabilities that can deliver substantial effects over transoceanic distances would also play key roles from the first hours. Particularly prominent are likely to be information warfare, cyber, counter-space, and related units.

There would also be much larger, heavily armed American units, such as carrier strike groups and some army divisions, that may take some time to deploy to the theater but could provide the Chinese with more readily identifiable targets. In the first days of a major war these forces, which are often described as "outside forces,"[3] would probably maneuver in greater depth, while delivering heavy firepower against enemy units operating in and around the first and second island chains.

In the first weeks and months of multi-domain combat, the contributions of the Indo-Pacific allies are likely to be exceptionally valuable. Many allied units are of high quality, intimately familiar with the complexities of the region, and well-practiced in operating with US forces and with each other.

A further strategic consequence of America's geographical remoteness from the primary theater of conflict is that, depending on the detailed conduct of the war, there is a risk that the US public may feel detached, remote, and almost disconnected from the conflict. Polling conducted in recent years suggests that in most circumstances Americans are heavily focused on immediate domestic affairs rather than on military operations conducted in distant theaters designed to secure long-term strategic interests. This lack of deep public engagement was a notable feature of US military operations in Vietnam, Iraq, and Afghanistan, and it had profound effects, not least on the morale of military personnel in the field. This mental detachment of the American public was summarized succinctly by an American lieutenant colonel in Baghdad in 2006 who remarked to a journalist that "we're at war; America's at the mall."[4] Over time this lack of strong public engagement undermined presidential and congressional commitment to the struggles in Iraq and Afghanistan and eroded American staying power.

Whether this limited public commitment would be evident in a US-China war would probably depend on the nature, scale, and geographic spread of Chinese operations. If, during the first days of a war, Chinese forces launched heavy attacks on American forces and bases causing high casualties, the United States public would draw parallels with Pearl Harbor, rally behind the president, and demand strong retribution. The outcry would be especially strong were China to launch attacks on Hawaii or the continental United States. However, if China avoided direct attacks on US and allied forces, the interest and involvement of the American public in military operations on the other side of the world may be weaker and less enduring.

The potential mental detachment of significant sections of the American public from the primary operating theaters of some categories of Indo-Pacific war contrasts starkly with the perceptions of the Chinese public. Most Chinese view Taiwan, the South China Sea, the Senkaku Islands, and large swathes of border country in India and Bhutan as being inalienable parts of their homeland. In consequence, American, Indian, and allied operations anywhere near these regions would be viewed by most Chinese citizens as an existential threat. The overwhelming Chinese view is that their leaders should not only strive to secure these and related territories but also must do so with all available resources. There is therefore a possibility that the two major protagonists in such a war may be worlds apart not only in physical geography but also in mental engagement and, ultimately, political will.

Indicator #2: Strategic Interests, Values, and Ideology

The declassified 2018 US Strategic Framework for the Indo-Pacific lists the top US interests in the theater as:

> Defend the homeland and American citizens abroad; prevent the spread of nuclear weapons and the means to deliver them;
>
> Preserve US economic, diplomatic, and military access to the most populous region of the world and more than one-third of the global economy;
>
> Enhance the credibility and effectiveness of our alliances; and
>
> Maintain US primacy in the region while protecting American core values and liberties at home.[5]

The US Strategic Framework then describes ten desired "end states" within the Indo-Pacific. Seven of the ten provide further insights into how the United States plans to approach any major conflict in the region. They emphasize the "maintenance of American diplomatic, economic, and military preeminence"; upholding the principles that have enabled US and regional prosperity and stability, including sovereignty, freedom of navigation and overflight, and so forth; the maintenance of free markets; the resolution of regional disputes lawfully without coercion; reinforcing the coordination of Association of Southeast Asian Nations (ASEAN) member states, strengthening the US strategic partnership with India; and working with international partners to resist Chinese attempts to undermine their sovereignty.

These priorities are those of a democratic status quo power. They do not portray the United States as a dominant and demanding hegemon. Prominence is certainly given to the maintenance of American strategic and economic power in the region. But the American role is described as being more that of a team leader that strives to uphold the sovereignty of independent states and their freedom from coercion according to international law.

These strategic priorities also reflect many of the underlying values and ideological foundations of the United States. The US Strategic Framework emphasizes the need to stand against those who seek to undermine individual human rights and liberties, engage in unfair business practices, and weaken, divide, and coerce regional states and communities. It explicitly states that a primary objective is to "promote US values throughout the region to maintain influence and counterbalance Chinese models of government."[6]

These references to many of the underlying principles and values of the founders of the United States republic speaks powerfully to most American citizens. Emphasizing American preparedness to fight not only for its strategic and economic interests but also for its deep ideological passions has certainly been a powerful driver of Americans in the past. As Princeton University professor Aaron Friedberg has stated, "historically what has moved and motivated the American people is a recognition that the principles on which their system is founded are under threat."[7]

These core interests, values and ideological principles provide the context for the US Strategic Framework's description of US military objectives and priority actions in the Indo-Pacific theater:

> **Objective:** Deter China from using military force against the United States and US allies and partners, and develop the capabilities and concepts to defeat Chinese actions across the spectrum of conflict.
>
> **Actions:** Enhance combat-credible US military presence and posture in the Indo-Pacific region to uphold US interests and security commitments.
>
> Devise and implement a defense strategy capable of, but not limited to: (1) denying China sustained air and sea dominance inside the "first island chain" in a conflict; (2) defending the first-island-chain nations, including Taiwan; and (3) dominating all domains outside the first island chain.
>
> Help our allies and partners improve their security posture, including military capabilities and interoperability, to ensure strategic independence and freedom from Chinese coercion.

> Expand partnerships and capabilities that limit China's ability to coerce allies and partners.[8]

The US National Defense Strategy of 2018 builds on these points by painting a larger vision for the country's strategic approach when it states:

> A long-term strategic competition requires the seamless integration of multiple elements of national power—diplomacy, information, economics, finance, intelligence, law enforcement, and military. More than any other nation, America can expand the competitive space, seizing the initiative to challenge our competitors where we possess advantages and they lack strength. A more lethal force, strong alliances and partnerships, American technological innovation, and a culture of performance will generate decisive and sustained US military advantages.[9]

The National Defense Strategy then talks about the US being "strategically predictable but operationally unpredictable" and "developing a lethal, agile and resilient force posture and employment."[10] In order to achieve these advances, it says that the US must:

> Foster a competitive mindset. To succeed in the emerging security environment, our Defense and Joint Force will have to out-think, out-maneuver, out-partner, and out-innovate revisionist powers, rogue regimes, terrorists and other threat actors.[11]

While these aspirations are highly relevant, there are questions about how much progress towards their achievement is being made and the outlook for their delivery during the coming decade.

Indicator #3: A Strong, Innovative Economy

The United States retains the world's largest national economy, the highest levels of productivity and, arguably, the most innovative and adaptive new-generation industries. It is also one of the more mature national economies, bringing with it sustained levels of moderate economic growth.

The US no longer leads the world in many types of mass manufacturing and heavy industry, with low levels of investment in these fields during the first decades of the twenty-first century.

The US economy is highly diversified and relatively self-sufficient. Trade as a percentage of GDP is only 23% compared to China's 35%.[12] Moreover, many of America's strategically sensitive imports are supplied by trusted allies and other international partners. While the US government and Congress are concerned about the vulnerability of some American supply chains, the economic security of the country is probably superior to that of any other major economy.

The United States also retains the status of being the world's preeminent financial center and its primary financial rule-maker. The US operates the world's leading stock market, and the US dollar is the world's most traded and trusted international currency. More than any other nation, the US is the center of the global economy. Most of these favored economic circumstances are unlikely to be seriously challenged during the coming decade.

In combination, these dimensions of American economic power provide the United States with many of the resources needed to fight and sustain a major war so long as the national leadership and the national citizenry remain supportive.

Indicator #4: Technological Leadership

While the United States has led the world in most technologies for over a century, its status as the global leader is now being contested by China and, in a more modest way, by some other countries. This change is evident in the numbers of patent applications submitted by various countries, the relative scale of advanced-technology industries, and changing market shares in everything from semiconductors to advanced telecommunications equipment and motor vehicles.

Exactly who is in the lead in particular areas is difficult to ascertain. The *Wall Street Journal* has reported that China is probably in the lead in 5G telecommunications, especially for modestly priced mass applications.[13] In artificial intelligence (AI), the Chinese are probably spending more money and publishing more research articles, but in many areas of applied AI they struggle to match the technological depth and the commercial agility of Microsoft, Alphabet's Google, and some other giant American corporations. In quantum technology, China may lead in some communications applications but the US and some of its allies almost certainly lead in quantum computing and a range of other applications.

In recent years successive US administrations, members of Congress, and business leaders have recognized the challenges to American technological leadership and launched initiatives designed to reinforce US preeminence.[14] However, given the scale of technology investments in China and other parts of the world, American leadership is being lost in some domains and cannot be taken for granted in other fields during the coming decade.

During past wars and other crises, the United States has demonstrated formidable abilities to invent, develop, and deploy highly creative strategies and systems that change the dynamics of a struggle. The first and second "offset strategies" are notable cases in point.[15] However, China is also working to develop "game-changing" capabilities and now possesses superior manufacturing capabilities to roll out many types of advanced systems quickly and on a large scale. Beijing can be expected to rapidly deploy some technological and other surprises during the course of a major war.

Indicator #5: Demographic and Educational Strength

At 334 million people, the United States has the world's third largest population, behind China and India. Moreover, the American population continues to grow. This is despite the fertility rate (children per female) falling in recent years to just below the level needed for population stability. Nevertheless, the momentum gained from earlier decades together with a steady immigration rate of about a million people each year means that the American population will continue to grow till at least the middle of the century.

While the rate of growth in the American population is slowing and the average age is rising, the demographic challenges faced by the United States are much less serious than those confronting China. With the American workforce still growing and the quality of the labor force high, US productivity per head continues to lead the world in most sectors.

This performance is partly a consequence of the contribution made by the American education system. The United States is home to many of the world's leading universities, schools, and other educational institutions. The standards at the elite institutions are high, and the performance of many graduates from these institutions is impressive.

However, this exceptional performance does not characterize the entire American education system, large parts of which are little better than average and suffering a further relative decline.[16] The international rankings for 15-year-old student performance show that American students ranked 11th in reading, just behind New Zealand and three spots ahead of Australia. In mathematics, American students ranked 37th compared to 29th for Australia and 18th for the United Kingdom. In science, American students ranked 18th, one place behind Australia, two behind Germany and thirteen behind Japan.[17]

Moreover, there are numerous indications that standard measures of educational performance do not capture qualitative declines in teaching and educational delivery, patterns of learning, and in post-educational functional performance. In at least some educational systems in the US, there appear to be declining standards of fact-based research, critical analysis, applied logic, and problem solving.[18]

Declining educational standards in most parts of the United States have serious consequences for the nation's economic growth and development.

They also have important consequences for national security. Large numbers of poorly or moderately educated people will constrain national performance and flexibility when the country is placed under pressure. They will significantly impact the quality of media performance, broader public assessment of national issues, and the standard and speed of decision-making in crises and wars. Importantly, they will also increase the vulnerability of the American people to the types of "dis-integration" operations now being conducted against the US by China and Russia.

It is certainly the case that American colleges and universities still produce some graduates with exceptional intellectual capabilities. This small elite will likely continue to have a disproportionate impact on the nation's performance in wars. However, it is doubtful that this can compensate fully for the broader societal decline in fact-based analysis, rigorous assessment, and rational, bias-free discourse, debate, and decision-making.

Indicator #6: Strong Alliance Network

One of the special strategic assets possessed by the United States is its network of alliances. Some eminent Americans have gone so far as to state that "the United States principal adversaries are more constrained by its network of alliances than by its [America's] military might."[19]

An argument periodically made is that the United States cannot provide optimal security for itself on its own. National and international security is best seen as a "team sport" played by a strong network of trusted allies that will almost always outflank even the most powerful authoritarian opponents who are forced to operate largely on their own. Henry Kissinger captured the special nature of America's alliance relationships when he said:

> Our ties with the great industrial democracies are ... not alliances of convenience but a union of principle in defense of values and a way of life.

> Our efforts to build peace and progress reflect our deep-seated belief in freedom and in the hope of a better future for all mankind. These are values we share with our closest allies, the great industrial democracies.[20]

Because America's alliance relationships are built on much more than shared interests in a particular issue but also on shared values, beliefs, and standards of behavior, deep trust has been developed, the depth and breadth of cooperation is exceptional, and the relationships are mostly enduring. In many cases, allied cooperation has been reinforced by frequent combined military operations and histories of even larger combined campaigns during past crises and wars. The passage of time has also fostered strong personal friendships between allied communities. Some allies even describe their partners as carrying a similar status to family.

There are many practical consequences for American power, especially in major conflict and war. Most obviously, the allies contribute substantial financial, industrial, military, and other resources to supplement US-led operations in nearly all theaters. Allies also routinely extend US production lines for priority military systems, thereby reducing unit costs for all participating countries and strengthening cross-alliance interoperability. An important consequence is that the defense forces of many allies can slip into even distant theaters to provide valuable reinforcement to American operations with little notice.

Allies often provide substantial intelligence, combat training, and logistic support services to deployed American forces. In most regions of strategic importance, local allied forces can share extensive operational experience, detailed knowledge, and strong networks of personal contacts. The intelligence and operational capabilities of some allies are of high quality.

Allies also provide access to strategically valuable territories, bases, logistic support assets, training areas, and much else besides. In the Indo-

Pacific, some allies and strategic partners are capable of providing much more extensive support to American forces when required. A notable case is Australia whose continental expanses provide extensive options for dispersed basing backed by quality civil infrastructure, advanced industrial capabilities, and a skilled, supportive workforce and public.

In recent years some Indo-Pacific allies and partners have launched major initiatives to expand their munitions and military equipment manufacturing, repair, and support capabilities. These new industrial capabilities will not only strengthen allied capacities to build and maintain local forces, but they are also capable of providing substantial support to visiting American units. Notable expansions of military industrial capabilities are underway in South Korea, Japan, Taiwan, Australia, and India.

In the event of a major conflict in the Indo-Pacific that stretched the industrial support capabilities of the United States and its local allies, there would probably be scope to also draw on the support capabilities of more distant allies and partners. In some categories of contingency, particularly important support could be provided by the advanced industries of Europe.

There are also many less tangible forms of assistance that allies can provide to the United States that, in some Indo-Pacific contingencies, could make a profound difference. Allies can contribute fresh thinking, surprisingly advanced technologies, innovative operational concepts, cultures of experimentation, habits of speedy implementation, and the rigorous testing of American concepts and systems. Allies can also make a disproportionate contribution to some categories of operational and campaign planning.

America's allies do not agree on everything. Indeed, there have been times in the past when Washington's management of alliance relationships has been demanding and difficult. However, nearly all Western officials and analysts agree that America's alliance network is a substantial strategic asset that is unmatched. This is particularly the case when planning to fight a major war in a theater as expansive, complex, and demanding as one in the Indo-Pacific.

Indicator #7: American Dominance of the Exterior Lines

When the forward projection of US forces into the Indo-Pacific is combined with the dispersed basing and forces of America's theater allies and partners, another important strategic advantage becomes clear: The United States and its allies are in a strong position to dominate the rimlands of the Eurasian landmass and, in any serious war, interdict most shipping and many aviation movements to and from China.

The thinking behind this key advantage has a resonance in the strategic debates of a much earlier era. In 1904 Sir Halford Mackinder published a paper in which he argued that the Eurasian landmass stretching from Eastern Europe and through central and East Asia bounded in the south by India and the Persian Gulf comprised the "global heartland."[21] Mackinder asserted that whoever dominated this "central location" would control what he called the "world island" and that whoever controlled the "world island" would dominate the planet. The parts of the world beyond his heartland he called the "outer crescent." His view was that the rest of Asia, Australasia, Africa, Western Europe, and the Americas were geographically and culturally alien to inner Eurasia and of far lower strategic importance.

While Mackinder's theory appeared to be confirmed by many of the events of the Second World War and the strength of the Soviet Union during the following four decades, a rival theory soon gained greater prominence. Nicholas J. Spykman argued in 1942 that Mackinder overstated the geopolitical significance of the heartland and that the "rimlands" surrounding the Eurasian heartland were the key to global domination.[22]

Developments in recent decades suggest that Spykman's argument has greater weight. Most of the world's population, most of its industry, and the bulk of its wealth are located within 200km of coastlines. A large proportion of the world's cities and many centers of government have been built in these littoral zones. Moreover, the increasing globalization of the international economy in recent decades has reinforced these trends. The scale of international trade, the vast tonnages involved, and the frequency of shipping and aircraft movements are unprecedented. The coastal rimlands of Eurasia together with the offshore islands and continents clearly have preeminent strategic value in the modern era, and these are dominated by the United States and its allies.

In the event of a major crisis or war, China has the capability to contest its closer rimlands in the Western Pacific, the mountainous regions to India's north, and parts of Central Asia. It also has the capability to launch selective strikes and disruptive operations further afield, including against the American homeland. However, its capability to interdict US and allied shipping and other trade in a sustained manner would be limited.

At the same time, the United States and its allies would dominate most of the rimlands from the outset. They are capable of establishing effective control over most international shipping and many aircraft movements with Chinese destinations. The only significant exceptions are likely to be movements in the immediate approaches to China's national territory and transits across China's long land borders with Russia, Mongolia, the central Asian republics, and Pakistan.

The Chinese are well aware of the country's heavy reliance on international trade, and Xi Jinping has launched numerous programs to strengthen China's self-reliance. Nevertheless, American dominance of the maritime and air rimlands continues to carry strong strategic deterrence and formidable wartime leverage.

Indicator #8: Strategic Nuclear Deterrence

A long-standing strategic advantage of the United States over China has been its capability to deter the vertical escalation of any major war because of its far superior strategic nuclear forces. The US continues to have a much larger and more mature strategic nuclear arsenal, and it maintains a strong deterrence posture. However, China has moved to modernize and expand its strategic nuclear arsenal in recent years, and there are indications that some American and allied assumptions about the role of Chinese nuclear forces in a major war warrant review.

The US strategic nuclear arsenal has three primary components. First, there are 400 Minuteman III missiles deployed in underground missile silos in the American midwest. Second, the US Navy operates fourteen Ohio-class ballistic-missile-firing submarines each of which can carry up to twenty Trident D5 missiles. Third, the US Air Force operates twenty B2 Spirit and forty-six B52H Stratofortress bombers that can launch nuclear tripped cruise missiles or drop gravity bombs. The US currently has a total of 1,467 operational strategic nuclear warheads deployed.

In recent years the United States has launched major programs to modernize all three legs of its strategic nuclear arsenal. First, a new land-based strategic missile—the Sentinel—is under development to replace the Minuteman III force. Second, the US Navy has ordered the production of a force of twelve new Columbia class ballistic missile-firing submarines. And third, the US Air Force has started to build some 100 new B21 strategic nuclear bombers.

China also now has three legs to its strategic nuclear arsenal. The first is a force of 104 intercontinental ballistic missiles of several types that are deployed either in underground missile silos or on large vehicles (called transporter erector launchers or TELs) for movement through extensive underground tunnel systems. Second, the PLA Navy operates six Jin-class ballistic-missile-firing submarines, each of which can carry up to twelve CH-SS-N-14 missiles. And third, China operates a small force of H-6N bombers that carry air-launched ballistic missiles.

China is also modernizing and extending its strategic nuclear arsenal. At least 200 new underground missile silos were reported to be under construction during 2021 in Western China and the Pentagon has reported that China is likely to deploy some 1,500 strategic nuclear warheads by 2035.[23] A new class of ballistic-missile-firing submarine is also believed to be in advanced development. In addition, China has a long-range strategic bomber in advanced development that is expected to greatly strengthen the third leg of China's strategic nuclear arsenal.

The superiority of the US strategic force and of US strategic nuclear deterrence appear likely to be maintained for the next several decades. However, there are at least four reasons to be concerned about such standard judgements.

First, Chinese strategic nuclear plans, programs, and doctrines are being developed within a largely opaque military-industrial complex. Many aspects of China's current and future nuclear development are hidden and uncertain. Moreover, because China has thus far refused to participate in strategic arms reduction talks, there have been few opportunities for extensive discussions on such matters with the United States and the West.

Second, there are indications that China may be developing some completely new types of ballistic missiles and other strategic weaponry that have the potential to be highly destabilizing and potentially lead to catastrophic misperceptions in future crises.[24]

Third, there is evidence that China has developed low-yield nuclear weapons and some elements of nuclear doctrine that envisage the early use of nuclear weaponry in combination with cyber and other instruments to win a substantial theater advantage in certain contingencies. As Andrew Krepinevich argues, these types of development have the potential to erode the long-standing "nuclear firebreak" between Chinese conventional operations and nuclear war.[25]

Fourth, the United States is now confronted by two potentially hostile major nuclear powers. Were Russia and China to coordinate their nuclear force development, deployment, and operational planning, the challenge for the maintenance of American and allied deterrence and defense would be greatly complicated.

The bottom line is that the United States currently possesses a clear advantage in strategic nuclear deterrence. However, China's military planning is moving in some new and potentially destabilizing directions that will likely force a serious review of American assumptions about the future for nuclear deterrence and warfighting.

Indicator #9: America Handicapped by Misperceptions About the Nature of Future War

American thinking about a major war in the Indo-Pacific is mostly very conventional. The US public assumes that a future war will be the business of the military but not a major concern for them. Even amongst military and national security professionals, the primary focus is on developing and deploying a conventional military force—albeit a high-technology one—for operations around the first and second island chains in the Western Pacific. In extremis, a large-scale, extended war is mostly conceptualized as a high-tech version of World War II. These widely held assumptions drive American war-planning and are the backbone of most American defense-capability-development decisions.

The main problem with this approach is that the shape of any war is not determined by one side but by at least two. And, as discussed in chapter 2, China is preparing to fight a different kind of war than that envisaged by most Americans. The Chinese conception of war emphasizes many non-kinetic, nonmilitary capabilities, designed to weaken, divide, mislead, confuse, and wear down the enemy well in advance of any kinetic exchanges, and these operations are also designed to be turbocharged through all violent phases of conflict until victory is won.

Several large Chinese government agencies undertake these operations often in a coordinated manner and with considerable professionalism. They use instruments and modes that extend far beyond those of standard influence, persuasion, propaganda, disinformation, and lawfare to include those that in the past have been labeled "active measures" such as coercion, bribery, corruption, kidnapping, and sabotage. The Chinese now employ all of these measures together with physical and cyber intrusions in creative combinations tailored for specific operational targets.

These types of operation have mostly been used in the past for intelligence gathering, recruiting foreign operatives and agents of influence, intimidating Chinese nationals abroad, and progressing Beijing's views on specific issues such as territorial claims in the South China Sea, the origins of COVID-19, and China's "reeducation" programs for China's Uyghur and Kazak minorities. In recent years, however, the Chinese have adopted some of the techniques pioneered by the Russians to take these operations to a new level of social manipulation. The intent of some more recent operations is not so much to achieve an immediate tactical objective for the Chinese Communist Party. It is rather to penetrate, mislead, divide, and confuse allied and other targeted societies, corrode and collapse their economic backbones, and discredit many of the key institutions that have been the primary upholders of community values, interests, cohesion, and national pride.

The Chinese do not usually create an issue in order to manipulate or disrupt a foreign society but rather monitor fringe groups or radicals, distill the gist of their arguments, generate strongly worded statements, slogans and/or fake stories, and then amplify the messaging dramatically using social media "regiments" and trolls. Two of the leading Chinese troll entities are the 50 Cent Army and the Cyber Army, but there are also large contractors involved. Some of the "people" conducting these social media operations are not even real—they are AI-driven automated bots geared to amplify disinformation, propaganda, and conspiracy theories.[26] A notable case is the reported Chinese campaign in social media to manipulate debates leading up to the 2022 US midterm elections.[27]

These operations are often supported by cyber activities and locally deployed agents. Foreign politically aligned journalists and community leaders will routinely join the fray, and traditional media organizations will often note the surge in social media commentary, report the story at face value, and give the controversy even greater prominence.

Promoting unconventional views in democratic states often triggers a strong reaction. Once early signs of community objections are observed, Chinese trolls may be directed to switch sides to goad the "reactors" at the other end of the spectrum into action. A further fake story or two and the sheer weight of thousands of troll messages may amplify the counteroffensive.

The staff of electronic, print, and other media organizations in allied countries sometimes push one side of the debate or another, and not infrequently politicians, senior business, trade union, church and other community leaders can be spurred to state strong positions and even join political arguments. The primary Chinese purpose of these operations is not to "win" an argument but rather to stir up dissent, division, and community polarization. Families grow more suspicious of the people next door, business colleagues engage in arguments on false premises, communities grow less trusting of the people in the next suburb, and the reputations and legitimacy of many traditionally neutral and widely supported community organizations, churches, and government agencies are seriously damaged. China's goal is to corrode American and allied societies over time, weaken their moral cohesion, strengthen divisions, undermine industrial strength and resilience, and markedly increase their vulnerability to manipulation and collapse in future crises.

The PLA calls these operations "enemy dis-integration work," and it trains personnel to conduct them in both "peacetime" and war. "Enemy dis-integration work" has always been a key PLA mission; it is codified in the PLA's "Political Work Regulations" and is a primary role of the PLA's 300,000-strong Strategic Support Force.[28] Admiral Philip Davidson stated in congressional testimony that when all agency staff and contractors are included, China's "vast disinformation machine" contains "nearly one million people."[29]

These operations have a long history in China. Weakening the adversary's cohesion and resolve were foundational elements of Mao Zedong's campaigns against the Kuomintang and the Japanese, and these are deeply etched into Chinese strategic doctrine. Xi Jinping grew up living and breathing "dis-integration work" because his father directed these political warfare operations for much of his career.[30] Now as CCP Secretary and president of China, Xi personally directs relevant Chinese agencies in these operations through his chairmanship of the Politburo Standing Committee and the Central Military Commission.

The current form of Chinese dis-integration operations can be seen particularly clearly in those currently being conducted against Taiwan. Michael J. Cole, editor of the *Taiwan Democracy Bulletin*, describes the objectives of these Chinese operations as:

- Corrode, bypass, and manipulate Taiwan's democratic institutions, elections, and public trust therein;
- Undermine Taiwan's morale and weaken resistance to Beijing's objectives by exacerbating feelings of abandonment, isolation and inevitability;
- Sow confusion, exacerbate divisions, and contradictions within society;
- Co-opt elites, businesspeople, politicians, retired military officers, civil society, and the media; and
- Coerce the CCP's opponents.[31]

In Taiwan and most allied countries, Chinese entities appear to have been experimenting with these types of highly corrosive and divisive campaigns. They have been developed and employed to deeply influence and shape the media, educational institutions, businesses, key government agencies, and others.

For example, CCP-affiliated entities have worked hard to monopolize Chinese-language media in allied countries and to build influence in the mainstream local press and electronic media. In an approach that the Chinese call "borrow a boat to go out on the ocean," regular articles, print supplements, television stories, and other media materials are provided for use in the US and elsewhere.[32] Many cash-strapped media organizations in the US and allied countries have welcomed this "assistance."

Chinese operations in educational institutions have been designed to closely monitor ethnic Chinese students and staff,[33] attack, marginalize and force the dismissal of staff who are critical of China,[34] shape curricula and activities in ways that favor the CCP,[35] steal valuable intellectual property,[36] and recruit potential agents.[37]

While most Americans are aware of some of these activities, few are well informed about their breadth and scale. An even smaller group of Americans realizes that China is conducting social-manipulation operations as part of a strategic campaign to threaten allied cohesion. The Chinese leadership aspires to use these dis-integration operations to have the war half won before a major kinetic conflict begins.

Because of the conventional nature of American strategic planning, little priority is being given to the danger posed by this Chinese manipulation. American security and defense attention is focused almost entirely on developing a new generation of conventional military capabilities that can reassert undisputed military dominance of the maritime Western Pacific.[38] These initiatives are important and relatively easy to progress because they fall neatly within the Pentagon's responsibility. However, effectively countering Chinese operations across Beijing's much broader canvas of political manipulation is rarely addressed comprehensively. American monitoring of these Chinese and Russian operations is fragmented and patchy. Responses are not coordinated by any national strategy, and there is no integrated countercampaign. Potential legal constraints have not been seriously addressed, and responsibilities and appropriate resources are yet to be allocated. This is a serious vulnerability. Chinese and Russian political warfare operations are sapping the strategic power of the United States, its allies, and its security partners.

Indicator #10: Political and Social Fragilities at Home

A primary driver of Chinese campaigns to "dis-integrate" American society is the Chinese Communist Party's strong conviction that the core of United States strategic power is the unity, cohesion, and resilience of the American people. Their judgement is that the United States will only be able to wage and sustain a major conflict in the Indo-Pacific if a substantial majority of the people endorse the need to commit forces to fight such a war, knowing that the casualties are likely to be high and the struggle prolonged. Although a major war in the Indo-Pacific would probably be very different to anything experienced by the US for many decades, the behavior of the American public in conflicts since the Second World War gives pause for thought.

If the Chinese attack American and allied forces and inflict significant casualties, there is a strong probability that the US public would rally to the cause and support powerful counteraction—at least for the first few months. However, there must be doubt about how long this strong united stance would be sustained. The experiences of Korea, Vietnam, Iraq, and Afghanistan suggest that Americans may be prepared to commit forces initially to secure priority interests on the other side of the Pacific but that such commitments over time may be difficult to sustain politically. Eventually, continuation of the struggle may prove to be impossible.

The basis for such doubts lies not only in US endurance during past conflicts but also on the substantial changes taking place in American society. Recent polling suggests that the American public has clear and consistent views on most international policy and security issues. For instance, during the last four decades, between 60 and 70% of the American public have regularly indicated that they believe it would be best for the United States to play an active part in world affairs rather than withdraw.[39]

There also appears to be a strengthening of American public support for international action in important Indo-Pacific contingencies. The results of a 2021 poll indicate that if North Korea invaded South Korea or if China invaded Taiwan, a clear majority of Americans favor the commitment of US troops.[40]

However, given the substantial increase in polarization and political partisanship that now characterizes the views of the US public on almost every issue, there must be serious questions about the resilience of the American public to stay the course in the face of heavy combat casualties when the issues at stake may be viewed by many as being the primary concern of countries on the other side of the world.

The Chinese and Russian regimes perceive the depth of political and social division in the US as a strategic weakness they can exploit. One measure of this division is the party approval ratings of new presidents a year after their election. As can be seen in figure 5, the partisan divide has almost tripled since the Eisenhower administration in the 1950s and the Johnson administration in the 1960s.[41]

In the 1950s and 1960s, the views of Democrat and Republican voters approving the president's performance in his first year were only 20–30% apart, no matter which party occupied the White House. By the 1980s, the gap between the supporters of the two parties on the president's performance in the first year had widened to 45%. During the Obama administration, it rose to 60%, in the Trump era it rose again to 80%, and then it receded a little under Biden to 70%. In the first year of the Biden administration 76% of Democrats approved of the president's performance whereas only 6% of Republicans did. The level of continuing political polarization is substantial.

Figure 6 shows that the support bases of the two parties have also become much more distinct in recent years. For example, 78% of white evangelicals vote Republican whereas only 17% vote Democrat, 62% of white non-college-educated men vote Republican whereas only 30% vote Democrat, 60% of rural southerners vote Republican but only 33% vote Democrat, and 57% of Americans who attend religious services weekly vote Republican but only 37% of these people vote Democrat.[42]

Figure 5. Percentage of Population Approving the President's Job During the First Year.

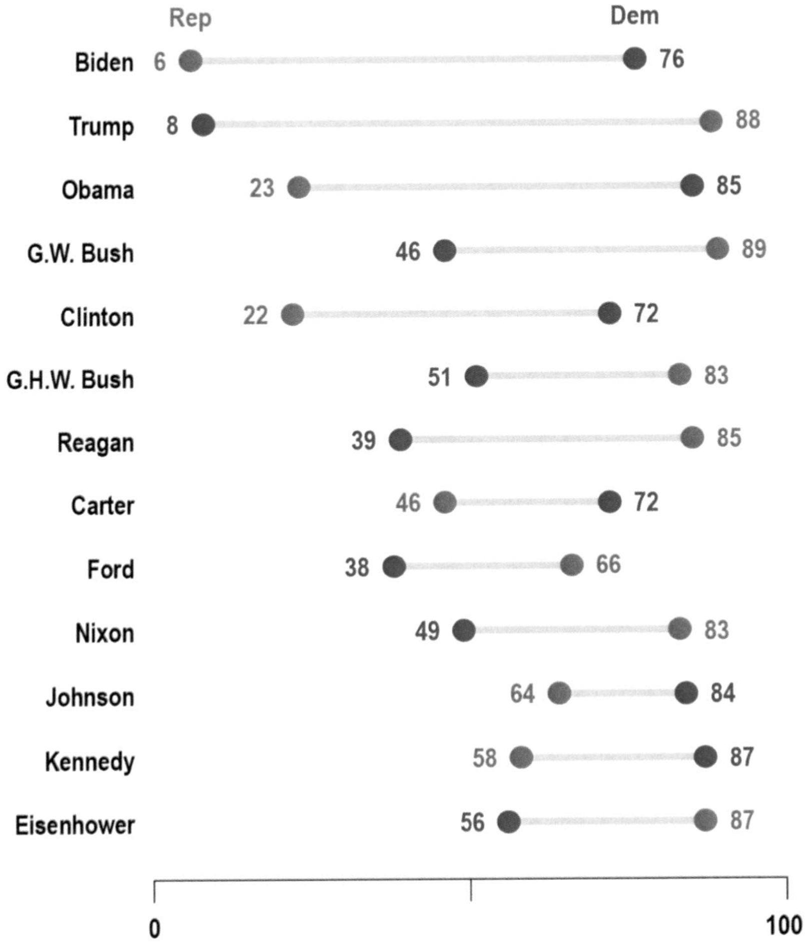

Source: Carroll Doherty, 'Key Takeaways on Americans' Growing Partisan Divide Over Political Issues' Pew Research Center, October 5, 2017, https://www.pewresearch.org/fact-tank/2017/10/05/takeaways-on-americans-growing-partisan-divide-over-political-values/.The original figure following President Biden's first year in office drawing on data from: "Biden Starts Year Two with Diminished Public Support and a Daunting List of Challenges," Pew Research Center, January 2022, https://www.pewresearch.org/politics/2022/01/25/biden-starts-year-two-with-diminished-public-support-and-a-daunting-list-of-challenges/.

Figure 6. Percentage of Voters in Subgroups Who Identify with Each Party.

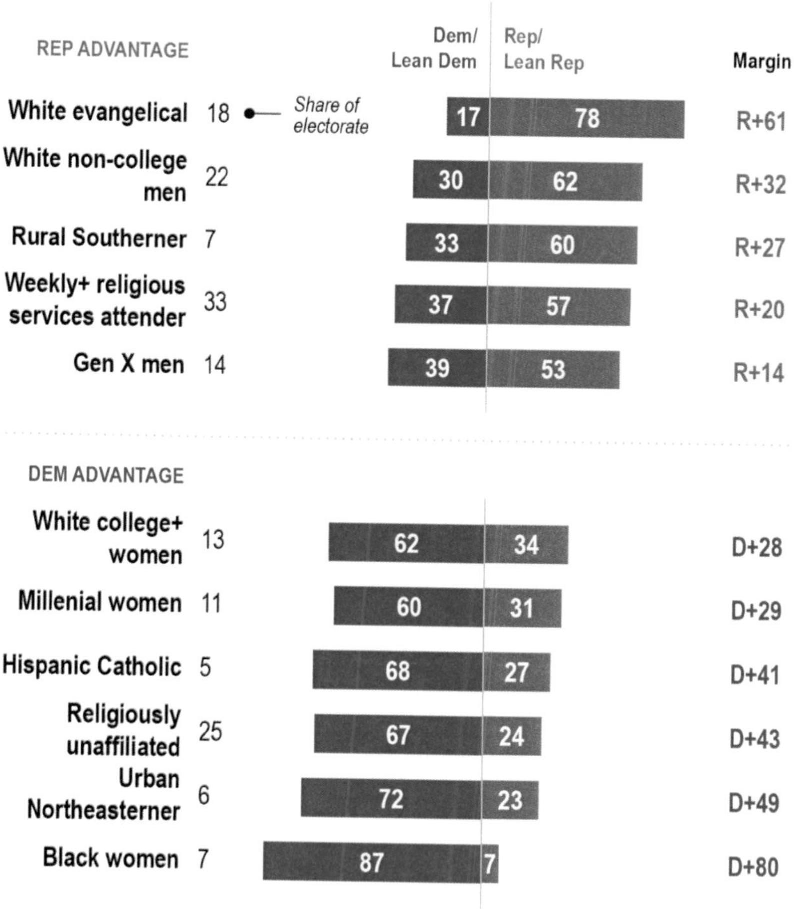

Source: Carroll Doherty, "Key Takeaways on Americans' Growing Partisan Divide Over Political Issues," Pew Research Center.

The statistics also show that 87% of black women vote Democrat against 7% who vote Republican, 72% of urban northeasterners vote Democrat and only 23% vote Republican, and 67% of Americans with no religious affiliation vote Democrat but only 24% vote Republican.

A further indicator of division is the steep rise in the numbers of anti-government demonstrations and riots against administrations of both political persuasions. From the late 1970s till 2005, the number of major anti-government demonstrations and riots never rose above five per year. However, from 2006 to 2018, there was a steep and uninterrupted rise in major anti-government demonstrations to 55 each year and a similar percentage rise in the number of riots to 11.[43] Dissent against administrations of both political colors rose to historic highs.

This deep political and social divide is now reflected in American opinions not only on domestic issues but also international issues. When Americans were asked in 2020 whether they had confidence in President Donald Trump doing the right thing in international affairs, 88% of Republicans responded positively but only 13% of Democrats did. When essentially the same question was asked of Americans a year later about whether they had confidence in President Biden doing the right thing in world affairs, only 27% of Republicans responded positively but 88% of Democrats did.[44] This suggests strongly that the American public's view on whether a president is doing a good job in managing international affairs is driven more strongly by the voter's party affiliation than by the quality of the job the president and his administration may actually be doing.

Similarly, the views of voters on some key international security issues differ by up to 38% between the parties. For instance, a Pew Research Center poll found that 63% of Republicans believed that limiting the power and influence of China "should be given top priority as a long-range foreign policy goal," whereas only 36% of Democrats did. And when asked whether "maintaining the US military advantage over all other countries" should be given top priority as a long-range foreign policy goal, 68% of Republicans responded affirmatively but only 30% of Democrats did.[45]

This analysis suggests that in the event of a major conflict in the Indo-Pacific, most of the American public would probably support the commitment of forces if major US interests were at stake. However, if the issues were not seen to be critical by most Americans, casualties were high, and the conflict was not ended quickly, significant dissent could be expected in months, possibly within weeks. Some of this dissent would likely be driven by rising concerns about the human, financial, and other costs of the war. But another and possibly even stronger driver is likely to be the deep distaste of half of the electorate in the person and the political party that happens to occupy the White House at the time.

On top of this, there would be another factor at play—the serious erosion of public trust in the US government in recent decades. When the American public was asked during the 1950s and early 1960s whether they trusted the government in Washington, over 70% responded positively. However, from the mid-1960s, public approval of the government fell steadily till it hit a low point of 30% during President Jimmy Carter's term in 1980 and then 20% in President Bill Clinton's early years. During the Obama administration, public trust fell again to around 15–18%, where it stayed during the Trump years and under Biden. So, in the 65 years from 1955 to 2019, public trust in the US government declined 55%.[46]

Other disturbing measures of American public sentiment were revealed in a November 2021 poll conducted by the firm Beacon Research. When a large sample of the public was asked whether they thought that "the greatest threats to the US come from outside the country or from within the country," 25% replied that the greatest threats came from outside, 41% said from inside the country, and 30% said both equally.[47] Then, when asked about their level of trust in the US military, 70% stated that they had a great deal of trust and confidence in 2018, but only 45% gave that answer in 2021.[48]

This combination of low public trust in the federal government, deep political polarization, a track record of limited political resilience in a number of conflicts, and Chinese and Russian dis-integration operations designed to magnify public divisions suggests that assumptions about how the US public and national leadership would behave in a major Indo-Pacific war need to be made with care.

The United States may no longer have a strong capability to sustain combat operations in a distant theater suffering significant losses when the issues at stake are not perceived by the mass of the American public to be vital. Any US administration that seeks to continue fighting such a war for an extended period is likely to encounter widespread public resistance.

Indicator #11: Stove-piped and Muscle-Bound Government Agencies Unprepared for Major War

Amongst the most serious challenges confronting American planning and preparations for major conflict are the muscle-bound and sometimes incoherent systems and processes of the US government. Some of this complexity is a function of the constitutional division of powers and the resulting vast number of organizations that operate in the national security field across the 50 states. Many federal departments and agencies are very large and sometimes have difficulty even coordinating their own views and providing coherent, timely input for national decisions.

A further complication is the churn of senior officials who are nominated by the winners of each presidential and state election to serve in each department and agency. The tenures of most senior officials are limited to four years, but in practice many serve for much shorter periods. This has serious consequences for the consistency and often for the quality and timeliness of decision-making.

Illustrative of the complexity of American national security decision-making is the dramatic growth in the National Security Council staff in the White House. This staff has become, in effect, a super department that reports directly to the president. As Ambassador Chas Freeman has pointed out, the National Security Council was very lean in its early days:

> Kennedy's initial NSC staff numbered six men...Twenty years later, when Ronald Reagan took office, the NSC staff had grown to around 50. By the time Barack Obama became president in 2009, it numbered 370, plus another 230 or so people off the books and on temporary duty, for a total of around 600.[49]

According to Fareed Zakaria, the national security staff then expanded even further: "Under Barack Obama, it had doubled again. Donald Trump shrunk it some, but President Biden has brought it back to more than 350, with lots of deputies, layers and complexity."[50]

The central point made by Freeman, Zakaria, and others is that unless very special circumstances apply, larger organizations tend to be more bureaucratic, internally focused, slower moving, and less agile. These challenges are multiplied when several much larger bureaucracies also have seats at the table. Too many people with veto power injecting too many divergent perspectives can distract from critical issues, weaken strategic logic, induce unnecessary hesitation, and cause serious decision-making delays.

These issues have particular salience when considering the quality and timeliness of decision-making in a fast-moving crisis in the Indo-Pacific. With the likelihood that Beijing would aim to take Washington by surprise in any major assault on Taiwan or another Indo-Pacific target, delays of even a few minutes could prove momentous.

These types of challenges are magnified in the largest agencies of the US government. For instance, while the US Department of Defense is notionally a single organization, it and the four armed services often act like a group of internally focused tribes that are competitive with each other, resistant to change, and highly risk averse. The dominant culture is bureaucratic and multiple-layered, strongly wedded to local rules, orderly and predictable processes, and the minimization of organizational risk. Senior retired officials report strains in civil-military relationships.[51] There is also often a heavy focus on inputs rather than the delivery of timely outputs or effects. Incentives for personal initiative, innovation, or for entrepreneurial "mission command" operations are limited.

The very poor and grossly uncompetitive performance of the US defense acquisition system was described in some frustration by Major General Cameron Holt, the Deputy Assistant Secretary of the Air Force for Acquisition, in July 2022. He stated that China was able to field new defense equipment "five or six times faster" than the United States and that:

> In purchasing power parity, they spend about one dollar to our 20 dollars to get the same capability... We're going to lose if we can't figure out how to drop the cost and increase the speed in our defense supply chains.[52]

The 2018 National Defense Strategy highlighted the need for serious reforms:

> Current processes are not responsive to need...We must transition to a culture of performance where results and accountability matter...The current bureaucratic approach, centered on exacting thoroughness and minimizing risk above all else, is proving to be increasingly unresponsive...
>
> The Department's management structure and processes are not written in stone, they are a means to an end—empowering the warfighter with the knowledge, equipment, and support systems to fight and win... If current structures hinder substantial increases in lethality or performance, it is expected that Service Secretaries and Agency heads will consolidate, eliminate, or restructure as needed.[53]

Indicator #12: No Clear and Agreed Strategy for Deterrence, Fighting, and Winning

Not only do many key American officials have an inaccurate perception of the likely shape of a major war in the Indo-Pacific and operate within an antiquated culture, but they also do not have a clear and agreed strategy yet for deterring and, if necessary, fighting and winning such a war. There are many American documents with titles that include the word "strategy," but there are no public documents that describe the central features of an agreed strategy or "game plan" for deterring and defeating a peer rival.

The declassified US Strategic Framework lists the "top interests of the United States in the Indo-Pacific," the "Desired End States," and the "Lines of Effort," but at no point does it make clear the key elements of the US strategy.

Similarly, the unclassified *Summary of the 2018 National Defense Strategy of the United States* lists four specific characteristics of the strategy and three priority lines of effort:

- Be strategically predictable, but operationally unpredictable...
- Integrate with US interagency [i.e. with other US government departments and agencies]. Effectively expanding the competitive space requires combined actions with the US interagency to employ all dimensions of national power...
- Counter coercion and subversion...
- Foster a competitive mindset...[54]

The 2022 Indo-Pacific Strategy of the United States lists five objectives and ten "lines of effort," but these describe broad foreign policy goals and general priorities for implementation. Similarly, the Biden administration's National Security Strategy simply describes broad investments in the underlying sources and tools of American power, building a strong coalition of allies and partners, and modernizing the military.[55] In consequence, even a generalized form of American defense strategy in the Indo-Pacific is not defined, at least in public. This is a serious problem. It is next to impossible for a large and widely scattered "team" to compete aggressively against a major power and be expected to win when there is no clearly articulated game plan beyond the most general descriptions of peacetime operations.

Indicator #13: Forces Refocusing on Fighting High-Technology Conventional War

Following two decades of combat operations in Afghanistan, Iraq, and Syria, the US Department of Defense has moved to focus more intently on the demands of deterring and, if necessary, fighting and defeating a peer competitor in the Indo-Pacific. These tasks are markedly different from the counterterrorism and counterinsurgency operations of recent years. New campaign strategies, new operational concepts, and several new military systems are needed quickly. Many complex skills must be learned or relearned in order to credibly confront a major power opponent.

Moreover, it is not just the tasking and the operational environment that has changed. As the Chairman of the Joint Chiefs of Staff, General Mark Milley, has emphasized, the United States and its close allies are also "right in the middle of a technological revolution—from ubiquitous surveillance to fielding long-range precision munitions—that will fundamentally change how we will fight."[56]

Appreciating the need to adapt and upgrade rapidly, the US armed services have critically reviewed their current capabilities and capacities for Western Pacific operations and have concluded that substantial changes are required. With a spirit of creative innovation, all four armed services have developed new concepts for effective operations, stress-tested key elements, and moved to acquire those new systems and skill sets that are of highest priority.

Former vice chairman of the US Joint Chiefs of Staff, General John Hyten, argued that "in the new environment if you concentrate, or aggregate forces, the opponent's long range fires coming at you from all directions will make you vulnerable."[57] The solution is to possess an exceptionally strong information advantage, disperse forces but be able to concentrate fires, and provide strong support to deployed units through a new, more agile, and difficult-to-target logistics system. Hyten called this war-fighting concept "Expanded Maneuver."[58]

The US Air Force has a particular challenge in conducting combat operations in the Western Pacific because as can be seen from figure 6, it normally operates from only seven air bases in the theater, two in South Korea, three in Japan, one in the Philippines, and one on Guam. However, because the high-capacity Anderson Air Force Base on Guam is located 1,700 miles from Taiwan—three or four times the average fighter aircraft's combat radius—air operations from that base would require extensive support from aerial tankers. Moreover, all seven US air bases are within range of China's theater ballistic and cruise missile forces and in the event of a serious conflict would likely suffer heavy damage in the first few hours.

Part of the US Air Force's solution is to disperse most air units to smaller military airfields, civilian airports and even temporary airstrips early in a crisis so that air operations can be maintained from these regional base clusters.[59] Special pre-positioning kits have been developed to support these dispersed air operations in the early phases of a war.[60]

The US Navy faces similar challenges in the theater. It plans to overwhelm an opponent by exploiting the vastness of the ocean in highly mobile operations to deliver several different types of strikes very rapidly using concepts and systems being developed in Project Overmatch. The US Chief of Naval Operations, Admiral Mike Gilday, explained:

> It's a big ocean, the Pacific. That's a lot of battle space... So, we want to come at a potential adversary from many different vectors, not just on the sea, but in the air, under the sea, on the land—the Marine Corps—in space and in cyberspace.[61]

General David Berger, Commandant of the Marine Corps, has been active in restructuring and retraining his units to operate as dispersed Stand-in Forces. These are mostly Littoral Regiments structured to defend the Western Pacific's first and second island chains and launch missile and other attacks against enemy forces operating in their vicinity. The first of these new Littoral Regiments was trialed in the major multinational exercise RIMPAC 22.[62] In order to facilitate this re-tasking, Berger took the controversial step of mothballing the Marine Corp's tank force and some of its helicopters. He is also promoting the early acquisition of a fleet of small amphibious ships to support the type of highly dispersed and difficult-to-target operations envisaged.[63] These focused plans have encountered some resistance from retired military officers and it is unclear how much of the commandant's restructuring will be funded by Congress.[64] Nevertheless, Berger has argued that in the event of war, his primary goal is to make enemy maritime operations in or near the two island chains very dangerous, if not untenable.

The US Army is also working to markedly improve its capability to operate in the Western Pacific. Much of the army's effort is being undertaken within the joint-service Project Convergence, a series of experiments designed to combine the digital data from multiple platforms on land, at sea, in the air, and in space to dramatically increase the speed and accuracy of targeting enemy forces across the full width of the theater. This work is designed partly to exploit the potential of the new wave of hypersonic and other missiles that are scheduled to enter service from 2023.

Above and beyond these initiatives of the US armed services, there is a number of portfolio-wide programs underway to rapidly strengthen American and allied combat capabilities in the Indo-Pacific. One of these is sometimes called Assault Breaker II. The original Assault Breaker program was launched in the late 1970s to detect, track, and attack Soviet armored formations advancing through Eastern Europe with stand-off sensor-fused munitions. American demonstrations of these capabilities helped convince Soviet leaders that they no longer had an option of launching a major land offensive through Western Europe to the English Channel. The intent of Assault Breaker II has yet to be revealed, but it appears designed to detect, track, and rapidly destroy an enemy's maritime forces in the Western Pacific within a matter of days.

An important conclusion is that the United States Department of Defense is designing, developing, testing, and planning to deploy greatly strengthened combat forces in the Indo-Pacific, especially within the first and second island chains. Funding for these changes has, however, been difficult to secure from Congress and progress has been slow. Nevertheless, by the mid-2020s some highly innovative operating concepts and a new generation of capabilities should be starting to have an impact on the military balance in the theater.

The primary focus of these initiatives is to prevent defeat in the first weeks of a major war and rapidly establish American and allied dominance of the Indo-Pacific's maritime domain. While these advances will probably strengthen theater deterrence and defensive capabilities, there must be doubts about whether they, on their own, would be sufficient to sustain combat operations for an extended period and ultimately force the regime in Beijing to give way.

Indicator #14: Pattern of Constrained Defense Expenditure

While the American military is moving to restructure their operating concepts, tactics, structures, and systems for combat operations in the Western Pacific, successive US administrations and congresses have been slow to support them with accelerated defense spending.

The pattern of US defense expenditure as a percentage of GDP displayed in figure 7 shows that while there was a modest rise in defense spending in the early 2010s, largely to fund operations in Afghnanistan and Iraq, there has really been no sustained growth in the national defense effort since 1980.

Figure 7. United States Defense Expenditure as a Percentage of GDP.

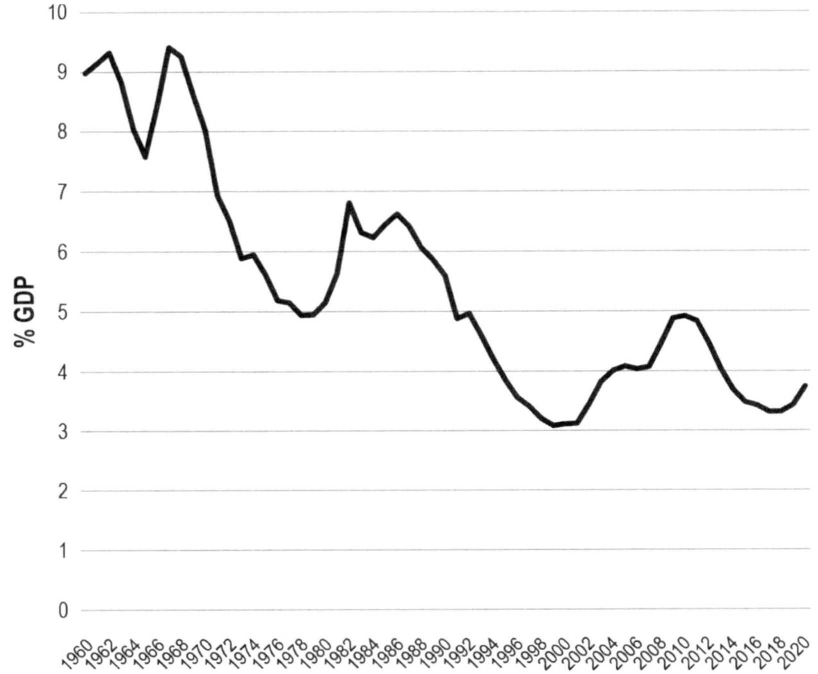

Source: SIPRI Yearbook, https://data.worldbank.org/indicator/MSMIL.XPEND.CD/Locations=US.

Despite a bipartisan consensus on the serious security challenges posed by China and Russia, recent congressional debates suggest that aside from some limited additional funds for Ukraine, there is little prospect of the Biden administration substantially boosting defense spending anytime soon. Meanwhile, inflation is eating away at the real purchasing power of the funds that are appropriated. There is a lack of urgency in Washington. Some senior security analysts have concluded that "the United States is rapidly reaching the point of strategic insolvency, with all of the resulting dangers."[65]

Michael Mazarr drew a similar stark conclusion in his major study of the rise and fall of great powers.

> The United States displays some of the characteristics of a once dominant power that has passed its competitive prime: by some measures, it is complacent, highly bureaucratized, and seeking short-term gains and rents rather than long-term productive breakthroughs. It is socially and politically divided, cognizant of the need for reforms yet unwilling or unable to make them, and suffering a loss of faith in the shared national project that once animated it....suggesting a once-dominant power congealing into immobility.[66]

Indicator #15: Relative Deindustrialization of the United States and its Allies

Another security challenge confronting the United States and its allies is the decline in their relative industrial capabilities and capacities. The shift in the manufacturing balance since the early 2000s is shown clearly in figure 8. In 2004 the manufacturing output of the United States was 2.5 times the size of China's. But by 2020 China's manufacturing output was double that of the United States. Moreover, there are numerous indications that China is attempting to power further ahead.

This extraordinary shift in global industrial power is a result of several forces. There has been a mix of pull and push factors at play. A primary pull factor has been the success of Chinese companies in exploiting lower costs of production (together with extensive government subsidies and other mercantilist policies) to make their products so attractive in international markets as to routinely outcompete American and other Western manufacturers. In consequence, Chinese companies now dominate many markets for manufactured goods and have driven numerous international competitors out of business. By 2018 China's factories produced 28 percent of the world's cars, 41 percent of ships, more than 60 percent of TVs, and 90 percent of the world's mobile phones.[67]

Figure 8. National Shares of Global Manufacturing (current US$).

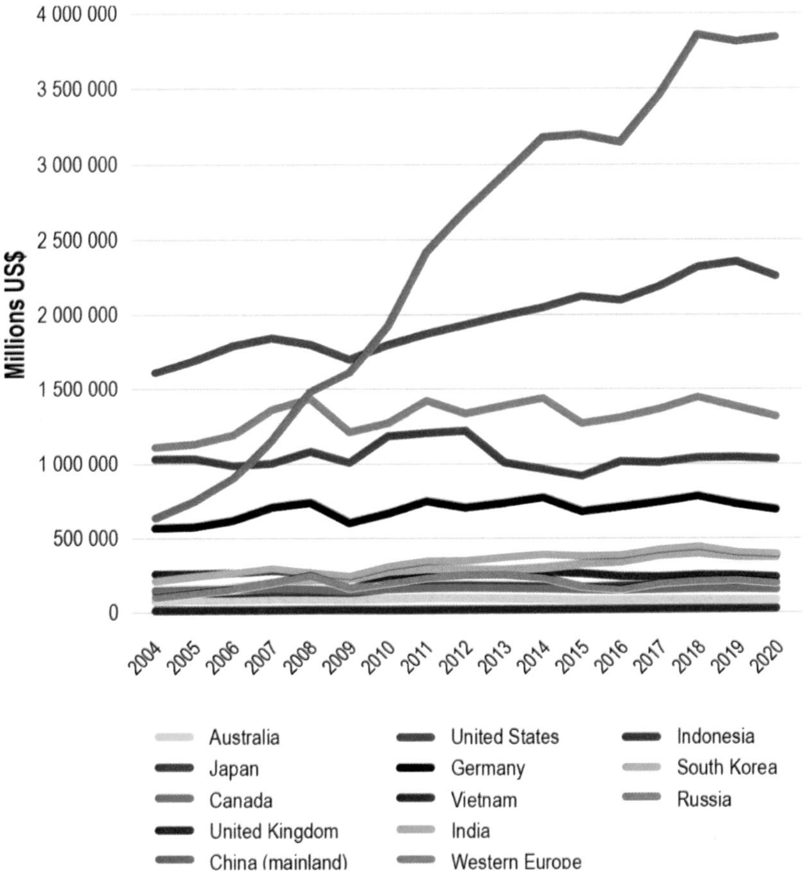

Source: UNSTATS SNA (System of National Accounts) database, https://unstats.un.org/unsd/snaama/CountryProfile.

A second pull factor has been a rising acceptance by international consumers of many categories of Chinese products. A third pull factor has been the almost universal acceptance of globalized production and distribution, along with low tariff and other barriers to trade. The economies of scale and relative efficiencies that can be achieved by globalized businesses have been mostly viewed in a very positive light, at least until COVID-19 forced some emergency re-shoring of priority production processes.

There have also been some strong push factors driving the relative deindustrialization of the West. For a start, there have been the strong incentives of Western businesses to use lower-cost Chinese products as a means of increasing their own market competitiveness and profit streams. Reinforcing these attractions, American and allied governments saw potential for efficiency gains from integrating their economies more closely with those of the developing world, and especially China. Michael Lind explains that while American and allied political and business leaders sold the vision of vast new markets for their exports, what was actually delivered was very different.

> Politicians pushing globalization like Clinton may have told the public that the purpose of NAFTA [the North American Free Trade Agreement] and of China's admission to the WTO [World Trade Organization] was to open the closed markets of Mexico and China to "American products made on American soil, everything from corn to chemicals to computers." But U.S. multinationals and their lobbyists 20 years ago knew that was not true. Their goal from the beginning was to transfer the production of many products from American soil to Mexican soil or Chinese soil, to take advantage of foreign low-wage, nonunion labor, and in some cases foreign government subsidies and other favors [...]
>
> The strategy of enacting trade treaties to make it easier for U.S. corporations to offshore industrial production to cheap-labor pools was sold by Clinton and others to the American public on the basis of two explicit promises. First, it was assumed that the Western factory workers who would be replaced by poorly paid, unfree Chinese workers would find better-paying and more prestigious jobs in a new, postindustrial "knowledge economy." Second, it

> was assumed that the Chinese regime would agree to the role assigned to it of low-value-added producer...
>
> Neither of the promises made by those like Clinton who promoted deep economic integration between the United States and China two decades ago have been fulfilled.[68]

Another strong push factor for deindustrialization has been the rise of powerful environmental and other voices in the US and other democratic states. They have frequently argued that heavy industry and most types of manufacturing are inherently dirty, emissions-heavy, and undesirable. Some of these groups have developed considerable influence in governments and more generally across societies. Politicians and officials have often responded by slowing down project approvals, adding new levels of regulation, and increasing costs and bureaucratic complexities for businesses.

Some of these environmental groups have also persuaded governments to offer substantial subsidies and other incentives to individuals and companies to invest in new forms of energy and resource production that push business costs even higher and deliver lower levels of system reliability and operational flexibility. The market distortions, system inefficiencies, and increased costs have seriously damaged the international competitiveness of many Western resource processors and manufacturers. Their capabilities to withstand the competitive pressures from Chinese-based companies that face few of the same cost, regulation, and supply burdens have been seriously undermined. To make matters worse, anti-industrial campaigning by special interest groups has built pressures on banks and other financial institutions to look with disfavor on many processing and manufacturing enterprises. There are reports that some organizations campaigning against US and allied industrial developments may be funded directly or indirectly by Chinese front organizations.[69] .

Filip Jirouš has described how Chinese intelligence agencies have manipulated both government and nongovernment environmental officials in the developed world to serve China's strategic interests:

> ...in the spirit of "do not destroy, repurpose," PRC influence agencies, as well as the Ministry of State Security, the PRC's main civilian intelligence agency, have been cultivating ties with the world's largest green non-governmental organizations (NGOs), as well as government environmental officials from the West. These efforts and NGO-regulations led to the current state when environmental foundations praise China and almost never criticize it, while the country remains one of the top world polluters. Thus, possibly with the best intentions, these institutions serve [the] PRC's propaganda and help legitimize the CCP in an area that had been Beijing's weak point both domestically and internationally, while also giving funds to the PRC....
>
> These activities are somewhat reminiscent of the USSR's exploitation of the world peace movement during the Cold War, through which Moscow sought to demilitarize its enemies by encouraging them to pursue a generally worthy goal. While their methods are similar, the focus of the CCP's "green cooption" efforts appear to be mainly to support its propaganda and political goals.[70]

The strategic effects of these Chinese operations have been to further handicap industrial development in the United States and its allies while removing any similar constraints on China's industrial and broader strategic development.

The combination of these and related activities has facilitated the vast transfer of industrial power from the US and its allies to China. However, this critical strategic development has so far attracted little focused attention by the Western media, by relevant governments, or even by defense departments. The new reality is that the overwhelming industrial superiority of the US and the other democracies that was so critical to winning victory in the two world wars is no more.

The United States and its allies can still design and build almost any type of manufactured product. But in many fields of strategic importance, they no longer run "hot" production lines, their costs are relatively high, and they cannot ramp up production of most military systems at scale without delays of many years.

In 2021, Mark Cancian published an assessment of the time required to replace America's current military system inventories.[71] Cancian concluded that replacing US defense equipment at surge production rates would take an average 8.4 years—about 5 years faster than the 13.5 years needed at peacetime production rates. Some systems have longer replacement times—especially space systems, missiles, crewed combat aircraft, and naval ships. Other systems with stronger technological links to the civilian economy—such as wheeled vehicles and C4I Systems—have shorter production times. Cancian also found that the US industrial base had become more brittle over time and that it would take longer for the US to replace its defense inventories at FY2020 production rates than at FY1990 production rates.

These concerns have been reinforced by the scale and pace of munitions use during the Ukraine war. Several observers have noted with dismay that Washington's supply of some types of missile to the Ukrainian Armed Forces during the first six months of the war depleted US stock holdings of those systems by about a third.[72] The munition requirements of a major war in the Indo-Pacific would likely be of a much larger scale.[73]

The transfer of US and allied manufacturing superiority to China and a general running down of the West's defense industrial base is a huge strategic loss. What we are witnessing is a serious undermining of the capabilities of the United States and its allies to fight, sustain, and win a future war against China and its partners. Some of the core economic foundations of American and allied global power are withering, and some are disappearing. If current trends continue into the 2030s, the economic and industrial demands of a major war may be beyond them.

Indicator #16: Struggle with the Security and Resilience of Supply Chains

A related challenge is the increased vulnerability of Western supply chains for many materials, manufactured items, and other goods that are essential for coping with major crises and wars. A small glimpse of some of the practical challenges was provided during the COVID-19 pandemic when many pharmaceutical ingredients required for vaccines and other priority medicines needed to be sourced from unreliable countries, especially China.[74] Recent reviews of US supply chains have revealed that during the first two decades of this century US vulnerabilities have increased in many strategic sectors. For instance, China supplies 60% of the world's processed lithium and 80% of the world's cobalt—both of which are essential for the manufacture of the types of high-capacity batteries that are critical for many defense, automotive, and other applications. In another strategic sector, the US share of global semiconductor production dropped from 37% in 1990 to 12% in 2021.[75]

While market forces have played a strong role in this global shift in manufacturing capability, so have the special government incentives that have been used extensively in China but also in a number of other countries. As a White House paper on supply chains noted:

> China stands out for its aggressive use of measures—many of which are well outside globally accepted fair trading practices—to stimulate domestic production and capture global market share in critical supply chains. The practice of "pumping and dumping" in which countries heavily subsidize an industry, gain market share, and then flood the market with cheaper products to wipe out competition, has been documented in a number of industries including pharmaceuticals and clean energy.[76]

In the face of these challenges, the Biden administration has announced some steps to restore US and allied industrial strength and resilience. For instance, the US State Department has launched a Minerals Security Initiative designed to funnel investment into the development of secure supply chains for strategically important minerals such as cobalt, lithium, and a range of rare earths.[77] Similarly, the bipartisan CHIPS Act authorizes the spending of $53 billion to develop the onshore domestic manufacture of semiconductors that are considered critical to US competitiveness and national security.

These are important initiatives but, in the broader context, only a modest start. An enormous amount remains to be done. In the absence of exceptional national leadership or the shock of a major international crisis, there appears to be little prospect of rapid progress being made in rebuilding American manufacturing and industrial strength.

Indicator #17: Defense Mobilization Weaknesses

While US industry, especially the manufacturing industry, has suffered a serious relative decline during the last two decades, American war planners are confronted by another closely related challenge. This is the neglected state of US mobilization planning and preparations.

In his landmark book on this topic, Harold Clem identifies four main categories of mobilization:

- Military preparations, training, and supply.
- Industrial production, supply, and stockholding
- Civil Defense, largely to protect the national leadership, the general population, and critical infrastructure and industries.
- Alliance activation to share the burdens of activating military units, trained personnel, system manufacturers and suppliers, logistic systems, and base structures.[78]

All four categories of mobilization were developed by the US and its allies during the Second World War and, for a time, during the Cold War. However, by the early 1980s many of these capabilities were viewed as being less relevant, some became excessively expensive to maintain, and others simply declined through neglect. This reduction in mobilization and industrial preparedness has been described by some experienced analysts as "structural disarmament."[79] Spending increases during the

Carter and Reagan administrations stemmed the decline for a few years, but following the end of the Cold War these capabilities were accorded lower priority and complacency became pervading. Indeed, at the start of the Clinton administration, the Federal Emergency Management Agency (FEMA) largely abandoned its mobilization role and focused instead on a much broader range of emergency contingencies with an all-hazards approach.

In recent years, the rapid growth of China's military capabilities and Beijing's aggressive international behavior have brought parts of the US and allied governments to focus more intently on the mobilization challenge. Some steps are being taken to strengthen the US National Technology and Industrial Base and to launch completely new initiatives such as AUKUS, the trilateral security pact between Australia, the United Kingdom, and the United States, announced on September 15, 2021. US allies have also conducted research into their own exposures to potentially hostile states, and a few have announced measures to enhance the security of key industrial sectors and supply chains.[80]

While some progress is being made in defense departments and related security agencies, very little of this thinking and planning has extended into other levels of government, civilian industries, educational institutions, or broader national communities.

It is difficult to see how US mobilization planning and supply chain security will be advanced rapidly until a federal administration makes it a high priority, a president argues the case persuasively, and a small high-powered task force, perhaps like President Dwight D. Eisenhower's Project Solarium group, is appointed to progress the necessary reforms with urgency.[81] None of this appears to be an early prospect although a bipartisan group of 15 US senators proposed a Solarium-like Grand Strategy Commission in October 2022.[82]

Primary Features of the War the United States Plans to Fight

American preparations for a major war in the Indo-Pacific are patchy and a work-in-progress. Largely because the reorientation of the United States security effort to the Indo-Pacific is relatively recent, much remains to be determined and even more remains to be funded and implemented. These efforts need to be turbo-charged if the US and its allies are to prevail in a major Indo-Pacific war.

Current American and allied planning suggests that fifteen key features will be prominent in the way the US fights any war with China in coming decades.

1. First, the US will have clear strategic goals. It will be strongly committed to the defense of its Indo-Pacific territories as well as those of its allies and security partners. It will also fight to maintain the principles of international law and especially of international maritime law. The US will work to progress a world order dominated by the liberal principles of individual freedoms, self-determination, and national sovereignty rather than those of coercion, predation, and authoritarian aggression.
2. There is a risk that the US government will find itself stumbling into a conflict without having first defined and implemented a clear strategy for fighting and winning a major war in the Indo-Pacific.
3. Timely and well-thought-out decision-making will be critical for American success in the lead up to, and during, such a conflict. The White House and relevant US agencies will need to be well prepared and practiced for the kinds of rapid-fire decisions that would be essential to seize and retain the initiative in such a crisis.
4. Most American planning and preparations for war with China assumes that it would take the form of a conventional military conflict, and this could mean that the US is outflanked because of the narrowness of its thinking. The initial American goal in such a war would be to win the battle for maritime supremacy in the Western Pacific. If the US and its allies won the initial exchanges at sea and possibly in space and cyberspace, most Americans would

assume that they were on the road to victory. But this would likely be an illusion. The CCP regime anticipates heavy losses in these domains and plans to dig in and fight a prolonged war through several stages until the United States and its allies collapse from political and industrial exhaustion.

5. America's options to deter China and, if necessary, to fight a major war will be constrained by the vast oceanic spaces that separate the continental United States from the primary Indo-Pacific conflict zones. Were war to break out with little or no notice, many of America's most potent capabilities could not be deployed quickly to the other side of the world.
6. A related complicating factor will be that American forces in the Indo-Pacific are normally located at a small number of difficult-to-defend bases. They are therefore vulnerable to surprise Chinese missile, aircraft, and special force strikes. Hence the timely dispersion and protection of these forward-deployed forces will be a US and allied priority.
7. American military planners will be able to exploit the theater's oceanic expanses to markedly reduce the threat posed by China's theater missile and air forces. Instead of rushing all available forces into the region at the commencement of a war, the US and its allies may choose to be very selective about what they deploy within range of China's theater-strike capabilities. In the initial phases of a war, when the PLA will be scouring the region for American aircraft carriers, other surface ships, and military aircraft concentrated on the ground, the allies may choose to keep most of those assets out of harm's way. They have the option of initially deploying forward only those forces that would be exceptionally hard for China to find and strike. In the first days of a war the allies could choose to emphasize cyber, space, underwater, and long-range air strikes together with modestly scaled ground-based missile and air units that would be widely dispersed, mobile, camouflaged, and protected. When combined with the deployment of decoys and other deceptive and disruptive measures, China's offensive operations could be thwarted. Many Chinese missiles would probably strike dummy targets, and some PLA forces might

also be lured into ambushes. The advanced networking of all relevant allied assets could make Chinese maritime operations exceedingly dangerous from the very beginning of hostilities. Once the initial Chinese missile salvoes and air strikes have been absorbed or deflected and China's reconnaissance, surveillance, communications, command, control, and related systems have been disrupted or destroyed, additional allied combat assets could be brought forward in relative safety to search out and neutralize other Chinese forces and provide enhanced protection to allied bases and communities in the theater.

8. In nearly every circumstance, neither side will want to escalate the conflict vertically—by using nuclear or most other weapons of mass destruction to gain an advantage. That would imperil the survival of both countries. However, it is very likely that both sides would escalate horizontally into new domains and new geographic theaters in order to exploit their opponent's vulnerabilities.
9. The US will have a tough time overcoming its seriously incomplete preparations for major war. Much will depend on whether the US government can vanquish the ponderous inflexibility, constrained innovation, risk-averse culture, and exceptionally long timeframes of the defense bureaucracy.
10. In the event of a major war, the US will pay a heavy price for neglecting mobilization planning and preparations. If America needs to fight for more than a very short period, it will face serious shortages of everything from trained personnel to missiles and spare parts. It would take at least two years for the full strategic weight of the American economy and society to be brought to bear. Battlefield losses and territories surrendered in the meantime could be substantial.
11. One notable weakness in American planning for major war is the apparent absence of a clear theory or concept of victory. What precisely would the US and its allies need to do to prevail and bring China to its knees? Posing this question brings a variety of answers, few of which give any sense of coherent logic, priorities, or plans. There appears to be unfinished work in this key area.

12. America's capacity to fight and win a major war will be seriously handicapped by its loss of manufacturing supremacy. Allied and security partner industrial capabilities will need to be networked and commissioned prior to a major crisis both to enhance deterrence and restore wartime production dominance.
13. A substantial American asset in any serious conflict will be its supporting set of allies and security partners. They would permit Washington to prepare its war plans as a strong team effort rather than as a solo campaign.
14. The many deep cleavages in American society have serious strategic consequences. The American people are not prepared psychologically, physically, or financially for a major war. In consequence, the initiation of such a conflict has the potential to cause shock, disorientation, confusion and, in some areas, defeatism. Worse still, while American and partner defense forces will be fighting to gain the upper hand in distant theaters, they may be forced—as they were in Vietnam, Iraq, and Afghanistan—to keep looking over their shoulders to check whether they are being undermined by a collapse of political will at home.
15. In the face of a surprise Chinese attack, the US population would probably rally strongly to support a powerful war effort. But whether this overwhelming public commitment to the war could be sustained for the full duration of an extended struggle remains an open question.

So while strong military capabilities would be essential to achieve victory, they would probably not be sufficient on their own. The outcome of such a conflict may be determined more by whether the fractured American society can restore its moral cohesion, rebuild its manufacturing base, reinforce its national resilience, and outlast the challenge from Beijing. Success in this great endeavor will require exceptional American leadership.[83]

NOTES

1. The US Military Sealift Command currently operates about 60 cargo vessels and tankers but most of these are already committed to fleet support. There is a Ready Reserve of about 40 additional ships but exercises reveal that less than 50% of these vessels are ready for operations. Another 60 ships in the US Maritime Security Program can be called for duty.
2. "Army Multi-Domain Transformation: Ready to Win in Competition and Conflict", Chief of Staff Paper #1, Headquarters, Department of the Army, March 16, 2021, pp. 6,7, https://api.army.mil/e2/c/downloads/2021/03/23/eeac3d01/20210319-csa-paper-1-signed-print-version.pdf; and Thomas G. Mahnken, "A Maritime Strategy to Deal with China," *US Naval Institute Proceedings*, 148, no. 2, February 2022, https://www.usni.org/magazines/proceedings/2022/february/maritime-strategy-deal-china.
3. Mahnken, "A Maritime Strategy to Deal with China." See also Commander Paul Giarra, Captain Gerry Roncolato, and Captain Bill Hamblet, U.S. Navy (Retired), "From 'Ends' to 'Ways' of Naval Strategy", *US Naval Institute Proceedings* 148, no. 4, issue 1430 (April 2022), https://www.usni.org/magazines/proceedings/2022/april/ends-ways-naval-strategy.
4. Greg Kandra, "We're at War; America's at the Mall," *CBS News*, September 8, 2006, https://www.cbsnews.com/news/were-at-war-americas-at-the-mall/.
5. *U.S. Strategic Framework for the Indo-Pacific* (declassified) (Washington, DC: The White House, May 2021), 1, https://www.documentcloud.org/documents/20455499-ips-final-declass_ocr.
6. Ibid., 7.
7. Quoted in Hal Brands and Zack Cooper, "U.S.-China Rivalry is a Battle Over Values," *Foreign Affairs*, March 16, 2021, https://www.foreignaffairs.com/articles/united-states/2021-03-16/us-china-rivalry-battle-over-values.
8. *U.S. Strategic Framework for the Indo-Pacific*, 7.
9. *Summary of the 2018 National Defense Strategy of The United States of America* (Washington, DC: US Department of Defense, 2018), 4, https://dod.defense.gov/Portals/1/Documents/pubs/2018-National-Defense-Strategy-Summary.pdf
10. Ibid., 5, 7.
11. Ibid., 5.

12. World Bank data at https://data.worldbank.org/indicator/NE.TRD.GNFS.ZS.
13. Asa Fitch and Stu Woo, "The U.S. vs. China: Who Is Winning the Key Technology Battles?," *Wall Street Journal*, April 12, 2020, https://www.wsj.com/articles/the-u-s-vs-china-who-is-winning-the-key-technology-battles-11586548597.
14. See, for example, Jodi Xu Klein, "As US-China Tech War rages, Washington debates steps beyond just blocking the competition," *South China Morning Post*, May 22, 2021, https://www.scmp.com/news/china/article/3134270/us-china-tech-war-rages-washington-debates-steps-beyond-just-block.
15. Robert Work, "The Third U.S. Offset Strategy and its Implications for Partners and Allies," (A speech delivered by the Deputy Secretary of Defense, Washington, DC, January 28, 2015), https://www.defense.gov/News/Speeches/Speech/Article/606641/the-third-us-offset-strategy-and-its-implications-for-partners-and-allies/.
16. For details, see Nicholas Eberstadt and Evan Abramsky, "America's Education Crisis is a National Security Threat," *Foreign Affairs*, September 20, 2022, https://www.foreignaffairs.com/world/america-education-crisis-national-security-threat.
17. Andreas Schleicher, *Program for International Student Assessment PISA 2018: Insights and Interpretations* (Paris: OECD, 2019), https://www.oecd.org/pisa/PISA%202018%20Insights%20and%20Interpretations%20FINAL%20PDF.pdf.
18. See these issues discussed in Douglas Belkin, "Test Finds College Graduates Lack Skills for White-Collar Jobs," *Wall Street Journal*, January 16, 2015, https://www.wsj.com/articles/test-finds-many-students-ill-prepared-to-enter-work-force-1421432744; and Hugo Sonnenschein, *Declining Standards in Higher Education* (College Community Index, Cyber College, University of Chicago, 2016), https://www.cybercollege.com/plume8.htm.
19. Kori Schake, Jim Mattis, Jim Ellis, and Joe Felter, "Defense in Depth," *Foreign Affairs*, November 23, 2020, https://www.foreignaffairs.com/articles/united-states/2020-11-23/defense-depth.
20. Henry Kissinger, "Excerpts From a Speech by Secretary Kissinger in Boston on U.S. Foreign Policy," *New York Times*, March 12, 1976, https://www.nytimes.com/1976/03/12/archives/excerpts-from-speech-by-secretary-kissinger-in-boston-on-us-foreign.html.

21. Halford John Mackinder, *The Geopolitical Pivot of History* (Kindle edition, Bookcrop, April 10, 2022).
22. Nicholas Spykman, *The Geography of Peace* (New York: Harcourt, Brace and Company, 1944).
23. U.S. Department of Defense, *Military and Security Developments Involving the People's Republic of China 2022*, Annual Report to Congress, IX.
24. See, for example: Timothy Wright, *Is China Gliding Towards a FOBS Capability?* (London: The International Institute for Strategic Studies, October 22, 2021).
25. Andrew F. Krepinevich, Jr., *The Decline of Deterrence* (Washington, DC: Hudson Institute, 2019), 34–46.
26. Samantha Bradshaw, "Influence Operations and Disinformation on Social Media," *Center for International Governance Innovation*, November 23, 2020, https://www.cigionline.org/articles/influence-operations-and-disinformation-social-media/.
27. Mark Scott, "China Influence Operation Targeted US Midterm Elections," *Politico*, September 27, 2022, https://www.politico.eu/article/china-us-midterm-election-influence-meta-facebook/ See also Ben Nimmo and Mike Torrey, *Taking Down Coordinated Inauthentic Behavior from Russia and China* (Menlo Park: Meta Company, September 2022); and Dustin Volz, "China-Linked Internet Trolls Try Fueling Divisions in US Midterms, Researchers Say", *Wall Street Journal*, October 26, 2022, https://www.wsj.com/articles/china-linked-internet-trolls-try-fueling-divisions-in-u-s-midterms-researchers-say-11666777403.
28. Minxin Pei, "China's Changing of the Guard: Contradictory Trends and Confusing Signals," *Journal of Democracy* 14, issue 1, January 2003, https://journalofdemocracy.org/articles/chinas-changing-of-the-guard-contradictory-trends-and-confusing-signals/ See also Terri Wu, "CCP's Political Warfare Left Unchecked in US, Experts Warn," *The Epoch Times*, November 8, 2021, https://www.theepochtimes.com/ccps-political-warfare-left-unchecked-in-us_4092950.html; and Scott W. Harold, Nathan Beauchanp-Mustafaga, and Jeffrey W. Hornung, *Chinese Disinformation Efforts on Social Media* (Santa Monica: Rand Corporation, 2021), https://www.rand.org/pubs/research_reports/RR4373z3.html.
29. Statement of Admiral Philip S. Davidson, Commander United States Indo-Pacific Command, *Stenographic Transcript before the Committee on Armed Services: Hearing to Receive Testimony on United States Indo-Pacific Command in Review of the Defense Authorization Request for Fiscal Year 2022 and the Future Years Defense Program*, United States Senate,

March 9, 2021, p.27, https://www.armed-services.senate.gov/imo/media/doc/21-10_03-09-2021.pdf
30. Gerry Groot, "The Rise and Rise of the United Front Work Department under Xi," Jamestown Foundation, *China Brief*, 18, issue 7, April 24, 2018, https://jamestown.org/program/the-rise-and-rise-of-the-united-front-work-department-under-xi/.
31. Michael J. Cole, "Taiwan and CCP Political Warfare," *Sinopsis*, December 27, 2019, https://sinopsis.cz/en/taiwan-and-ccp-political-warfare-a-blueprint/.
32. Anne-Marie Brady, *Magic Weapons: China's Political Influence Activities Under Xi Jinping* (Conference paper delivered at the Wilson Center, Washington, DC, on September 16, 2017), 10, https://www.wilsoncenter.org/sites/default/files/media/documents/article/magic_weapons.pdf.
33. Hamilton, *Silent Invasion,* 213–227.
34. Ibid., 195–200.
35. Ibid.
36. Ibid., 200–213.
37. "US Department of Justice, "Chinese Intelligence Officers Charged with Using Academic Cover to Target Individuals in United States: Four Chinese Nationals Charged with Conspiring to Act in the United States as Agents of the Chinese Government," The United States Attorney's Office, District of New Jersey, October 24, 2022, https://www.justice.gov/usao-nj/pr/chinese-intelligence-officers-charged-using-academic-cover-target-individuals-united.
38. See, for example: Robert Haddick, "Defeat China's Navy, Defeat China's War Plan," *War on the Rocks*, September 21, 2022, https://warontherocks.com/2022/09/defeat-chinas-navy-defeat-chinas-war-plan/.
39. Dina Smeltz, Ivo Daalder, Karl Friedhoff, Craig Kafura, and Emily Sullivan, *A Foreign Policy for the Middle Class—What Americans Think* (Chicago: Chicago Council on Global Affairs, 2021), 8.
40. Ibid., 31.
41. Carroll Doherty, "Key Takeaways on Americans' Growing Partisan Divide Over Political Issues," Pew Research Center, October 5, 2017, https://www.pewresearch.org/fact-tank/2017/10/05/takeaways-on-americans-growing-partisan-divide-over-political-values/.
42. "In Changing U.S. Electorate, Race and Education Remain Stark Dividing Lines," Pew Research Center, June 2, 2020, https://www.pewresearch.org/politics/2020/06/02/in-changing-u-s-electorate-race-and-education-remain-stark-dividing-lines/.

43. Peter Turchin and Andrey Korotayev, "The 2010 Structural-Demographic Forecast for the 2010–2020 Decade: A Retrospective Assessment," *Plos One*, August 17, 2020, https://doi.org/10.1371/journal.pone.0237458.
44. "Majority of Americans Confident in Biden's Handling of Foreign Policy as Term Begins," Pew Research Center, February 24, 2021, 10, https://www.pewresearch.org/politics/2021/02/24/majority-of-americans-confident-in-bidens-handling-of-foreign-policy-as-term-begins/.
45. Ibid., 17.
46. "Public Trust in Government 1958–2022," Pew Research Center, June 6, 2022, https://www.pewresearch.org/politics/2022/06/06/public-trust-in-government-1958-2022/.
47. "U.S. National Survey of Defense Attitudes on behalf of the Ronald Reagan Foundation – Final Topline Results," Beacon Research, BR #9593, November 2021, 10, https://www.reaganfoundation.org/media/358081/reagan-foundation-november-2021-survey-topline-results.pdf.
48. Ibid.
49. Chas W. Freeman, Jr, "The End of the American Empire," *War on the Rocks*, April 11, 2016, https://warontherocks.com/2016/04/the-end-of-the-american-empire/.
50. Fareed Zakaria, "Here's why the U.S. National Security Apparatus Keeps Producing Failures," *The Washington Post*, August 19, 2021, https://www.washingtonpost.com/opinions/2021/08/19/heres-why-us-national-security-apparatus-keeps-producing-failures/.
51. See, for example, Dan Lamothe, "Past Pentagon Leaders Warn of Strains on Civil-Military Relations," *Washington Post*, September 6, 2022, https://www.washingtonpost.com/national-security/2022/09/06/pentagon-civilian-military-relations/?utm_source=sailthru&utm_medium=email&utm_campaign=dfn-ebb&SToverlay=2002c2d9- https://www.washingtonpost.com/national-security/2022/09/06/pentagon-civilian-military-relations/?utm_source=sailthru&utm_medium=email&utm_campaign=dfn-ebb&SToverlay=2002c2d9-.
52. Thomas Newdick, "China Acquiring New Weapons Five Times Faster Than U.S. Warns Top Official," *The War Zone*, July 6, 2022, https://www.thedrive.com/the-war-zone/china-acquiring-new-weapons-five-times-faster-than-u-s-warns-top-official.
53. US Department of Defense, *Summary of the Defense Strategy of the United States of America* (Washington, DC: Department of Defense, 2018), 10.
54. Ibid., 5.

55. The White House, *National Security Strategy*, October 2022, https://www.whitehouse.gov/wp-content/uploads/2022/10/Biden-Harris-Administrations-National-Security-Strategy-10.2022.pdf.
56. Cited in John Grady, "Milley: NATO in Forefront of Change of 'How We Fight,'" *USNI News*, July 16, 2021, https://news.usni.org/2021/07/16/milley-nato-in-forefront-of-change-of-how-we-fight.
57. For details see Theresa Hitchens, "The Joint Warfighting Concept Failed, Until it Focused on Space and Cyber," *Breaking Defense*, July 26, 2021, https://breakingdefense.com/2021/07/the-joint-warfighting-concept-failed-until-it-focused-on-space-and-cyber/.
58. Ibid.
59. Maj. Scott D. Adamson and Maj. Shane "Axl" Praiswater, "With Air Bases at Risk, Agile Combat Employment Must Mature," *Defense News*, November 12, 2020, https://www.defensenews.com/opinion/commentary/2020/11/12/air-bases-are-at-risk-without-the-agile-combat-employment-approach/.
60. Ibid.
61. Chief of Naval Operations Public Affairs, "CNO Speaks with Local Media in Hawaii Aboard USS Carl Vinson," *America's Navy*, August 16, 2021, https://www.navy.mil/Press-Office/Press-Briefings/display-pressbriefing/Article/2733185/cno-speaks-with-local-media-in-hawaii-aboard-uss-carl-vinson/.
62. Gidget Fuentes, "New Marine Littoral Regiment Will Make Debut in This Year's RIMPAC Drills," *USNI News*, June 6, 2022, https://news.usni.org/2022/06/06/new-marine-littoral-regiment-will-make-debut-in-this-years-rimpac-drills.
63. Gen. David H. Berger and Ryan Evans, "General David H. Berger on the Marine Corps of the Future," *War on the Rocks*, January 2, 2022, https://warontherocks.com/2022/01/general-berger-on-the-marine-corps-of-the-future/.
64. See these issues discussed in Owen West, "Are the Marines Investing in the Edsel or the Mustang?," *War on the Rocks*, May 27, 2022, https://warontherocks.com/2022/05/are-the-marines-inventing-the-edsel-or-the-mustang/.
65. Hal Brands and Eric Edelman, "The Military Buildup We Need," *The Weekly Standard*, March 1, 2017, https://www.washingtonexaminer.com/weekly-standard/the-military-buildup-we-need.

66. Michael J. Mazarr, "What Makes a Power Great – The Real Drivers of Rise and Fall," *Foreign Affairs*, July/August 2022, https://www.foreignaffairs.com/articles/united-states/2022-06-21/what-makes-a-power-great.
67. U.S. Department of Defense, *Assessing and Strengthening the Manufacturing and Defense Industrial Base and Supply Chain Resiliency of the United States: Report to President Donald J. Trump by the Interagency Task Force in Fulfillment of Executive Order 13806*, September 2018. https://www.dni.gov/files/NCSC/documents/supplychain/20190325-Executive-Order-Assessing-Strengthening.pdf.
68. Michael Lind, "The China Question," *Tablet*, May 20, 2020, https://www.tabletmag.com/sections/news/articles/china-strategy-trade-lind
69. Lee Edwards, China's "Soft" War Against America, Commentary Asia, The Heritage Foundation, February 22, 2021; and Patricia Adams *The Red and the Green: China's Useful Idiots* (London: The Global Warming Policy Foundation, 2020), Briefing 51.
70. Filip Jirouš, "Make the Green Serve China: PRC Influence Operations Target International Environmentalism," Jamestown Foundation, *China Brief* 22, issue 16 September 9, 2022, https://jamestown.org/program/make-the-green-serve-china-prc-influence-operations-target-international-environmentalism/.
71. Mark F. Cancian, *Industrial Mobilization: Assessing Surge Capabilities, Wartime Risk and System Brittleness* (Washington, DC: Center for Strategic and International Studies, 2021), https://csis-website-prod.s3.amazonaws.com/s3fs-public/publication/210108_Cancian_Industrial_Mobilization.pdf.
72. Joe Gould, "Lockheed, Aiming to Double Javelin Production, Seeks Supply Chain 'Crank Up,'" *Defense News*, May 9, 2022, https://www.defensenews.com/industry/2022/05/09/lockheed-aiming-to-double-javelin-production-seeks-supply-chain-crank-up/.
73. Conrad Crane, "Too Fragile to Fight: Could the U.S. Military Withstand a War of Attrition?," *War on the Rocks*, May 9, 2022, https://warontherocks.com/2022/05/too-fragile-to-fight-could-the-u-s-military-withstand-a-war-of-attrition/; Gordon Lubold, Nancy A. Youssev and Ben Kesling, "Ukraine War is Depleting U.S. Ammunition Stockpiles, Sparking Pentagon Concern," *Wall Street Journal*, August 28, 2022, https://www.wsj.com/articles/ukraine-war-depleting-u-s-ammunition-stockpiles-sparking-pentagon-concern-11661792188.

74. Semiconductor Industry Association, *2021: State of the U.S. Semiconductor Industry,* 2021, https://www.semiconductors.org/state-of-the-u-s-semiconductor-industry/.
75. The White House, *Building Resilient Supply Chains, Revitalizing Manufacturing, and Fostering Broad-Based Growth* (Washington, DC: The White House, June 2021), 9, https://www.whitehouse.gov/wp-content/uploads/2021/06/100-day-supply-chain-review-report.pdf.
76. Ibid., 11.
77. Ian Marlow, "New US Program Targets Rare Minerals Needed for Evs and Solar Panels," Bloomberg *News*, June 25, 2022, https://www.bloomberg.com/news/articles/2022-06-24/us-seeks-to-bolster-lithium-cobalt-supply-chains-beyond-china.
78. Harold Clem, *Mobilization Preparedness* (Washington, DC: National Defense University, 1983).
79. Thomas A. Callaghan, Jr., "The Structural Disarmament of the West: Our Most Critical Defense Industrial Challenge," in *Industrial Capacity and Defense Planning*, eds. Lee D. Olvey, Henry A. Leonard, and Bruce E. Arlinghaus (Lexington: Lexington Books, 1983), 3–22.
80. See, for example, a statement by the Hon. Karen Andrews, Minister for Home Affairs, "New Voluntary Principles to Protect Australia's Critical Technology Supply Chains," Department of Home Affairs, November 15, 2021, https://minister.homeaffairs.gov.au/KarenAndrews/Pages/voluntary-principles-to-protect-australia-critical-technology-supply-chains.aspx.
81. Dr Richard Weitz, "A New Project Solarium," *Second Line of Defense*, September 20, 2011, https://sldinfo.com/2011/09/a-new-project-solarium/.
82. For details, see Bryant Harris, "Senators Propose China 'Grand Strategy' commission to Guide US Policy," *Defense News*, October 1, 2022, https://www.defensenews.com/congress/2022/09/30/senators-propose-china-grand-strategy-commission-to-guide-us-policy/.
83. There are many excellent books that address the current strategic circumstances of the United States and its allies. Those that I have found valuable include Hal Brands and Michael Beckley, *Danger Zone* (New York: W.W. Norton & Company, 2022); Hal Brands and Charles Edel, *The Lessons of Tragedy* (New Haven: Yale University Press, 2019); and Elbridge A Colby, *The Strategy of Denial* (New Haven, Yale University Press, 2021).

Chapter 4

What Kind of War?

The Complexities of an Indo-Pacific War

This chapter turns from Chinese and American planning for major war in the Indo-Pacific to focus on the nature of such a conflict. Contrary to the assumptions of many, the progress of such a war is likely to be multilayered and far more complex than a simple transition from peace to war. It would probably pass through several phases, possibly as many as six or seven. The character of each phase would differ in terms of its nature, operational demands, deployed elements, and its duration. The economic, social, military, and political impacts across the theater would also change as the conflict progresses from one phase to the next. Understanding these complexities and preparing for the significantly different demands of each conflict layer will be essential if defeat is to be avoided and victory won.

The Layers and Phases of a Major US-China War

How a major war between China and its supporters and the United States and its allies would begin, progress, and end is impossible to determine with precision in advance. However, the research into the planning and preparations of the two sides that is summarized in chapters 2 and 3 provides strong indicators of how such a war might start, the form it is most likely to take, and the duration that should be anticipated.

There are two main categories of warfare that would feature in any serious conflict between China and the United States: non-kinetic (largely nonviolent) operations and kinetic (violent) fighting. As we have seen in chapter 2, China is already conducting non-kinetic operations against the US, its allies and a range of other countries and intensified activities of these types are likely to play key roles in the lead-up to the kinetic phases of a major war. Indeed, non-kinetic operations would probably continue, supplement all kinetic phases of such a war, and likely be maintained for some time after the cessation of formal hostilities.

The primary phases likely to feature in a major US-China war are displayed in figure 9. On the lower part of this figure are the non-kinetic operations that are very active at the beginning of the conflict and continue in varying modes in support of the kinetic operations portrayed in the upper segments of the figure. The conflict phases that are purely non-kinetic are displayed as phases 1A, 1B, and 4.

There are four distinct phases of kinetic operations (2A, 2B, 3A, and 3B) that are displayed in the upper part of the figure. The main characteristics of all phases are described briefly next.

Phase 1A: Political Warfare Operations

Phase 1A operations would almost certainly be conducted by the Chinese at the commencement of any major conflict. These are expected to be an upgraded and sharpened version of the information, propaganda, manipulation, coercion, disruption, and dis-integration operations that several Chinese agencies and their contractors have been conducting against the US and its allies and partners for several years.[1] Key priorities would likely be the penetration, exploration, targeting, and accelerated exploitation of strategically relevant systems and organizations. Anticipated physical activities would include break-ins, system theft, bribery, coercion, and blackmail.

Figure 9. Probable Phases of a US-China War.

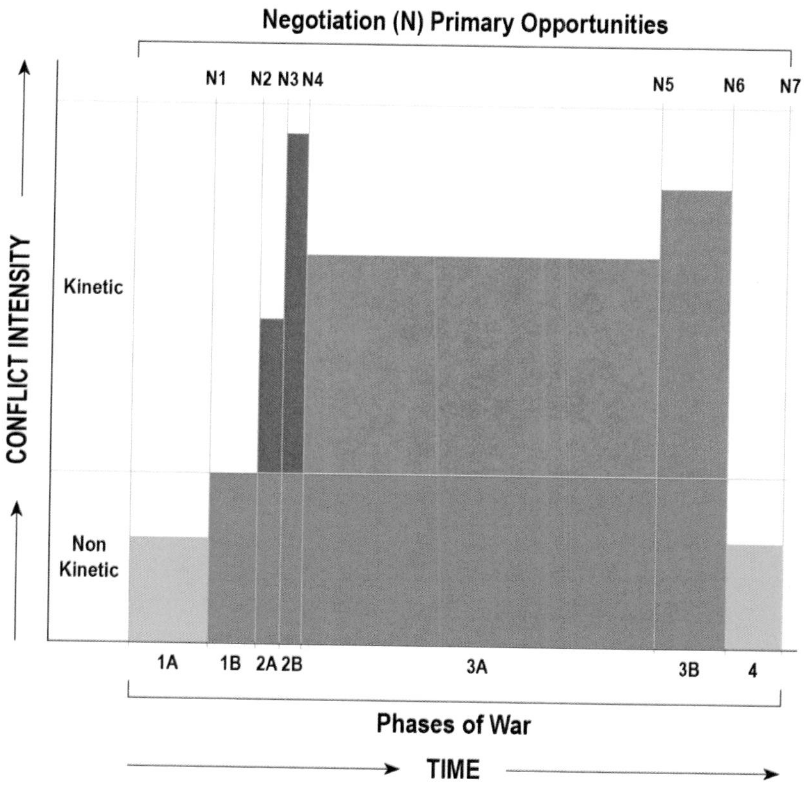

Information operations would manipulate allied media, insert fake news, attack dissenting views, and distort public and official perceptions. In this phase, cyber intrusions would be sharpened to occasionally trigger electricity, gas, water, and transport disruptions; push the US and its allies off balance; cause confusion; and slow down processes of decision-making. Some cyber and subversion operations would probably be designed to prepare the way for a much stronger intensification of political warfare operations that are planned to follow in phase 1B.

The political warfare operations in phase 1A would be targeted not just against the United States and its allies. They would be especially intense in those countries that are located in the Western Pacific and the Indian Oceans. As Admiral Philip Davidson, the former Commander US Indo-Pacific Command, briefed Congress: "China's pernicious approach to the region includes a whole-of-party effort to coerce, corrupt, and collapse governments, businesses, organizations, and the people of the Indo-Pacific."[2]

During the last two decades the PLA has been developed, equipped, and postured primarily to invade Taiwan.[3] Especially notable is the exceptionally strong force of theater ballistic and cruise missiles, air and naval strike forces, and marine and airborne assault units supported by a network of bases in adjacent mainland provinces. As part of its coercive campaign the PLA and associated paramilitary forces have been training for an invasion by practicing assaults on full-sized replicas of key Taiwanese buildings and other installations .[4] Repeated Chinese force penetrations of Taiwanese air and sea space during recent years appear to have rehearsed several phases of such an assault.[5] Chinese agencies have also conducted extensive cyber operations against Taiwan's government, military, and broader electronic infrastructures.[6]

Nevertheless, despite China's intense focus on Taiwan, it is possible that Beijing's priority in the initial phases of a major war in the Indo-Pacific might be elsewhere—such as the Senkaku Islands and Japan, part of the South China Sea, the Philippines, or Vietnam. There is also a possibility that intensified phase 1A operations could be focused initially on India's northern borders, Bhutan, or Nepal. Whatever the immediate target, China's political warfare operations would be designed to pressure the primary target to wilt, collapse politically, and effectively surrender—and for all of this to happen without substantive US and allied intervention.

Throughout this phase, Beijing would warn the US and its allies not to interfere in "China's legitimate strategic interests" or to ramp up a "new cold war." Chinese media and members of the regime would threaten a range of retaliatory measures in a coordinated campaign to coerce allied passivity. Chinese agents, sympathizers, and naïve civil activists in the United States and most Western countries would warn of the dangers of "provoking China" and the first "anti-war" protests would be organized on the streets of some allied capitals. CCP political warfare would also aim to sow confusion about the causes of the conflict and try to disguise China as the aggressor by "blaming the victim."

As a strategic operation, phase 1A would be designed to shape the theater, weaken, and encourage the collapse of "enemy states" that stand in Beijing's way and persuade US and allied decision-makers to turn away and stand aloof. Towards the end of this phase Beijing might choose to intensify political warfare operations further by escalating their scale and intensity (i.e. vertical escalation), expanding the conflict into new physical or virtual domains (horizontal escalation), or suing for peace and terminating the conflict. This negotiation option is displayed in figure 9 as vertical line N1.

Phase 1B: Intensified Political Warfare Operations

Towards the end of phase 1A, Beijing may realize that the immediately targeted state or states are unlikely to collapse quickly. Indeed, there is a strong possibility that China's political warfare operations would harden target state resolve and strengthen allied and partner determination to stare down China's coercive behavior and dis-integration operations. In this situation, the CCP leadership is unlikely to be in a mood to back down.

This would lead to phase 1B, in which the Chinese party-state would greatly intensify its political warfare operations to intimidate, weaken, and dis-integrate decision-making and broader communities in the immediately targeted state(s), the United States, and key allies. The regime would likely whip up nationalist sentiment across China and generate a hostile environment for the diplomatic missions of targeted countries and for most foreign-owned enterprises. Demonstrations may be organized in Chinese cities, boycotts launched against Western companies, some

American and allied personnel may be arrested on trumped-up charges, and physical attacks launched, possibly injuring expatriate citizens and damaging local facilities.

Within the locally threatened state(s), the United States, and other targeted countries, Chinese agencies, front organizations, and other entities would double down and greatly expand the scope, scale, reach, and intensity of their political warfare campaigns. The primary goals would be to exacerbate domestic divisions, mislead communities, generate confusion and, where possible, create a sense of helplessness. Chinese agencies would manipulate and sometimes directly threaten individuals, media organizations, and key commercial and government entities. Funding would flow from unconventional sources to "peace" movements and other dissident organizations. Disinformation would proliferate, and the staff of some US and allied enterprises would be encouraged to strike against their governments' actions. Thousands of protesters would hit the streets in the US and allied countries, with a prevailing sense of crisis and foreboding fostered.

The divisive stresses in most of the targeted countries would be amplified by deeply polarized media ecosystems. Normal democratic debates would often degenerate into arguments and in some cases into violent clashes. National and allied will to resist the Chinese political warfare offensive would fracture with some prominent individuals and groups arguing for various forms of appeasement and strategic retreat.

To exacerbate the challenges in targeted countries Chinese entities would probably make expanded use of cyber and other means to incapacitate a wide range of physical, electronic, and virtual services in the utility, transport, media, health, and other sectors.

In this confused environment, the governments of the US and allied countries would be seriously challenged to maintain coherent counternarratives, economic stability, and national responses. In some communities, the primary focus would shift from countering China's political warfare offensive to the protection and continued operation of local services.

Some targeted societies may struggle to maintain cohesion, national direction, and democratic processes. A rise in hopelessness, defeatism, and isolationist sentiment could follow.

During the course of phase 1B, it would probably become clear that the Chinese regime was not acting alone in the conduct of some of its intensified political warfare operations. China and Russia share an interest in undermining and weakening the US and its allies. Indeed, the two authoritarian regimes have exchanged views and have probably already cooperated in some political warfare operations.[7] Hence, in the event of a developing crisis between China and the US, some Russian involvement should be anticipated. A small number of other authoritarian regimes could also be expected to contribute to the campaign. North Korea and Iran could view participation to be in their interests.

Phase 2A: China Launches a Military Assault on a Targeted Local State

At some stage during phase 1B, the Chinese regime may conclude that intensified political warfare operations on their own would neither trigger the collapse of the targeted regional state nor prevent the US and its allies from strengthening their security operations in the Indo-Pacific. In those circumstances, Beijing would have some tough choices to make. It could back down under the cover of a face-saving narrative. This is indicated as negotiation point 2 (N2) in figure 9. Alternatively, Beijing might choose to continue its intensified political warfare operations indefinitely in the hope that its opponents would eventually become so weakened and exhausted that they yield under the guise of a tension-reduction agreement or peace deal. A third option (indicated as phase 2A) would be to maintain the political warfare offensive but supplement it with a carefully calibrated military operation designed to seize the targeted local state (e.g., Taiwan) without triggering meaningful US and allied intervention. In theory, this might be achieved by a slow-paced international blockade, the sequential capture of Taiwan's outer islands, or a leisurely paced, phased military assault. However, because these approaches would provide plenty of time for Washington and allied capitals to respond with large-scale redeployments and the application of substantial force, they are unlikely to be favored by Beijing. A more attractive option would probably be a lightning military assault against the targeted local state that catches the US and its allies off guard and achieves a speedy fait accompli.

The Chinese leadership would appreciate that all of these options carry substantial risk. In particular, they would worry that a limited kinetic operation against Taiwan or another targeted state may not be possible without triggering an immediate and very forceful intervention by American and allied forces, possibly resulting in a serious Chinese military defeat. That type of outcome could be catastrophic for the Chinese Communist Party, not least for its domestic legitimacy and continued rule.

Nevertheless, there is a strong possibility that Xi Jinping and his colleagues would be convinced that the PLA could deliver what they call the "three dominances": localized command of the sea, command of the air, and command of information.[8] China's coordinated multi-domain planning would need to be of an exceptionally high standard, and the operation would need to be undertaken with great speed and skill. If the leadership believed that the PLA and relevant supporting agencies had achieved a sufficient level of proficiency, they might be given a green light to launch a fait accompli operation against the targeted state.

In order for this type of attack to be given the best chance of success, Beijing would make extensive use of subterfuge and deception. Taiwan, the US, and its allies would be encouraged to believe that any change in Chinese readiness states, unit deployments, and other activities in preceding weeks were routine operations. When the primary assault is about to be launched, key allied surveillance and intelligence assets would be misled and/or blinded, possibly under the cover of cascading power outages or other relatively innocent events.[9] Cyber operators and political warfare agencies would spread credible stories to deceive intelligence agencies and delay US and allied decision-making.

A likely approach would be for the PLA to conduct a large multi-domain exercise in the targeted region and then, in a surprise change of focus, elite special force units would be inserted into the targeted state to seize the highest-priority people and facilities. Then, within 2–3 hours, powerful missile strikes, bombing, and other attacks would destroy or disrupt key command and control sites and combat units in the targeted country before they are able to deploy for operations. The larger PLA air and seaborne units would race to the scene shortly thereafter. One well-connected Chinese commentator has stated that the PLA plans to achieve its primary operational objectives in Taiwan within 14 hours.[10] The goal would be to shock the targeted government, the military, and most of the society into immediate submission. By the time that allied agencies gain a clear picture of the operation, the scope for intervention may have evaporated.

Were the Chinese to succeed with this type of surprise assault on Taiwan, the strategic impact would be profound. A large hole will have been punched through the first island chain—the primary allied defensive line in the Western Pacific. The seizure of Taiwan would give the PLA the freedom to develop bases and deploy missile, air, and naval forces that would directly threaten Japan, especially the Ryukyu Island chain in the country's southern region.

An even bigger strategic impact of a successful Chinese assault of this kind would be the loss of American credibility. The US would be seen to be unwilling and unable to defend a partner democracy, despite having been aware of the Chinese threat for several decades. Many of America's closest allies would be brought to question the deterrence and defensive value of their strategic relationships with the United States. In order for Washington to avoid this disaster, time would be of the essence. If the White House hesitates to intervene on the earliest indications of a Chinese invasion or decides to turn away and avoid a major war at all costs, America and its allies could suffer their greatest defeat since the Second World War.

Were this failure to occur, the options for recovering the situation would be daunting. While the United States might be capable of raising, training, and deploying the substantial forces that would be required to recapture Taiwan, it would take at least two years to prepare and would necessitate a very large war with China. Substantial US, allied, and local casualties would be inevitable. Such an operation would also confront the real prospect of Beijing using tactical nuclear weapons to defend their newly won territory. The dilemmas for the allies would be acute. America and its allies may have lost their long-held escalation dominance. Meanwhile, Chinese and probably Russian political warfare organizations would continue to be active in dividing, undermining, and dis-integrating American and allied political will. This situation is described in greater detail in phase 2B.

Another possibility is that when confronted by such flagrant aggression, the allies decide to turn the tables on Beijing immediately by launching a major counteroffensive to destroy most of China's navy and much of its theater missile and tactical air strike forces. Part of the logic would be that the US and the allies should fight with their strongest and most immediately deployable weapons—mostly in the maritime, cyber, and space domains—and follow up with crippling economic and political warfare offensives. The goals would be to exact a terrible price on the Chinese regime and force the PLA to withdraw all of its forces to the mainland.

Conducting kinetic strikes against the Chinese mainland would carry significant risks, especially if the missile, air force, and naval base targets played important roles in supporting China's nuclear strategic deterrent forces. In consequence, there is likely to be support in some allied capitals for a more cautious approach. This might entail a sustained effort to defeat Chinese political warfare operations and ramp up allied offensive political, economic, and ideological operations to isolate, undermine, weaken, and eventually topple the CCP regime in Beijing. This type of campaign would likely take decades, pose huge challenges for the development and maintenance of allied unity and resilience, and ultimately be of uncertain value. Much of the international community, including large numbers of American and allied citizens, would likely view such a response as appeasement and a serious strategic defeat.

In Beijing the Chinese leadership may weigh these and other possible scenarios and decide that the risks of a fait accompli attack are acceptable and approve the operation for launch. Alternatively, the regime may conclude that despite the attractions of a lightning invasion of Taiwan (or maybe the Philippines), such a major operation could not be launched without triggering an immediate American and allied intervention. Their assessment could be that the risks of a Chinese failure would simply be too high. In that event, Chinese Communist Party leadership may discard phase 2A and move to achieve their goals by launching a surprise full-scale conventional war against the US and its core allies. This alternative campaign is described in phase 2B.

Phase 2B: A Full-Scale Conventional War Between China and the US and its Allies

At first glance, it would appear unlikely that Xi Jinping and his colleagues would rationally choose to launch a full-scale conventional war against the United States and its allies. Such a course would carry very serious risks; it would almost inevitably result in the death of a large number of Chinese citizens and would likely trigger far-reaching economic sanctions. However, when one considers this option within the framework of what is known about how Xi Jinping thinks, it starts to look like a credible possibility.

There are at least six reasons why Xi Jinping might launch a major conventional war against the US and its allies. First, Xi and his colleagues talk frequently about how China is growing in strength and the United States is failing. A common refrain is that "The East is rising and the

West is declining."[11] Indeed, Chinese spokespeople and commentators sometimes engage in deeper criticism of the American model of democracy, the failure of successive US administrations to develop a strong, united society, and Washington's allegedly poor record of delivering prosperity to its citizens.[12] At least in public, Xi exudes a high level of self-confidence. As Elizabeth Economy has written, Xi appears to be "a leader convinced that the world is there for China's taking."[13] There is a risk that Xi might believe too much of his own propaganda.

A second reason why Xi Jinping could favor launching a major war against the US alliance is that he appears to have a strong sense of his own destiny. He may see winning a war against the US as his best chance of delivering the China Dream, achieving full "rejuvenation of the Chinese nation," and securing an honored place in the annals of Chinese history.

A third reason why Xi might prefer to launch a major war is that he may believe that Chinese society is well prepared ideologically, politically, and industrially to prevail in a major war. He has certainly given these issues a great deal of attention since his ascension to the leadership, and he may feel that the party's strong internal security apparatus is well placed to maintain social cohesion and morale even under the most extreme external pressure. His personal experience of the privations during the Cultural Revolution may have also led him to believe that Chinese society is inherently more resilient than those in the West.

Fourth, the PLA has been developed, structured, and trained to fight such a war. The Chinese leadership knows that in many respects the PLA outnumbers and outguns US and allied forces in the Western Pacific. Further, if Xi wishes to launch a major war or if he feels that such a war is inevitable, he has strong incentives to strike first. Xi knows that if he moves early by launching devastating missile, bombing, and special force strikes against the allies' concentrated bases and forces in the Western Pacific, it will be very difficult for the US and its allies to recover in the short term and vastly expensive in the long term. He may believe that a decisive victory could be won quickly.

Fifth, it is possible that China may initially plan to confine a conflict to the seizure of Taiwan or another limited goal (as described in the discussion of phase 2A) but be surprised by the speed and force of the US and allied response. Xi might suddenly find himself with the options of suing for peace and withdrawing in humiliating defeat or escalating the fight into a full-scale war. In those circumstances, he may choose full-scale war.

Finally, Xi Jinping and his colleagues appear not to be easily deterred by elevated levels of risk. On several occasions, Xi has launched undertakings—such as the ones in the South China Sea, against the Japanese Senkaku Islands, and into northern India—that would never be seriously contemplated by a Western democracy. Initiating a major war against the US and its allies would entail a high level of risk, but Xi may believe that China's prospects are good and that taking decisive action to install communist China as the dominant power in the Indo-Pacific is the nation's manifest destiny.

When such a major war starts and is underway, the pace of operations would probably be very rapid for the first few weeks. Chinese forces would attempt to capitalize on any initial surprise by doing as much damage as possible to the allies' forward bases and deployed forces. Powerful cyber and space operations would also be launched very early to degrade allied situational awareness and damage theater communications, command and control, and other systems.

China would also aim to conduct offensive operations against some targets that are farther from the Western Pacific. Allied ports and shipping might be attacked on American and allied coasts, special force raids may strike distant facilities, and sleeper cells may be activated in several countries to assassinate,[14] kidnap, and hold hostage government ministers, senior officials, and business leaders.[15]

Chinese political warfare operations would strive to dominate and further manipulate prevailing narratives in the deeply shocked allied communities. Prominent themes would likely be the dramatization of allied losses, the supreme power and confidence of the PLA, and the hopelessness of further resistance. Some political warfare operations would also be designed to deepen domestic divisions in allied societies and foster resistance to emergency measures launched by allied governments. Additional disruptions would be caused by cyber strikes against public utilities, large corporations, media outlets, and many educational and community organizations. Some domestic sabotage operations would likely reinforce the sense of crisis.

In the event of this type of major conventional war, Russia could be expected to continue its political warfare and dis-integration operations against the US and some allies, probably in close coordination with China's operations in this field. Moscow might also see the war in the East as an opportunity to win further control over its western and southern border regions, extend its Ukraine operations by launching assaults on one or more of the Baltic republics, prize one or more countries away from NATO and the EU, and further erode American power and confidence.[16] In the medium term, the Western allies may view the possibility of a two-front war as a persistent risk.

Chinese and allied forces would likely suffer heavy losses in the first few days. The PLA would soon start to deplete its large, albeit finite, stocks of theater ballistic and cruise missiles and start to run out of operationally significant targets in the main areas of operation. The United States and its allies would work hard to disperse, hide, and protect their forward-deployed assets. In and around the first island chain, allied forces would launch powerful strikes against Chinese maritime targets. These would be supplemented by cyber, space, and underwater units and by long-range air assaults launched from distant locations, including from the US mainland.

However, the pace of operations would likely slow within 4–6 weeks and phase 2B would draw to a close. Although both sides would probably be badly bruised and bleeding, neither side is likely to have been able to deliver a knockout blow. Both sides have such strategic depth and scale as to render that prospect remote.

Another possibility is that one or both sides could call for a ceasefire, negotiate an armistice, or even conclude a peace agreement. This possibility of conflict negotiation and termination is indicated by the N4 vertical line in figure 9. However, on balance this would seem to be unlikely at such an early stage of the war. A more credible prospect is that once commenced, the war would continue in an evolving style and for a much longer period in phase 3A.

Phase 3A: Extended Conventional War Between China and the US Alliance

In phase 3A the two sides would recalibrate, review their strategies, work frantically to recover from their initial losses, mobilize large parts of their economies, and prepare to fight for many months and, more likely, several years.

China would maintain and probably extend its intensive political warfare offensive and conduct more military, cyber, space, economic warfare, and other operations against the allies. While these would cause further damage, they would mostly be designed to undermine American confidence, convince the US public that the war was a lost cause, and collapse allied political will to continue the fight. Beijing would use all of the resources at its disposal to encourage US leaders to negotiate a ceasefire and withdraw from the Western Pacific.

The United States, for its part, would look to impose crippling military, economic and reputational costs on Beijing and force the regime to negotiate major concessions or face a serious risk of China fracturing and collapsing under the strain.

One focus of the US alliance would be to inflict a succession of serious defeats on the PLA. Chinese military command-and-control systems would be disrupted; most of the PLA Navy would be sunk, damaged, or locked up in closed ports; large numbers of PLA aircraft would be destroyed or incapacitated; and those parts of the PLA theater missile force located in the coastal provinces would be suppressed. In addition, many of China's power, water, and transport systems would be damaged and critical-defense-production capabilities would be starved of critical components and raw materials.

These military operations would be supported by a multi-layered economic warfare campaign against China. The allies and their coalition partners would likely impose a blockade on external supplies of almost all technologies, along with most categories of manufactured goods, energy supplies, and raw materials. They would do this by working to prevent most China-bound cargoes loading and leaving ports or airports of origin. Another layer of the campaign would interdict, redirect, or arrest China-bound ships on the high seas and aircraft in international airspace. Those ships and aircraft that manage to reach China regardless would be banned from engaging in further international trade. Many ships and aircraft would be effectively locked into their ports or airports of arrival for the duration of the conflict. Special operations would also be undertaken to damage and disrupt overland supply routes.

In order to limit the electronic transfer of military, technological, economic, and other strategically relevant information, international communication links to China would be severely disrupted. Reinforcing all of these initiatives, the allies would rapidly build their political warfare capabilities in a belated attempt to compete more effectively with Beijing in that domain. The impact of these and related allied operations would be felt in most parts of China within weeks, with serious impacts on rates of production and many areas of civilian life within three months.

During the course of phase 3A, there would be limited periods of intense combat interspersed with long periods of lower-intensity operations. The Chinese would aim to launch periodic surprise strikes against the US and its allies in unexpected locations and using unconventional modes.[17] Some would be raids or assaults against targets in allied homelands and could involve the use of chemical, biological, or radiological weaponry. All of

RUSSIA, IRAN,

these operations would be framed within Beijing's continuing political warfare offensive and be designed to drive home the perception that China cannot be defeated and further allied resistance would be futile.

As with earlier phases of the struggle, there is a strong prospect that Russia and some other authoritarian states would assist China in fighting such a war. Moscow is almost certain to continue political warfare, cyber, and subversive operations against the US and its allies and would probably upgrade its intelligence flows to Beijing. Russia could also be expected to supply China not only with large quantities of oil, gas, and food but probably also some military equipment, spare parts, and components. For the regime in Beijing, a close partnership with Moscow and, to a lesser extent, with Tehran, Pyongyang, and Islamabad would extend China's strategic depth and, hence, its campaign endurance and resilience.

During the course of this long and costly phase, the core nature of the struggle would change. Combat operations would continue to be important. But the primary focus of the contest would likely shift over time to the two sides' economic, societal, and political resilience. In this type of war, victory often goes to the side that remains united, coherent, and resolutely standing on its feet.

In the later stages of phase 3A, both sides would have options for what happens next. It is possible that one side would be so exhausted that it decides to make significant concessions and sue for peace. That negotiation option is illustrated by the vertical line N5 in figure 9.

However, it is also possible that neither side wishes to concede and that the fighting in multiple domains extends phase 3A for a further period. Eventually however, one or both sides are likely to detect signs of wilting on the other side and decide to accelerate the enemy's collapse. There would be a number of options for attempting to bring the war to an end, most of which would require a period of intensified operations. This final drive for victory is the logic for phase 3B.

It is very possible that the phases of an Indo-Pacific war shown in figure 9 might not unfold in the sequence and manner portrayed. The leadership in Beijing might perceive a need to escalate quickly from 1A to 2A or even to 2B—essentially skipping some phases to inflict powerful preemptive damage on allied forces and shock them into an early withdrawal from the theater. At each phase, there is also a possibility that one side or the other might call for a ceasefire and head for the negotiating table. If such negotiations produce an outcome that is acceptable to both sides, kinetic hostilities might halt immediately.

Phase 3B: Intensified Operations to Seize Victory

Many signs of severe stress and exhaustion would be obvious in both China and the United States during phase 3A. China would probably have lost nearly all of the PLA Navy and most of its capability for long-range surveillance and intelligence in the Pacific and Indian Oceans. Worse still, the Chinese economy would probably be seriously damaged, with a significant part of the power grid offline as well as overland transport, the construction sector, and most nonmilitary manufacturing running well below prewar levels.

The challenges confronting Beijing would likely be further complicated by the probability of severe weather at some stage during this very long phase causing serious food shortages. In normal times, the effects of drought, flood, and extreme cold weather are ameliorated by greatly expanded imports of food, energy, and other critical supplies and large shipments across the Chinese landmass. Unfortunately, during phase 3A, those operations are likely to be greatly curtailed. In consequence, the war would probably deliver extreme privations to the Chinese people, including periods of widespread starvation.[18] Many migrant workers would be forced out of the cities and into country areas in efforts to boost food and subsistence production. The most vulnerable communities would likely be in the northern and western provinces, but there would be serious challenges for all parts of the country.

The stresses experienced by Chinese citizens would be exacerbated by the ongoing need to defend local communities and installations from sustained allied cyberattacks and periodic missile, air, and special force strikes. PLA and the People's Armed Police units would need to maintain a high degree of readiness in depth.

The economic, psychological, and social costs would be draining, and the security implications for the regime would be far-reaching. Domestic disturbances would probably increase, and there would likely be local strikes of workers and struggling communities. Anti-regime and anti-war sentiment may grow. However, the Peoples' Armed Police and other elements of the domestic security apparatus would detect such troubles early and would likely be ruthless in suppressing disturbances. Ringleaders would be arrested quickly, charged with sedition, and probably executed as traitors.

The level of distress experienced in some communities might lead to desertions in military and police units and possibly even to an attempted coup. However, the prospects of any dramatic change in the CCP regime would probably be low, except possibly if phase 3B were to bring China's society to almost complete collapse.

The long-running phase 3A would also see increasing strains in the United States and most of its allies. American and allied bases in the Western Pacific are likely to have been seriously damaged, and forward deployed military units would probably have suffered heavy losses. By the end of this phase, allied military casualties could run to tens of thousands, with an even larger number of civilians killed, but US and allied forces would probably dominate most areas of the Indo-Pacific that are more than 1,000 miles from Chinese territory.

Within the US and allied countries, there may have been some shortages of food, energy, and other essential items during the first few months of the war. But the bigger challenge is likely to be the rise of domestic dissent, especially in the fractured American society. Mostly sparked by genuine concerns but fanned by intense Chinese and Russian political warfare operations, anti-war movements would likely grow strongly during phase 3A. "Peace" demonstrations could be expected to proliferate and grow in size. There might also be anti-war strikes by some corporate staffs and widespread disruption in some cities. While most of these actions would be peaceful, violent clashes could be expected on some occasions as police and national guard units struggle to maintain control.

After several years of phase 3A, the stresses on the US Congress, the American mass media, and broader parts of society may be much more obvious. There are likely to be debates in some communities about whether the war should be continued or called to a halt. This would be the context for the leaderships of China and/or the United States deciding to intensify pressure on the other side in efforts to short-circuit the war and force their enemies to collapse.

The Chinese approach to pressuring the United States to give way would almost certainly be to exploit America's key weaknesses. The main Chinese effort would be to further intensify their political warfare and cyber operations to divide, weaken, confuse, and dis-integrate US society and its key institutions. These operations may be supplemented by a rash of sabotage and possibly some "terrorist strikes" against US and allied personnel in their homelands and citizens living in other parts of the world. Another possibility would be the release of a new type of lethal virus in allied homelands.

The PLA would likely launch further surprise operations, in part to demonstrate that it was not a spent force and that few locations were beyond its reach. But Beijing's primary goal would be to drive home to American and allied decision-makers that a clear victory is unachievable and that an early retreat to the negotiating table is the most sensible way forward.

Washington's options for intensifying pressure on Beijing would probably look rather different to those considered by the Chinese. While the US and its allies may have attempted to punch holes through China's Great Firewall to facilitate direct communication with the Chinese people, these operations would probably have had little success. In consequence, the allies would likely work to exploit their relative advantages in maritime military capabilities and democratic frameworks to further tighten the economic and political isolation of China. To those ends, further efforts may be made to draw additional neutral states into the allied coalition.

In phase 3B, US and allied forces would probably sharpen and intensify their attacks on key economic sectors and on core systems of CCP control. While these operations would inflict further pain on the regime and the Chinese people, their strategic impact so late in the war may be limited.

The results of the intensified operations on both sides in phase 3B would probably be inconclusive. It is possible that there could be a coup or other dramatic change in the regime in Beijing. It is also possible that a "peace" candidate could win the next American presidential election. However, on balance, it is more likely that neither side would make much progress and that both would eventually reconcile themselves to the inevitability of a negotiated outcome, indicated by vertical line N6 in figure 9. When that happens, discussions would probably begin via secret channels.

Phase 4: Negotiated Settlement but Political Warfare Continues

This final phase assumes that China and the United States eventually negotiate a ceasefire and then an armistice or peace agreement. This may not happen quickly. The experience of the wars in Vietnam, Afghanistan, and other theaters is that peace talks may get underway while fighting continues, but the negotiations may drag on for many months.

Once the formal fighting stops and both sides become convinced that an agreement will be honored, all parties would start to turn their attention to postwar reconstruction. The economic challenges would be substantial. However, once a degree of normality is restored, some or all parties could expect periods of moderate or even rapid economic growth.

Whether prewar patterns of economic trade, finance, and other economic interactions between the two camps would be restored is doubtful. The primary drivers of economic globalization would have been seriously damaged, and trust between the two sides would be difficult to rebuild.

Further complicating the situation is that powerful interests in both camps are likely to consider any peace settlement to be temporary and the wartime struggle to remain unfinished business. Unless there is a regime change in Beijing, there would almost certainly be a strong Chinese desire to maintain active political warfare operations against the United States, it allies and partners, and most neutral states. These operations and the substantial organizations that manage them have an enduring place in the Chinese Communist Party's strategic culture and are likely to have an ongoing role in the pursuit of the party's interests internationally and at home.

The United States and most allied and partner countries would have strong incentives to remain detached from China economically, technologically, politically, and ideologically. In the postwar era, indicated as phase 4, the Chinese Communist Party would probably be viewed by most of the world with disdain. Hence while the kinetic fighting may have ceased, the scene may be set for the struggle to continue in another guise—a new long-running "warm war."

The Critical Dimensions of Fighting a Major Indo-Pacific War

A major war between China and the United States and their respective allies would be much more complex and demanding than most analysts and practitioners assume. Viewing the challenge as a simple transition from peace to a military-dominated war is oversimplified and misleading.

In reality there would likely be several distinct phases of such a war. Each phase would have its own characteristics, require tailored operational concepts and campaign plans, different or substantially modified tool kits, and at least some specialized skill sets. Moreover, each phase would operate within its own timeframes. Getting the mixes of capabilities and capacities right and in place in appropriate timescales would be essential to deliver optimal effects, to gain the upper hand, and eventually to attain victory.

There are four primary categories of capability that would be critical to success:

1. **Military capabilities** of substantial size, operating with a relevant mix of multi-domain systems, driven by appropriate theater strategies and operational concepts, staffed by well-trained, experienced, and disciplined personnel directed by exceptional commanders and all tied together by a well-designed and very resilient command-and-control system.
2. **Geostrategic positioning** involving the building of trusted and deeply collegiate alliances and security partnerships with like-minded countries and international agencies. Diplomatic and broader relationship-building capabilities would play a strong role here and in arranging the pre-positioning of forces and capabilities in appropriate locations with resilient local support.
3. **Economic-industrial capabilities** of substantial size and relevant diversity possessing highly innovative cultures and practices. They would include advanced design and manufacturing capabilities supported by very resilient finance, energy, logistics, and transport networks.
4. **Social and political unity and cohesion** driven by shared values, deep ideological foundations, and agreed security goals. All of these factors should generate steely national will and strong resilience. Exceptional leadership would be required.

Strength in all four categories would be essential for success in any major Indo-Pacific war. Dominance in only one or two categories would probably not be sufficient. Likewise, chronic weakness in just one of these key categories could be crippling and may lead to defeat.

While all four categories of capability would be needed in every phase of a major war, their relative priority for each side would change as the conflict progressed. For instance, in the initial kinetic phases (2A and 2B), military and economic-industrial requirements are likely to be the top priorities, together with continuing efforts to bind up social and political unity and cohesion.

Phase 3A would probably be the longest and most draining of the kinetic phases and could run for several years. While this phase would continue to place pressure on military resources, an even higher priority, as the struggle drags on, would probably be economic-industrial capabilities and the demands of social and political unity and coherence.

The development and rebalancing of priorities during the progression of a major war could not be managed effectively by a single government department or probably even a conglomerate of departments and agencies. The diversity of domains, the complexities of the systems, the knowledge bases, and levels of experience to manage activities across all four critical categories in short timeframes would be exceptionally demanding. Diverse business, media, logistic, and many other skills would need to be harnessed. Whole-of-government and, in most phases of the war, whole-of-alliance assessments and decisions would be required of types that have rarely, if ever, been necessary in the past.

The imperatives of adapting effectively to the demands of a major war are strong. Peacetime systems and habits of operation would not be adequate. Given that there is a possibility of a major war erupting in the Indo-Pacific at short notice, an early priority should be the design, structuring, and testing of highly skilled, robust, and resilient national and allied command-and-control arrangements tailored for the task.

The Probable Shape of a Major Indo-Pacific War

In summary then, the primary features of a war between China and the United States in the Indo-Pacific would likely be as follows:

1. There would be two combatant camps and a large number of neutral countries.
2. Intensified political warfare and cyber operations are likely to be launched against the US and its allies prior to the initiation of kinetic attacks.
3. There are four primary scenarios that may trigger a major kinetic war between China and the United States:
   - China launches a deliberate attack on contested territory, most likely Taiwan, resulting in rapid escalation and major war.
   - China launches a deliberate, massive, and multi-layered attack on American and allied forces in the Western Pacific in an attempt to knock US forces out of the war, and the theater, by swift preemptive action.
   - With the United States and its allies suffering fierce Chinese and Russian political warfare and cyberattacks and sensing the imminence of follow-on kinetic attacks, Washington may decide to launch kinetic strikes first, primarily against China's communications, command, control, and intelligence systems and its key maritime capabilities.
   - During a period of heightened tension, an accidental clash between the two sides escalates into major war.
4. The use of tactical nuclear weapons in such a war is possible. A strong case can be made that some aspects of nuclear deterrence are eroding.[19] Even limited use would have strong psychological impacts and force national leaderships to recalibrate their strategic and theater campaign plans. The shock could increase the incentives for both sides to negotiate an early ceasefire. But on balance, nuclear use would probably be avoided by both sides. It is more likely that the kinetic phases of a major Indo-Pacific war would be conventional, supplemented by some hybrid terrorist-like operations. Nevertheless, care is needed with these assumptions. If one side is losing badly or suffering huge losses in the later phases of such a war, the probability of nuclear use could rise substantially.

5. Cyber and counter-space operations would feature prominently. There may also be some limited use of chemical and biological weapons.
6. While both sides would like to win such a war quickly, this is unlikely to happen. Both sides possess great strategic depth and scale, and neither is likely to be able to deliver a speedy knock-out blow.
7. A major war in the Indo-Pacific would probably become a lengthy struggle in which both sides suffer substantial human, military, economic, and social losses.
8. There will be few, if any, sanctuaries on earth in a major Indo-Pacific war.
9. A major war in this theater would probably progress through several phases, each of which would have significantly different characteristics and requirements.
10. China and the United States are both preparing for the possibility of having to fight a major war in the Indo-Pacific. However, their investment patterns have quite different emphases. On the US side the primary focus is on improving military capabilities and geostrategic positioning. On the Chinese side, by contrast, the preparations are on a larger scale and of a more wide-ranging nature. They spread across all four critical dimensions with especially heavy investments in social and political cohesion, economic resilience, and in many categories of military capability.
11. If a major US-China war broke out in the mid-2020s, the American and Chinese sides would possess capabilities that are dissimilar but of broadly comparable strength.
12. The American and allied publics cannot outsource the fighting of a major war against China to their military and defense organizations and expect a successful outcome. In this sense, the current American and allied conception of major war is too narrow. It is vulnerable to being outflanked by China's use of a broader range of domains and instruments and Beijing's much heavier focus on

social-political, economic-industrial, and geostrategic leverage. In order for the allied coalition to prevail in this type of contest they would need to mobilize a much broader range of resources. And these resources would need to be available to support the war effort for an extended period.

13. Even after a long struggle, the result would probably not be a decisive victory by either side. While it is possible that the stresses of a drawn-out war might cause the political collapse of one side, the deep resilience of both camps when subjected to great pressure means that the more likely endpoint would be a negotiated settlement, with one side then having the upper hand and dictating the primary terms.
14. In the final phases of a major Indo-Pacific war, the corrosive effects of China's ever-present political warfare and cyber campaigns would likely have a powerful influence on the outcome. Ultimately, such a conflict would probably be a struggle not so much over which side has the strongest military forces or even the strongest economy. It would more probably be a battle to determine which side has the strongest, most united, and most resilient society.[20]

NOTES

1. These operations are detailed at length in Ross Babbage, *Winning Without Fighting: Chinese and Russian Political Warfare Campaigns and How the West Can Prevail*, vols 1 and 2. See also Nathan Beauchamp-Mustafaga, "Cognitive Domain Operations: The PLA's New Holistic Concept for Influence Operations," Jamestown Foundation, *China Brief* 19, 16, September 6, 2019, https://jamestown.org/program/cognitive-domain-operations-the-plas-new-holistic-concept-for-influence-operations/.
2. Statement of Admiral Philip S. Davidson, Commander United States Indo-Pacific Command, *Stenographic Transcript before the Committee on Armed Services*, 14, https://www.armed-services.senate.gov/imo/media/doc/21-10_03-09-2021.pdf.
3. Office of the Secretary of Defense, *Military and Security Developments Involving the People's Republic of China 2021*, 45, 161–163. See also Mallory Shelbourne, "Davidson: China Could Try to Take Control of Taiwan in the 'Next Six Years,'" *USNI News*, March 9, 2021, https://news.usni.org/2021/03/09/davidson-china-could-try-to-take-control-of-taiwan-in-next-six-years.
4. For photos and other details, see Joseph Trevithick, "China's Largest Base Has Replicas of Taiwan's Presidential Building, Eiffel Tower," *The War Zone*, May 27, 2020, https://www.thedrive.com/the-war-zone/33591/chinas-biggest-base-has-huge-replicas-of-taiwans-presidential-building-and-the-eiffel-tower.
5. Demetri Sevastopulo, "US Defence Chief Warns of China 'Rehearsals' for Attack on Taiwan," *Financial Times*, December 5, 2021, https://www.ft.com/content/21711040-5123-4077-a5ec-b76731fcba1e.
6. Bill Gerz, "U.S. Pacific Intel Chief: Coming Chinese Attack on Taiwan Could Target Other Countries," *Washington Times*, July 8, 2021, https://www.washingtontimes.com/news/2021/jul/8/us-pacific-intel-chief-coming-chinese-attack-taiwan/.
7. Michael Kofman, "The Emperors League: Understanding Sino-Russian Defense Cooperation," *War on the Rocks*, August 6, 2020, https://warontherocks.com/2020/08/the-emperors-league-understanding-sino-russian-defense-cooperation/. Note that President Putin and Xi Jinping set down a clear marker for the future of their security relationship at their Summit in Beijing on February 4, 2022. Their joint statement stated,

in part: "They [the two parties] reaffirm that the new inter-State relations between Russia and China are superior to political and military alliances of the Cold War era. Friendship between the two States has no limits, there are no 'forbidden' areas of cooperation...." *Joint Statement of the Russian Federation and the People's Republic of China on the International Relations Entering a New Era and the Global Sustainable Development*, February 4, 2022, http://en.kremlin.ru/supplement/5770#sel=1:21:S5F,1:37:3jE.

8. Jared M. McKinney and Peter Harris, "Broken Nest: Deterring China from Invading Taiwan," *The US Army War College Quarterly: Parameters* 51, no. 4 (November 17, 2021, 27, https://press.armywarcollege.edu/cgi/viewcontent.cgi?article=3089&context=parameters.
9. See this discussed in Samson Ellis and Cindy Wang, "Taiwan Warns China Can 'Paralyze' Island's Defenses in Conflict," Bloomberg, September 1, 2021, https://www.bloomberg.com/news/articles/2021-09-01/taiwan-warns-of-china-s-ability-to-paralyze-island-s-defenses.
10. McKinney and Harris, "Broken Nest," 25.
11. See this and related issues discussed in Elizabeth Economy, "China's Inconvenient Truth."
12. Ibid.
13. Elizabeth Economy, "Xi Jinping's New World Order," *Foreign Affairs*, January/February 2022, https://www.foreignaffairs.com/articles/china/2021-12-09/xi-jinpings-new-world-order.
14. Chinese doctrine and debates include many references to "assassin's mace" operations that include physical assassinations of enemy leaders. See Jason E. Bruzdzinski, "Demystifying Shashoujian: China's Assassin's Mace Concept" in *Change in China*, eds. Andrew Scobell and Larry Wortzell, (Carlisle: US Army War College, 2004), https://www.jstor.org/stable/resrep11969.13?seq=1.
15. Ibid. Chinese military doctrine and debates make reference to "assassin's mace" that refer to assassinations and other operations to incapacitate or destroy an enemy's leadership.
16. *Joint Statement of the Russian Federation and the People's Republic of China on the International Relations Entering a New Era and the Global Sustainable Development*, February 4, 2022.
17. See several of these possibilities discussed in Robert O. Work and Greg Grant, *Beating the Americans at their Own Game: An Offset Strategy with Chinese Characteristics* (Washington, DC: Center for a New American Security, 2019).

18. The Chinese leadership is deeply concerned about the security of essential supplies such as energy, grains and minerals in future crises and Xi Jinping has discussed these challenges openly on a number of occasions. See Orange Wang, "Xi Jinping Says China Must be 'Self-sufficient' in Energy, Food and Minerals Amid Global Challenges," *South China Morning Post*, December 13, 2021, https://www.scmp.com/economy/china-economy/article/3159522/xi-jinping-says-china-must-be-self-sufficient-energy-food-and; and Orange Wang, "China Must Beware 'Grey Rhino' of Primary Commodities Shortage, Top Policymaker Warns," *South China Morning Post*, December 11, 2021, https://www.scmp.com/economy/china-economy/article/3159354/china-must-beware-grey-rhino-primary-commodities-shortage-top. On the potential for serious food shortages, see "$2.6.tn Could Evaporate from Global Economy in Taiwan Emergency," *Nikkei Asia,* August 22, 2022, https://asia.nikkei.com/static/vdata/infographics/2-dot-6tn-dollars-could-evaporate-from-global-economy-in-taiwan-emergency/.
19. See Krepinevich, *The Decline of Deterrence*, 34–46.
20. The books and reports that have been helpful in developing this analysis on the shape for a future major war include Andrew F. Krepinevich Jr., *Protracted Great Power War* (Washington, DC: Center for New American Security, 2020); Graham Allison, *Destined for War* (Boston: Mariner Books, 2018); Kerry K. Gershaneck, *Media Warfare* (Washington, DC: Center for Security Policy, 2021); Andrew F. Krepinevich Jr., *The Decline of Deterrence* (Washington, DC: Hudson Institute, 2019); and Bob Davis and Lingling Wei, *Superpower Showdown* (New York: Harper Collins Business, 2020).

Chapter 5

The Economic Context for Major War

What would be the economic dimensions of a major conflict between China and the United States? To answer this question, it is necessary to first understand the complex economic dynamics of the Indo-Pacific as they exist today, why these dynamics have developed, and how specialization and globalization have created both wealth and vulnerabilities. An understanding of these powerful economic systems is essential to plan effectively for major security crises and wars.

The major countries in the Indo-Pacific each possesses an inherent degree of economic resilience, but they are all dependent to varying degrees on the flow of trade and the associated exchange of money. Each country relies on the external supply of essential inputs and access to international markets to sell significant parts of their production. In peacetime, they transact with each other both out of preference and of necessity. But in a major war, these linkages would be placed under great stress or broken and the resilience of each nation would be severely tested.

This chapter examines current patterns of trade and finance in an era of "peace" but with rising tension at both the superpower and local levels and outlines seven key characteristics:

- **Regional and global trade linkages**, how these have formed, and how they are changing as political, technological, and commercial dynamics evolve.
- **The cross-border financial flows** that enable these trade links, and how financial positions form between countries.
- **The complexities of the supply chains** that facilitate trade across the region, emphasizing the development of global value chains that span multiple countries to produce the most sophisticated items.
- **The comparative advantages** of the region's countries, revealed in their net trade balances in different categories of products, and what they mean for each nation's resilience and vulnerability.
- **Supply chain interdependencies** between nations, and how they perceive their resulting power and vulnerabilities.
- **The scope for trade and other economic redirection** away from current patterns, and how much would be possible in the event of major war.
- **The levels of resilience in the major economies** of the Indo-Pacific, and how they could be strengthened in a major conflict.

Regional and Global Trade Linkages

On November 15, 2020, the Regional Comprehensive Economic Partnership (RCEP) free trade agreement was announced. By mid-2022, this agreement spanned fifteen partner countries: Australia, Brunei, Cambodia, China, Indonesia, Japan, South Korea, Laos, Malaysia, Myanmar, New Zealand, the Philippines, Singapore, Thailand, and Vietnam. The Joint Leaders' statement at the launch ceremony stated that RCEP would "cover a market of 2.2 billion people, or almost 30% of the world's population, generating a combined GDP of US$26.2 trillion or about 30% of global GDP, and account for nearly 28% of global trade (based on 2019 figures)."[1] Although the RCEP introduces few deep reforms to the trading system, its creation is testament to the region's self-perceived coherence as an economic bloc, broadly comparable to multinational projects in Europe and North America.

The extent of the region's economic integration can be seen in the calculations of the Asian Development Bank, which show that the bloc's internal or intraregional trade is about 58% of the region's total international trade—far higher than that in North America (40%) but slightly below that of the European Union (63%).[2] The trading patterns of the region's major economies are tightly intertwined with each other, and for many products they form a common supply chain serving the rest of the world. This effect is sometimes referred to as "Factory Asia."

The Indo-Pacific is also becoming more Sino-centric as China's proportion of direct trade with other parts of the world falls. In 1990, the biggest external trading partners of Asia (excluding China) were North America (with 25%), followed by the EU (18%). By 2019 their shares had slipped to 13% and 11%, respectively. During the same period China's share (if considered as an external counterpart) had grown from 5% of the region's trade to 25%. China is inserting itself into regional trade either as an aggregator (i.e., final assembler) or as an end customer. Of the 58% of Indo-Pacific trade that is intraregional, China alone contributes about one-third, according to the Asian Development Bank.

China has now won a dominant position as both a customer and supplier for the region. China (plus Hong Kong) buys roughly the same amount of ASEAN exports as the US and EU combined. Indeed, the ASEAN bloc is now China's largest trading partner. This development has generated much favorable commentary about ASEAN's strategic weight, but it is notable that for most ASEAN countries, China is a bigger market than all of the other bloc's members combined. The levels of export dependency of South Korea, Taiwan, and Australia on China are greater still. Even Japan, despite its very close direct trading relationship with the United States, now counts China as its top export customer.

The same is true of the Persian Gulf states. Of the Indo-Pacific's major economies, only India is less reliant on exports to the Chinese market.

Figure 10. China's Importance to Indo-Pacific Trade Partners.

	Exports to China*		Imports from China*		Balance
2019	*$bn*	%	*$bn*	%	
Japan	168.3	24%	171.3	24%	(3.0)
Korea	168.1	31%	109.0	22%	59.1
Taiwan	151.8	43%	57.3	22%	94.5
India	28.8	9%	85.8	18%	(57.0)
Australia	108.2	41%	57.4	26%	50.8
Singapore	96.0	25%	52.5	15%	43.5
Malaysia	49.8	21%	45.8	22%	4.0
Thailand	39.1	17%	48.4	22%	(9.3)
Indonesia	30.5	18%	48.1	28%	(17.6)
Vietnam	48.6	18%	76.8	30%	(28.2)

Source: Compiled from *World in Trade Statistics (WITS)* by the World Bank, https://wits.worldbank.org/countrystats.aspx?lang=en.

As seen in figure 10, the situation with imports is similar. China is the largest supplier to Indonesia, Australia, South Korea, and Taiwan by a comfortable margin—more than 50% larger than their next largest trading partner. Remarkably too, Japan and India import twice as much from China as from the US and EU, respectively, their second-ranked suppliers. And for ASEAN, imports from China are not far short of the bloc's total imports from the EU, the US, and Japan combined.

The Indo-Pacific's trade networks reflect the patterns of commerce developed over decades of relatively benign geo-economic conditions. These networks are efficient but often logistically complex, reliant on cheap transport, abundant labor, and the spare production capacities of regional states. The steady improvement of trade conditions in recent decades has lowered average global industrial tariffs from 20–30% after the Second World War to less than 10% today, a period during which world trade volumes have multiplied about 40 times.[3] The COVID-19 pandemic halted the rise of merchandise trade but only for a single year. Today's intricate trading networks are the product of the "long peace."

Formal cross-border trade in services is one-fifth of global trade, but services can account for as much as three-quarters of domestic economic activity in the most industrialized nations. Most of this activity is digitally connected. Global electronic communication bandwidth grows by about 30% every year. By some estimates, 93% of all data moves around the world via undersea cables.[4] Chinese firms are increasingly prominent builders and operators of this global network.[5]

Average global trade intensity (exports as a percentage of GDP) peaked at 30% in 2008 and has since stagnated. A major factor contributing to this decline has been a halving of China's trade intensity, with its exports falling from 36% to 18% of GDP. From 2010 to 2020, China's growth also slowed steadily and is expected to slow further. Despite this, China's economic power has continued to rise with its firms and workers becoming more skillful and innovative. China's domestic economy is now nearing the scale of the US and Europe; China is experiencing a burst of capital and capacity accumulation unmatched in history. However, at the same time as China's global market share has risen and it displaces competitors in overseas markets, its economy has become more closed and its supply lines have been drawn in. As a McKinsey report concluded: "China has been reducing its exposure to the world, while the world's exposure to China has risen."[6]

It is normal for large continental countries to trade relatively less than smaller ones because they possess substantial domestic economies. But in China's case, a strong mercantilist campaign has been underway featuring vast state subsidies and aggressive protectionist and other measures to ensure that key international markets are won and foreign competitors handicapped and often driven out of business. The result has been that China's exports have risen quickly, but its trade intensity has fallen because its domestic output has grown even faster.

Beijing's policy of dual circulation—to internalize its own huge market and to globalize selectively from a position of strength—is not merely an aspiration. It describes what actually occurred between 2005 and 2020. What is made in China is increasingly built and sold by local firms to meet domestic demand. Dual circulation does not reject globalization *per se*. Beijing wants local firms to continue to "go out" into export markets, and it welcomes inbound foreign investment so long as it is useful. Dual circulation is essentially a reframing of the 1980s mantra of "two markets, two resources" when Beijing policymakers viewed the domestic market as a resource to protect and insulate, while foreign markets were to be penetrated and exploited.[7] Driven by both anxiety and ambition, China's decoupling from the global economy was underway well before the debate on this subject began in the Western world.

Concerns over potential trade vulnerability and resilience are not new in the Indo-Pacific. Japanese firms, with their large overseas production networks, began developing sophisticated supply chain management systems from the 1970s and 1980s to mitigate against disruptions. Most major countries maintain controls on the supply chains of sensitive goods and services. Yet for all the talk of international decoupling, diversification, and diversion, progress has so far been limited. The result is that China's merchandise trade balance surged during the COVID-19 pandemic, especially its surplus with America, and so China and the EU are now the world's two largest exporters, with roughly a 15% global share each. Armed with an array of industrial policy tools, including the Made in China 2025 program, Beijing's leaders have no intention of relinquishing China's manufacturing power.[8]

Nevertheless, not all of the Indo-Pacific economy is exposed to international pressures. Most Indo-Pacific countries strive for a degree of domestic self-sufficiency and resilience. That is one of the main reasons why providers of utilities (e.g., electricity, water, telecommunications) and other vital service providers are usually owned and operated within national borders. Other notable exemplars are the national financial systems.

Cross-Border Financial Flows

Total global financial assets are in the order of $400 trillion, of which about 40% resides in the Indo-Pacific region.[9] Financial assets do not represent the entire capital stock of nations (there are other sources of non-monetized wealth such as sovereign land, natural resources, and human and social capital), but they are a fair measure of a country's disposable economic power. To give an idea of financial interconnectedness, consider that four categories—(1) foreign direct investment (FDI), (2) cross-border lending, (3) international equity portfolios (share holdings), and (4) international bond portfolios—are each about $35–40 trillion in size and total $140 trillion. Therefore, the world is about 35% financially globalized to some degree, either owned or owed across international borders. This is a remarkably high figure.

There are three essential observations about the nature of international financial stocks and flows, and the system that facilitates them. First, despite the apparently high level of financial globalization, the bulk of every major nation's capital is owned and invested domestically. Nearly all countries have domestic financial systems designed to capture and invest the savings of their populations at home. These systems can be relatively closed and self-sustaining. It is only on the margins that nations trade, lend, and borrow, pay for imports, or invest abroad.

Second, the region's cross-border financial positions can be surveyed as they stand today, but in a crisis, flows would matter more than stocks—and gross flows matter more than net flows. To explain why, consider that any two countries may lend to and invest in each other. Under normal circumstances, they will each honor their mutual obligations. Confidence that their positions will be squared is how the international financial system underwrites the flow of commerce in peacetime. However, this practice would likely be terminated in war. Bilateral flows would be subjected to a high degree of scrutiny and restriction. In a major crisis, counterparties jealously guard their treasuries and each payment. This is an extreme form of the paradox of financial liquidity: it is absent when most needed.

Third, it is necessary to distinguish between "real" and "financial" exchanges. Real exchanges are actual transactions, namely trade and direct investment. Financial exchanges facilitate the real ones, and the three principal types are claims, currency exchanges, and payments.

For example, real investment across borders (such as foreign direct investment in factories, farms, and other productive assets) creates productive capital in overseas territories, which is in extremis vulnerable to confiscation and operation behind enemy lines. Financial claims are "paper" instruments (such as shares, bonds, debts owed, or bank accounts) which, at worst, might be forfeited. Each of these variables would experience different effects and would change in varying ways during the course of a multiphase war.

Foreign Direct Investment (FDI)

FDI is arguably the most sensitive form of finance. It is the highest-powered form of investment because it is permanent equity. FDI is usually invested by multinational corporations in the most profitable and sophisticated parts of global value chains, such as mines, factories, research centers, retail, and infrastructure networks. About half of all global trade is directly attributable to the international production networks of multinationals.[10] There is an accumulated stock of about $36 trillion of FDI worldwide, of which the EU and the US combined account for over half, and about a quarter is located in the Indo-Pacific region.[11]

FDI has slowed markedly since the early 2010s relative to GDP and trade. Countries are not investing in each other with the same enthusiasm as before. Although this measure is volatile and cyclical, there has been a clear downward trend in global FDI from a peak of 5% of global GDP before the Global Financial Crisis of 2009 to 2% in 2019.[12]

This decline in FDI intensity suggests that multinational companies, the main actors in cross-border investment, are growing more cautious about investing abroad. Political and geopolitical factors as well as business motives are at play. Chinese firms have become more reticent about (or restricted from) sending FDI abroad, preferring instead to invest at home.[13] Yet the experience of 2020 tells a very different story. Despite the pandemic, strategic tensions, and fears of decoupling, FDI from other countries continued to surge into China, and total portfolio inflows rose to record levels.[14] Many multinational corporations and Wall Street investment managers rushed into China while they were still able.

However, foreign operations in China are de facto on a pathway to becoming more like local Chinese entities rather than being integrated into global networks.[15] International firms are "not decoupling from China, but rather decoupling their China operations from their global ones."[16] They are increasingly being torn between the idiosyncratic demands of the Chinese market and the need to diversify production elsewhere. Some are already forming separate red and blue supply chains.[17] "Companies are battening down the hatches [in China]. It is not that the world is leaving China; more that China is becoming a world unto itself."[18]

In contrast, the relatively open ASEAN economies have accumulated $2.7 trillion in investments from foreign enterprises and continue to attract new flows. Because they are close to China, ASEAN countries play a key role in the Factory Asia complex. They are a natural choice for multinationals seeking to diversify manufacturing to a "China+1" footprint. Moreover, some of China's own firms are now investing in ASEAN countries too, notably in infrastructure.

Figure 11 shows outbound and inbound foreign direct investment stocks for selected economies. These figures are only rough estimates because of a number of measurement uncertainties (such as the scope for some double counting).

Figure 11. Total Foreign Direct Investment Inflows and Outflows for Selected Regions and Countries (2020) in US$ billion.

2020		Outward	Inward
World		39,246	41,354
North America		10,093	11,905
Europe		17,686	16,066
Indo-Pac		10,370	10,172
	China*	4,306	3,804
	Japan	1,982	243
	Korea	501	265
	India	101	480
	Australia	627	791
	ASEAN	1,671	2,913
	Taiwan	382	110

Source: Compiled from *Beyond 20/20 WDS*, UNCTAD, https://unctadstat.unctad.org/wds/ReportFolders/reportFolders.aspx?sCS_ChosenLang=en.

International Equity and Bond Portfolios

The difficulty of counting cross-border financial flows is most acute in the categories of equity (i.e., shares) and bond securities (held individually or through investment funds). Figure 12 also shows that European and American investors hold a lot of each other's stock markets and that the US runs a substantial net national bond liability due to US Treasury issuance.

The survey also reveals that entities in three offshore financial jurisdictions (Cayman Islands, Ireland, and Luxembourg) have alone issued "equity" to foreign investors valued at almost $11 trillion. Individuals, corporations, and banks are exploiting these offshore financial centers to gain tax benefits, regulatory work-arounds, and other advantages. The most prominent user of such havens is the Chinese technology sector, which uses complex structures to get beneficiary interests into the hands of investors abroad without violating foreign ownership rules. Because these mechanisms have little regard for national interests, regulators in Washington and Beijing have been racing each other to force the delisting of these firms from American stock exchanges.

Figure 12. Total Foreign Equity and Bond Portfolio Investments for Selected Countries (First Quarter 2021) in US$ billion.

International Equity Portfolios			
		Assets	Liabilities
World		39,471	39,471
Americas	US	10,490	9,077
	Canada	1,753	953
	Cayman	2,874	4,444
Europe	UK	2,078	2,126
	Lux	1,879	3,947
	France	1,730	1,443
	Germany	2,304	1,273
	Ireland	1,055	2,524
	Neth	1,254	948
Indo-Pac	China*	2,125	1,981
	Japan	1,429	2,037
	Korea	464	619
	India	5	591
	Australia	697	489
	ASEAN	1,009	176
	Taiwan	303	573

International Bond Portfolios			
		Assets	Liabilities
World		36,846	36,846
Americas	US	3,868	10,328
	Canada	501	1,218
	Cayman	1,897	1,253
Europe	Lux	2,997	1,063
	Ireland	2,584	778
	Germany	2,635	2,783
	UK	1,622	2,168
	France	2,255	691
	Neth	1,217	1,742
Indo-Pac	China*	1,125	680
	Japan	2,996	2,837
	Korea	242	231
	India	5	85
	Australia	328	807
	ASEAN	770	198
	Taiwan	-	6

Source: Compiled from IMF Coordinated Portfolio Investment Survey (CPIS), https://data.imf.org/?sk=b981b4e3-4e58-467e-9b90-9de0c3367363.

Meanwhile, Chinese firms in many other industries dominate the registries of the British Caribbean offshore financial centers where they face little scrutiny.[19] Probably the most prolific of these entities are Chinese state-owned enterprises. The party-state leviathan is "a complex, diversified, and politicized commercial system... [in which] the average size of the largest 100 conglomerates in China increased from 500 companies in 1995 to more than 15,000 companies in 2015."[20] Chinese state-owned enterprises still account for about 40% of the national economy. They monopolize many of the country's most strategic industries, and they generate 4.5% of global GDP, an economic mass larger than India's total economy. Chinese state interests own and operate strategic assets and infrastructure in many parts of the world. The ruling Chinese Communist Party is increasingly embedded in these businesses, blurring the distinction between public and private ownership and control.

A final feature of China's hybrid economy is its extensive use of special economic zones at home and in other countries, which rely heavily on government subsidies and tax breaks and feature varying degrees of transparency. There are now 6,500 of these zones globally, of which 2,500 are located in China itself.[21]

In summary then, China's annual external financial balance is in robust surplus and its stated net international investment position is over $4 trillion, more than that of Japan or Germany—but the overall picture is murky. China's ownership and influence in international finance might be underestimated, and it is almost certainly the world's largest undeclared creditor.[22] There is substantial evidence that state and private interests have discreetly stashed huge amounts of capital overseas as investment, lending, securities, and official reserves.[23] In a global crisis, some of this funding that is located overseas could be utilized to support the regime's strategic interests.

Supply Chain Complexities

Most global economic activity takes place domestically, and this is especially true in large economies. Approximately 80% of global value-added content involves the production of goods or services at home which are *not* traded but used to meet domestic demands.[24] This underscores the potential resilience of most nations to external disruptions. Most basic needs of national citizens can be met by local resources.

The simplest type of cross-border trade involves products made completely by domestic factors for export (i.e., factor content crosses a national boundary once for direct consumption). This is known as a *traditional* global value chain. *Simple* global value chains are imports or exports of goods that cross borders for further processing and then again for final consumption. If that processed item is, in turn, exported again to other countries, then the factor content crosses a national border at least twice, and is known as *complex* global value chain activity.

Many factors determine the shape of supply chains. They are usually intricate networks ("spiders") rather than vertical chains ("snakes"). Each industry's supply chains have unique characteristics. The degree of internationalization (measured by gross exports as a share of global output) is 75–85% for electronics, machinery, textiles, and automobiles, but it is less than 15% for banking, retailing, and agriculture.[25] Mining, chemicals, pharmaceuticals, and food occupy the middle ground at between 35% and 60%. Importantly, the highest technology industries are also the most internationalized. They use multiple production-sharing steps, within multinational corporations and local contractors, across carefully chosen sets of countries. Complex activity accounts for about half of all world trade.

After 2008, economists observed a distinct shift from globalization towards regionalization, reversing the pattern of the prior two decades. This move to regionalization has been most pronounced in the Indo-Pacific, especially in complex global value chain networks. Electronics is the prime example, where production-sharing occurs between a concentrated cluster of East Asian countries. Because they are close to each other, they can transact at just-in-time speed. They have developed highly skilled workforces, huge economies of scale, and specialized production processes and product sets that have become formidable barriers to entry for other parties wishing to participate.

Multinational corporations have been keen to plug into Factory Asia, reinforcing East Asia's manufacturing primacy. In the famous case of the iPhone, Americans may generate most of the profits upstream from design services and downstream from retail services (the "smile curve"), but only Factory Asia can provide the volume manufacturing that actually builds the product. The rising centrality of China in the region that is observed at the macro trade level can also be seen in specific industries and supply networks. Characteristically, Apple's iPhone is still built mainly in China, although in recent years Apple has attempted to diversify production. In the meantime Chinese firms have learned how to develop their own brands of cell phones and other electronic products for sale at home and as exports, and further strengthened their lock-hold on the global market for key components.

This explains the stalling of global trade intensity and the rising regionalism in Asia. It also explains why foreign direct investment, at the vanguard of international financial integration, has slowed. China is growing more self-sufficient in the factors of production, including knowhow and capital. In many sectors, China now also has an abundance of production capacity and is exporting its surplus products, creating problems for many industries worldwide.

China's massive domestic service industries, especially its sophisticated digital services sector, are mostly closed to outsiders but these are now venturing into neighboring countries such as in ASEAN. Huawei alone has 56 active cloud projects worldwide, and another 13 are planned.[26] Meanwhile multinational corporations are treading warily in China for geopolitical and other reasons. America's listed corporate sector derives

25% of its total revenues from China, but local competition and political interference are rising.[27]

Discussions about modern trade tend to focus on the high-profile manufactured goods sector and particularly the production of complex global value chains such as cars, electronics, or pharmaceuticals. But all economies need upstream basic material inputs and downstream service sectors too. This leads to three general observations about the nature of supply chains in the Indo-Pacific today.

1. Basic Materials

Physical flows of primary goods or commodities in the region are immense. Eleven billion tons are shipped by ocean transport worldwide each year, which is 85% of all world trade by weight. Of this, roughly 40% is transported by shipping containers, 30% by tanker, and 30% by bulk ships carrying commodity materials in dry solid form.[28] The most valuable items are often shipped by air freight, which transports more than 35% of world trade by value.[29]

The Indo-Pacific's geography is more suited to maritime than terrestrial freight. That is why the region handles the loading and unloading of about half of the world's seaborne trade. Ocean transport delivers vital primary supplies to nearly all of the region's economies. The region's ports also handle 64% of global container throughput. Asian companies own over half of the world's shipping tonnage and three countries—China, South Korea, and Japan—command 93% of shipbuilding output.

While containers convey much of the world's complex global value chain trade, tankers and dry bulk ships still dominate fleet tonnage and cargo ton-miles. China's imports of crude oil doubled during the 2010s and now account for 22% of all global oil imports, a little less than Europe's 24%. Imports of oil into India also surged 60% during that decade. Indeed, the entire Indo-Pacific region accounts for 55% of all crude imports, and this share is rising as US import demand has fallen.[30] Of the three major bulk categories, China accounts for 72% of world iron ore imports; China,

Japan, and India together account for 52% of coal imports; and the Indo-Pacific region as a whole accounts for 46% of grain imports.

China imports one billion tons of iron ore annually, the raw feedstock for the largest urbanization enterprise in history. The value of urban property sales by China's local governments each year exceeds the entire GDP of Australia.[31] Property construction and related services account for 29% of China's GDP.[32] Together with infrastructure, this means that the "fixed asset formation" complex accounts for much of China's GDP. In order to supply this domestic industry, China now generates 56% of the word's steel output and roughly 60% of global cement production. State-owned enterprises are prominent in this sector.

China is also a mining superpower, extracting 51% of the world's coal and dominating the mining of a vast range of metals, such as tungsten (82% of global output), gallium (94%), and the processing of others, such as magnesium (89%) and rare earths (80%).[33] The reason China imports so much iron ore is because its own reserves are of low quality.

As China has rapidly modernized and its citizens have acquired homes in cities, they have naturally sought the conveniences of urban life: cars, appliances, furniture and furnishings, household goods, apparel, education, healthcare, and so on. Local companies have been the most responsive to meet these demands, building extensive supply chains inside the country from the mine to the shopfloor. Regional countries (e.g., Australia and major oil exporters) fortunate enough to possess what China lacks have benefited greatly from this development boom. But they have become dependent to varying degrees on the rapid growth of the Chinese materials market, and China in turn is dependent on them. A key question is whether, when, and how the resource bonanza might end.

2. Manufacturing Global Value Chains

The Indo-Pacific is pivotal in making the world's essential, advanced, and innovative goods. As early as 2013, the region accounted for about 45% of manufacturing global value addition, and this figure has continued to rise.[34] Moreover, Factory Asia is becoming more internally integrated, in contrast to Europe and North America where *intra*-regional activity in global value chains has actually declined.[35] Although world trade intensity seems to have peaked, Europe and North America are now trading more with Asia than internally. This explains why "decoupling" the Western world's economies from China would be very challenging.

This does not mean that Europe and America are losing relevance to global value chains because in many cases they are playing lesser but more specialized roles, for instance in supplying key technological inputs. Europe and America are still the headquarters of the world's largest multinational corporations, the apex companies that coordinate the production-sharing arrangements of most complex global value chains. Even in China, multinationals still account for 36% of exports, though this share is steadily declining.[36] Importantly, China is becoming more prominent as the customer of global value chains. An analysis of the period 2000–2017 showed that "China played an increasingly important role both as a supply and demand hub in traditional trade and simple value chain activities, while the US and Germany remained the most important hubs in complex value chain networks."[37]

Consider the electronics industry, where China displaced Japan as the world's top exporter around 2005. There are huge two-way flows of electronics between China on the one hand and South Korea and Taiwan on the other. For instance, foundries in South Korea and Taiwan fabricate semiconductors, send the wafers to China for packaging, and receive assemblies or modules back. China is the top electronics module supplier to most of the region. There are some notable exceptions such as Singapore, Malaysia, and Vietnam (where the US sends its wafers for packaging) and Thailand and the Philippines (where Japan sends its wafers for packaging). But China's overall ascendence in electronics manufacturing is so comprehensive that it now commands 80% or more of the final assembly of electronics and key components such as printed circuit boards.

Thus, China is not just a big supplier. It is also the main recipient of electronics (or typically intermediate components like modules) for the entire region. It is therefore at the crux of the electronics industry, as it is in many other sectors. Again, the most striking features here are the bilateral dependencies between China and South Korea as well as between China and Taiwan. Those two dyads are the most important in the entire electronics industry. Without the dispatch of semiconductor wafers (by air) throughout the Western Pacific, the world's IT sector would quickly come to a crashing halt.

3. Services Supply Chains

Each year, trade generates about 20% of global value-added content, and services (such as banking, telecommunications, tourism, transport, and construction) constitute about 20% of trade. Therefore, services trade across borders is nominally only 4% of the world's economic activity. But this understates the real role of services in international commerce. Alternate estimates stand at about $6 trillion, or 7% of global GDP.[38] These revisions recognize that services such as sharing research and development and transfers of intellectual property between corporate affiliates around the world play important roles, but these transactions mostly go untracked or underpriced. Another reason services are undervalued is when they are free. Most notably, the internet delivers trillions of dollars of value (information, communication, entertainment, navigation, etc.) without charge. A proper accounting of services in trade might double or triple its official value.[39]

The COVID-19 pandemic threw the world's dependence on the internet's contribution to economic activity into stark relief. Although the true economic costs were immense, governments around the world were able to keep their populations at home with remarkably little social upheaval. This would have been unimaginable a generation earlier. These days, employees are expected to continue to work and students to attend classes online. This is the global digital supply chain in action. It is only possible because of an electronic worldwide utility that operates at low cost, is mostly interoperable between countries, and has continued without interruption for years. But it is conceivable that this network will be splintered in the future and, in consequence, become less efficient and prone to degradation by cyber and other forms of attack. Connected by hundreds of undersea fiber cables worldwide, it is also physically vulnerable.

The other strategic global service supply chain is finance. Trade, investment, and other real transactions across borders are enabled by financial ones (claims, currency, and payments). Every purchase order is underwritten by invoices, receipts, and letters of credit. At the apex of this network are the interbank communication and clearing systems. One European consortium (SWIFT) messages about half of the world's international payments and together with the US systems (CHIPS and Fedwire) clear almost all dollar-denominated trade, which is 80% of global trade.[40] These systems are interoperable, with 70% of CHIPS transactions originating from SWIFT.[41]

This long-dominant Western system will be challenged in the period ahead. Through a variety of means, China is working to reduce its dependencies even as it cements its place at the center of the global trade order.[42] Extra urgency has been generated by the consequences facing Russia, which was largely excommunicated from the world financial system following its invasion of Ukraine.[43]

However, Beijing's attempts to promote its own financial order, centered around its trade and lending with neighboring and developing countries, has so far made scant progress in displacing the dollar and the euro.[44] Precisely because China's regulators are wary of foreign liabilities, they maintain tight control over the country's capital account, so the renminbi national currency is not easily convertible and it is not yet suitable as a liquid reserve currency. This has limited the currency "internationalization" project to a few bilateral projects with select partners, notably including Russia.

Comparative Advantage

Nations are net exporters when their products have a comparative advantage, and they are net importers where they do not. Comparative advantage is not a theoretical concept; it is the basis of national survival. Every country must import products and pay for these with foreign exchange earned from exports. Without a balancing of payments, they will become indebted or insolvent, so they must find export activities in which they are competitive. Their sources of comparative advantage may be structural (e.g., in the form of unique natural resource endowments) and they may become entrenched (e.g., exceptional industrial capacity with high entry barriers, or expertise that cannot be copied). The large degree of industrial specialization that has resulted makes any potential disruption to these complex supply chains a major risk.

The four major economies of East Asia run net trade surpluses in a distinctive set of categories. As can be seen in figure 13, vehicles and machinery make up 42% and 28% of Japan's net exports. For South Korea, electronics, vehicles, and chemicals provide 39%, 29%, and 16% of the nation's surplus. Taiwan's comparative advantage is even more concentrated with 70% of net export income earned from electronics alone. China has a broader mix, with the electronics, machinery, and textiles sectors each comprising about 30% of net exports. These four countries are all metal processors as well. They are also large importers of energy, ores, and agricultural commodities. In the case of China, tourism services, purchased when Chinese residents travel overseas, are a substantial offsetting item.[45]

Figure 13. Share of Net Trade Surplus and Net Trade Deficit by Key Categories, For East Asia (2019).

Key net imports, % of total net imports

	Japan	Korea	Taiwan	China
Ore	6%	7%	3%	13%
Energy	35%	37%	39%	25%
Agri	28%	18%	23%	10%
Chemicals				
Metals				
Textiles	16%	7%	5%	
Electronics				
Vehicles				
Machinery				
Pharma	4%	1%	4%	2%
Services	4%	17%	7%	39%

Key net exports, % of total net exports

	Japan	Korea	Taiwan	China
Ore				
Energy				
Agri				
Chemicals	9%	16%	6%	3%
Metals	6%	5%	9%	7%
Textiles				30%
Electronics	9%	39%	70%	30%
Vehicles	42%	29%		2%
Machinery	28%	11%	10%	28%
Pharma				
Services				

Source: Compiled from *Atlas of Economic Complexity*, https://atlas.cid.harvard.edu/.

Figure 14. Share of Net Trade Surplus and Net Trade Deficit by Key Categories, For Selected Maritime Countries (2019).

Key net imports, % of total net imports				
	India	Australia	US	Indo
Ore				
Energy	37%		1%	
Agri				
Chemicals	7%	12%	7%	16%
Metals			2%	
Textiles		11%	20%	
Electronics	14%	17%	16%	17%
Vehicles	3%	27%	16%	
Machinery	9%	30%	15%	39%
Pharma		3%	7%	
Services				15%

Key net exports, % of total net exports				
	India	Australia	US	Indo
Ore	1%	32%	1%	3%
Energy		29%		16%
Agri	11%	13%	13%	48%
Chemicals				
Metals	4%	4%		3%
Textiles	20%			8%
Electronics				
Vehicles				2%
Machinery				
Pharma	7%			
Services	40%	6%	80%	

Source: Compiled from *Atlas of Economic Complexity*, https://atlas.cid.harvard.edu/.

Figure 14 shows that the big maritime nations (US, India, Indonesia, and Australia) are the mirror image of the East Asian states, creating an interlocking set of dependencies. Australia and Indonesia are powers in agricultural, energy, and minerals exports. Remarkably, within their net surplus categories, the United States and India derived 80% and 40% of their income from services, respectively. The US and Australia both run substantial deficits in all five categories where East Asia is strongest—electronics, vehicles, machinery, chemicals, and textiles.

Figure 15. Share of Gross Trade Surplus and Gross Trade Deficit by Key Categories, For East Asia (2019).

Key gross imports, % of total gross imports				
	Japan	Korea	Taiwan	China
Ore	2%	2%	1%	6%
Energy	15%	18%	14%	13%
Agri	10%	7%	7%	8%
Chemicals	9%	9%	13%	9%
Metals	4%	6%	7%	4%
Textiles	6%	4%	3%	2%
Electronics	9%	13%	26%	15%
Vehicles	4%	3%	4%	4%
Machinery	11%	12%	20%	11%
Pharma	2%		1%	1%
Services	26%	22%	3%	23%

Key gross exports, % of total gross exports				
	Japan	Korea	Taiwan	China
Ore				
Energy	2%	6%	3%	2%
Agri	2%	2%	2%	6%
Chemicals	11%	14%	12%	9%
Metals	6%	7%	8%	7%
Textiles	1%	2%	3%	15%
Electronics	12%	25%	48%	25%
Vehicles	18%	12%	3%	4%
Machinery	20%	14%	19%	21%
Pharma	1%	1%		
Services	23%	16%	1%	9%

Source: Compiled from *Atlas of Economic Complexity*, https://atlas.cid.harvard.edu/.

The comparative advantage of Southeast Asia (Indonesia, Singapore, Malaysia, Thailand, Vietnam, Cambodia, Laos, Philippines, Brunei, Myanmar, Timor Leste) lies somewhere in the middle. These nations play processing roles in global value chains, are resource exporters in agricultural products, and some have major service sectors in select areas such as finance (Singapore) and tourism (Thailand). Notwithstanding its vital role, this ASEAN bloc has only half the scale of trade of the US, India, and Australia combined and only a third that of the East Asian quartet.

Figure 15 shows the *gross* sectoral trade flows for East Asia. There are very sizeable trade flows in the electronics and machinery categories in particular, characteristic of the complex global value chains across multiple countries. Clearly visible in the electronics and machinery chains are the special roles of Japan, South Korea, and Taiwan in supplying China with advanced components as well as the roles that China's Southeast Asian neighbors play in supplying intermediate products. China is a giant converter of a variety of primary inputs, intermediates, and advanced manufactured components and services to get its products to the world market.

Seven states in the region play major parts in the electronics global value chain. At the cutting edge of the industry, Taiwan and South Korea (supplied with equipment and chemicals from Japan) each have one semiconductor giant exporting advanced integrated circuits, either directly to China (which accounts for 56% and 51% of their gross exports, respectively) or via packaging and testing operations in Malaysia, Singapore, and Vietnam. These modules in turn are mostly fed into China's hypercompetitive manufacturing sector for the final assembly of products. A map of the industry would show China as the central "hub" in both the demand and supply of electronics. The only pockets of the industry which lie outside the China-centered global value chain are South Korean production centers in Vietnam, the outsourcing of fabrication and packaging by US firms to Singapore, Malaysia, and Vietnam, and specialty contributions made by US and European suppliers.

Figure 16. Flows of Gross Electronics Trade for Selected Countries (2019).

US$ bln		Exporter										
Importer		Japan	Korea	Taiwan	China	Sing	Malay	Thai	Viet	US	Europe*	World
EA4	Japan		4	11	**33**	1	4	5	4	5	5	80
	Korea	6		9	**37**	2	2	1	8	5	5	81
	Taiwan	9	5		**24**	5	4	1	2	4	4	69
	China	**41**	**81**	**94**		**38**	**38**	**7**	**40**	**24**	**47**	460
SE4	Sing	3	3	13	**16**		13	1	1	4	4	66
	Malay	3	2	6	**14**	8		1	1	4	4	48
	Thai	5	1	2	**10**	2	3		1	2	2	33
	Viet	4	25	2	**31**	3	2	1		2	1	73
US		16	12	11	**103**	2	20	6	17		35	314
Europe*		11	10	10	**92**	3	12	4	16	24		248
World		111	159	167	715	76	109	33	117	169	127	

Source: Compiled from *Atlas of Economic Complexity*, https://atlas.cid.harvard.edu/.

The situation is similar in the machinery sector, where China operates an expansive industry whose exports match those of the US and Europe combined. Japan and South Korea are advanced machine makers in certain niches. They also provide high-end components into this global value chain, as do Europe, the US and Southeast Asian states. The ASEAN countries are also prolific machinery suppliers with almost $200 billion in gross exports. By comparison, Australia's machinery sales abroad were only valued at $7 billion.[46]

Figure 17. Flows of Gross Machinery Trade, for Selected Countries (2019).

US$ bln		*Exporter*								
Importer		Japan	Korea	Taiwan	China	ASEAN*	US	India	Europe*	World
EA4	Japan		4	4	36	9	15	1	16	97
	Korea	12		1	19	7	10	1	16	71
	Taiwan	11	2		11	5	8	1	10	52
	China	44	33	25		25	22	1	71	231
ASEAN*		36	11	6	57		14	4	30	147
US		43	15	16	115	32		5	122	484
India		4	3	1	18	3	5		10	54
Europe*		32	13	8	150	35	84	6		216
World		188	93	65	609	186	316	26	291	

Source: Compiled from *Atlas of Economic Complexity*, https://atlas.cid.harvard.edu/.

To summarize, East Asia imports oil, gas, ore, and food from the Persian Gulf, Australia, and Indonesia; it converts these primary inputs (via global value chains) into manufactured products, which are exported to the US and the rest of the world; and America supervises the international financial system and the internet in which India is also a major provider of services. Southeast Asia plays an adjunct role. In peacetime the international financial system allows countries to fund their deficits with their surpluses, with cross-border claims bridging any gaps. Participants in the global value chains import and export intermediate items, so they require multiple gross exchanges of goods and services (and payments) across national borders in order to develop and maintain their standards of living.

Supply Chain Interdependencies

Factory Asia has a paradox at its heart: the states that have the most fraught security relations with China also have the richest commercial ties with it. The most acute example is Taiwan, on which China depends heavily for semiconductors. The problem is replicated to a lesser degree with Australia, Japan, and South Korea, all of which enjoy military protection afforded by the United States and its close allies. ASEAN and Europe in turn profit handsomely from their economic ties with China while harboring concerns about its geopolitical aims.

How vulnerable is the world to these global and regional supply chain interdependencies? The canon of globalization is economic progress, low prices, consumer choice, and "peace through interdependence." By this thinking, no party would seriously seek to upend these beneficial arrangements. China would not attack Taiwan's "silicon shield" lest it lose access to the island's semiconductors and/or the American, Japanese, and European precision tools to make them. This belief has bred complacency on the part of industry executives and investors alike.[47] Most of the world's advanced semiconductor production takes place in a handful of fabrication plants (fabs) in locations just minutes by jet (to Taiwan) or an hour at most (to South Korea) from China's eastern seaboard. Even if those facilities were to remain intact during the initial phases of a kinetic war, they would be shut down within days if the airspace over them were contested because they rely on the regular supply and dispatch of wafers by commercial airfreight.

China "needs" very advanced chips from South Korea and Taiwan only to the extent that the world "needs" regular upgrades of smartphones and similar products—and in reality, the world doesn't. Moreover, the leaders in Beijing appear to give a higher priority to political sovereignty, national self-reliance, and geopolitical expansion than to broader economic priorities. Hence, they might consider large-scale industrial and commercial damage an acceptable price for personal, regime, and national strategic gain. Shutting down the consumer electronics global value chain would certainly deal a devastating economic blow to both China and some of its trading partners. But it might be survivable for China, at least for a while, through a combination of its domestic wafer fabrication capability, inventories, access to global distribution channels, and its ability to scavenge its vast stock of electronic devices for parts. The US- directed export controls imposed on Huawei demonstrate that China is reliant on microelectronics from abroad, but it also showed that China can adapt quickly. Huawei has been forced to totally reconfigure its business lines, but it nevertheless remains a formidable technology supplier.

The high-technology sector is a principal arena for strategic economic competition between the US and China. The resulting "tech war" can best be understood as an attempt by both countries to reduce their bilateral supply chain dependency. Because information technologies reach far into the security domains of these states, both Washington and Beijing are uncomfortable with the prospect of relying on each other. China has long pursued indigenous innovation strategies ("techno-nationalism") and in 2013 accelerated its efforts to rid itself of reliance on US suppliers in electronics and software.[48] US technology firms are now often facing China as their largest supplier, customer, competitor, and/or investment opportunity.[49]

Because technology is advancing rapidly, financial rewards accrue mostly to the leading players, creating a self-reinforcing "racing" dynamic. Taiwan and South Korea find themselves at the frontlines of this competition because their prowess in semiconductors now rivals or exceeds that of the US and China, and they are both trying to play strong roles in the two largest markets.

The machinery supply chain introduces an additional complexity. Machinery, far more than electronics, requires massive material inputs from the two other major processing sectors—metals and chemicals—where East Asia, especially China, run significant trade surpluses. These industrial powers are in turn importing feedstocks (ores and energy) to operate their smelting and refining enterprises.

The balance of payments is maintained by the circulation of maritime and airborne trade. If the sea lanes were denied to the tankers and bulk ships carrying basic materials inbound and the containerships outbound, that would present an existential challenge to the region's major economies, especially China's. Likewise, air corridors carry the just-in-time parts vital for complex global value chains. Although China is the most powerful and commercially diverse state in the Indo-Pacific trading system, it has an extreme requirement for both raw materials and components due to the high share of construction and exports in its economy. No other country makes even one-tenth of China's steel output, and this results in an outsized exposure to seaborne iron ore trade through the Indonesian archipelago from northern Australia. And, as discussed, China depends heavily on Taiwan and South Korea for high-end chips. Just these two cases of semiconductors and steel demonstrate the region's sensitivity to disruption.

Several countries have undertaken studies to examine the resilience and vulnerability of their supply chains and especially the potential risks of supplier and customer concentration.[50] These reports highlight dependence on China for many items that are critical for both civilian and military operations. Unsurprisingly, China is found to be problematically dominant in certain categories of electronics (e.g., PCs, handsets, printed circuit boards, transformers, batteries), machinery (e.g., winches, jacks, cranes, conveyors, containers, marine goods, metallurgical equipment), chemicals (e.g., aromatics, carboxylic acids, hydroxides and peroxides), and processed metals and alloys (e.g., manganese, magnesium, and various others). The COVID-19 crisis demonstrated that China's primacy also extends to healthcare products (e.g., active pharmaceutical ingredients, antibiotics, biocides, medical, protective, and safety equipment) and even food nutrition (e.g., vitamins). Chinese firms have cornered the market for a large number of product categories.

A demonstration of the resulting risks was provided in 2021 when Chinese power rationing caused a worldwide shortage of magnesium, a material which features in most vulnerability reports. China produces 89% of the world's magnesium metal, which is refined via power-intensive electrolysis.[51] Magnesium has an irreplaceable role as an alloying element in aluminum, and China has a 57% share of the world's smelting of aluminum. As discussed earlier, China imports huge amounts of iron ore for its steel industry and it relies on a mix of other domestic and imported ores, such as alumina and copper, which it processes for upstream supply to a wide range of manufacturing processes. China's main comparative advantage is in energy-intensive conversion. With its mega-scale power generation grid, China is the world's foremost "electrostate."

Chinese officials often talk about carbon and other potentially harmful emissions, and they even sign international agreements to reduce these. However, its dominant industrial priority continues to be the generation of vast quantities of cheap baseload power, which is achieved by continuing to build (a new one about every 10 days) and operate large numbers of modern coal and gas-fired power stations as well as some nuclear power plants.[52] Most of the processed metal that results was intended to feed the building boom at home. Once China's excess production flooded international markets, most Western countries shut their smelters and refineries and chose to rely on Chinese imports. China's industrial ascendancy accelerated the processes of decline in the rust belt regions in the United States and most of its allies.

The overall result is that China is *dependent* on the world for iron ore, *interdependent* with the world in other major metals such as aluminum and copper, and *independent* when it comes to materials such as processed rare earth elements where it has a commanding share of world production and control over most of the global supply chain.

China does, however, have its own concerns about supply chain security. It faces a high concentration of suppliers in important categories such as iron ore and natural gas (Australia), soybeans (Brazil), and semiconductors (Taiwan and South Korea). China is also a very large gross importer of chemicals and machinery, both categories in which

Japan and South Korea play strong roles. Figure 18 displays China's major import items by origin.

Policymakers in Beijing are keenly aware of the risks of interdependence. They have taken many steps to reinforce China's strengths and to mitigate its vulnerabilities. The United States, Japan, South Korea, and Australia have also launched initiatives to build more independent and competitive supply chains in some priority sectors.

One supply chain of rising importance is the battery industry, in which China has industrial primacy and other nations are scrambling to offset its lead in lithium and cobalt processing, electrolytic materials, and battery assembly and recycling.[53] Batteries are one of four strategic industries (along with rare earths, semiconductors, and pharmaceuticals) the US government has identified as being at risk of Chinese dominance.[54] In Xi Jinping's own words, a key industrial policy objective is to "enhance the global value chain's dependence on China and develop powerful retaliation and deterrence capabilities against supply cut-offs by foreign parties."[55]

The international economy is circular, with the flows of trade and money continuously cycling between partners. Interdependence runs both ways, and all major countries in the region have extensive bilateral trade interactions with each other. For example, Australia relies on a range of mining-related chemicals from China, which are in turn used in the processing and supply of metal ores to China. Economic planners in other Asian capitals have noted the same complex two-way interactions in their leading industries, whether one is considering industrial machinery, electronics, or agriculture.[56]

Figure 18. China's Largest Import Categories, for Selected Countries (2019).

Ore	5.98%	
Iron ore	3.58%	Aus (60%), Braz (21%)
Copper ore	1.35%	Chile (33%), Peru (25%), Mong (6%), Mex (5%), Aus (5%)
Energy	13.17%	
Crude oil	8.97%	Rus (15%), Irq (11%), Braz (8%), Ang (8%), Oman (7%), UAE (6%)
Natural gas	1.98%	Aus (26%), Turkm (14%), Qtr (11%), US (7%), Rus (6%)
Agriculture	8.23%	
Soybeans	1.44%	Braz (63%), USA (27%), Arg (7%)
Chemicals	9.47%	
Plastics	2.87%	Kor 17%), Jpn (14%), Twn (12%), US (8%), Saudi (7%), Sing (6%), Thai (6%), Iran (5%), Ger (5%). Mal (4%)
Organic chemicals	2.45%	Kor (21%), Jpn (12%), Saudi (10%), Twn (9%), India (6%), Sing (5%), US (5%), other ASEAN (8%), Europe (12%)
Metals	3.88%	
Copper	1.66%	Kor (32%), Ger (21%), Jpn (12%), Thai (10%), Twn (8%)
Textiles	1.71%	
Electronics	14.47%	Twn (20%), Kor (18%), Viet (11%), Mal (8%), Jpn (9%), Ger (5%), US (5%), other ASEAN (7%)
Integrated circuits	8.04%	Twn (35%), Kor (20%), Mal (9%), Jpn (5%), US (4%)
Vehicles	4.22%	
Cars	2.02%	Ger (30%), Jpn (23%), US (19%), Slvk (11%), UK (8%)
Auto parts	1.09%	Ger (33%), Jpn (23%), US (8.4%), Kor (5%), Mex (5%)
Machinery	10.73%	
Industrial machinery	6.51%	Jpn (21%), Ger (16%), Kor (13%), Twn (8%), US (7%), other EUK (14%), all ASEAN (15%)
Specialty machinery	3.94%	Jpn (18%), Kor (14%), US (14%), Twn (12%), Ger (11%), Sing (5%), other ASEAN (5%), other EUK (13%)
Pharmaceutical	1.17%	Ger (18%), US (16%), Switz (10%), UK (7%), Swe (7%), Ire (7%) France (6%), Jpn (5%), other Eur (15%)
Services	23.53%	of which travel/tourism (13.97%), transport (5.77%), telecom (3.05%), finance (0.74%) (partners not specified)

Source: Compiled from *Atlas of Economic Complexity*, https://atlas.cid.harvard.edu/ and ITC Trade Map (2020).

Nobody can be sure of the effects of a potential rupture in regional affairs. Parties that trade profitably during peacetime may find themselves mutually vulnerable in times of conflict, experiencing shortages of the items that they do not produce and a lack of demand for those they do. This would cause a complex and unpredictable cascading effect as every economy scrambles to adapt. If the crisis were prolonged, shortages of some items combined with huge surpluses in others would likely produce inflation, sectoral unemployment, and other wrenching macroeconomic disturbances that would challenge national policymakers.

Scope for Trade and Other Redirection

How easily could regional supply chains be reconfigured in the event of major war? Specifically, how could allied states maintain their resilience while denying the benefits of trade to their adversaries? There would be many factors at play, including economics, logistics, and finance.

Economics

Because comparative advantage is acquired over decades, it is exceedingly difficult for countries to revert to producing a full array of products at short notice. The strengths of Asian countries in complex global value chains have been built patiently, systematically, and expensively. For example, Chinese chemical companies have built a near monopoly in active pharmaceutical ingredients or drug precursors. Western countries, largely because of their stringent environmental and other regulations, have outsourced most of their production to China. This deindustrialization process has taken place over three decades. The consequences are many and profound. In the middle of the COVID-19 crisis, the US government was forced to make emergency loans to domestic chemical firms to restart the production of some basic pharmaceutical compounds.[57] But even this may take years, as the generic drug makers in India have learned.[58] At the same time, Beijing has long sought to reduce its reliance on imported semiconductors where Taiwan and South Korea continue to maintain a powerful lead.[59] It will take at least a decade for China to match them and, even then, it may lag because it currently lacks experience with some key production processes.[60] China's task will be made even more difficult as the US and its allies proceed with tighter export restrictions on the most advanced semiconductor manufacturing systems and the US bars its citizens and entities from working with Chinese chip producers except with specific approval.[61]

Logistics

The dispersed and complex geography of the Indo-Pacific, with a number of island, peninsular, and archipelagic nations, makes the region highly reliant on a number of oceanic corridors. According to the Center for Strategic and International Studies (CSIS), about 21% of global trade passes through the South China Sea.[62] Because China's southern ports adjoin this sea, about 64% of its maritime traffic (by volume) transits the waterway at some point. For Japan the figure is 42%.[63] However, the Malacca Strait is not the only access point to the South China Sea. It is possible to divert shipping to bypass this chokepoint and, if necessary, the sea entirely. Ultimately, if ships need to be diverted, they can be. A minor detour through the Sunda Strait would incur extra freight costs of only 0.1% of total cargo value.[64] Longer detours around the southern coast of Australia are also quite feasible.

In an effort to circumvent possible logistical constraints, China's Belt and Road Initiative is making a concerted effort to bolster terrestrial transport routes into the Eurasian continent (the "economic belt") in addition to building marine infrastructure (the "maritime silk road"). Many of the Chinese-funded roads, railways, and pipelines traverse China-friendly countries such as Russia, Iran, and Pakistan, affording Beijing alternative access points to vital markets. Malaysia's strategic location straddling the Indian and Pacific Oceans makes it an important potential corridor to bypass the Malacca Strait. Its three main seaports all have associated "dry-port" facilities connecting maritime traffic with hinterland road-rail links (i.e., down the peninsular to Singapore and Malacca and northwards into Thailand and beyond). Chinese freight to and from Thailand must traverse Laos or Myanmar by land or more commonly by shipping on the Mekong or Irrawaddy Rivers. This strategic logic has driven China to make extensive infrastructure investments in these countries in recent years.

China is a maritime great power.[65] It has the world's largest ports and shipyards, a powerful merchant marine and by far the most numerous fishing fleet, supported by a formidable armada of paramilitary vessels. China also has a financial stake in nearly two-thirds of the world's 50 largest ports. China's own ports handle 245 million containers each year.[66] China's Ministry of Transport operates a ubiquitous global maritime and intermodal information platform known as LOGINK which connects 15 of the world's largest ports and comprehensively tracks ship, cargo, and customer data.[67] These ports span the sea lanes from the Indo-Pacific to Western Europe, including Malaysia's Klang Harbor close to the Malacca Strait. LOGINK is reported to be offering participation to Singapore and Indonesia. According to one research institute senior fellow, Beijing's control of the system enables China to "cement international information superiority and control... and also gives it power to deny and coerce" because of the network's integration with the PLAN's military systems.[68]

Finance

In the event of a major crisis in the region, financial markets would react quickly. Shipping insurance costs would spike. In localized security crises (such as the Somali pirate raids in 2008 and Iran's 2019 ship seizures), marine war premiums rose tenfold. Weekly premiums rose to 0.5% of hull value, with extra charges to cover cargo value.[69] In the more serious 2022 Russia-Ukraine conflict, the war risk premium of making a single round trip across the Black Sea rose to 10% of hull value, making insurance more expensive than the actual cost of chartering and operating the vessel itself.[70] Such prohibitive costs effectively close off these routes to commercial passage altogether. The Russia-Ukraine conflict has also highlighted the role that sanctions on banks and other entities can play in altering the flow of international trade. It is clear that economic and financial measures can be weapons of war as much as military personnel and armaments.

Levels of Resilience of the Main Economies

The Indo-Pacific region contains some of the world's most dynamic and well-organized societies. Because of their large and dense populations and comparatively limited natural resource endowments (Australia being an exception), these nations need to excel in manufacturing and trade in order to survive, requiring them to establish high-quality institutions. This has fostered a series of remarkable economic and political transformations. Some of these countries have been battered by natural and man-made disasters, but they have demonstrated a high capacity to mobilize and endure adversity.

Any assessment of a nation's resilience must start with primary energy. Japan, with almost total reliance on seaborne fossil fuel imports, has historically given the security of these supplies very high priority. In the words of one analyst, "barring a technological breakthrough in energy production releasing it from dependence on imported hydrocarbons, any serious and sustained disruption to in-bound shipping flows would inevitably be perceived by the Japanese authorities as a threat to national survival."[71]

Like Japan, South Korea and Taiwan rely almost entirely on imported energy. In fact, their predicaments may be even more acute, because they face more proximate security threats than Japan. South Korea imports 100% of its crude oil and is home to three of the world's ten largest oil refineries. A major exporter of petroleum products, South Korea has six LNG terminals, including the world's largest regassifier, located at Incheon, twenty miles from the Demilitarized Zone that marks the effective border with North Korea. It is no wonder that South Korea's civilian economy is assessed to be "fragile."[72] Taiwan is reliant on imported fossil fuels for 93% of its primary energy needs. It also has a substantial petrochemical industry and imports growing quantities of natural gas.[73]

Still, these three advanced economies in Northeast Asia are innovative and disciplined societies. Provided their essential infrastructure remains intact and they receive a base level of energy imports, they should be able to respond and adapt effectively even to major disruptions.

At the other extreme, Australia is rich in natural resources but is under-industrialized. Australia is one of the world's principal exporters of coal, natural gas, and uranium, but its transport fleet relies partly upon imports of refined petroleum products, all of which are sourced from the Indo-Pacific. India is a huge importer of crude oil with most of its supplies coming from the Persian Gulf. India has the world's largest oil refinery, so it is also a net exporter of petroleum products.

For China, energy security is critical. Xi Jinping has stated that "as a major manufacturing power, China has to secure its energy supply in our own hands."[74] China relies increasingly on crude oil and natural gas imports, but it has Russia and Central Asia accessible across land borders and, like India, it is mostly self-sufficient in coal. China has some domestic oil production, a colossal coal industry, and a large renewable energy sector. Nonetheless, its deficits in primary energy, iron ore, and grains have increased substantially since 2000.

Conclusions

The national resilience of Indo-Pacific countries depends in large part on the balance each has struck between internal self-sufficiency and trade with their neighbors and the wider world. While China has taken numerous steps to reduce its perceived economic vulnerabilities, many other countries, including the United States and most of its allies, have embraced economic integration and interdependence and, until recently, ignored the greatly increased dangers that would be posed by a major security crisis.

There must be doubt about the sustainability of the highly integrated Indo-Pacific economy. Friction is rising in the regional commercial system. This is partly a pushback against Beijing's aggressive mercantilist policies. The US and China are locked in a "trade war," a dispute which fundamentally is about the compatibility of Chinese party-state capitalism with long-established global trading rules. There is increasing concern about the economic and security implications of a techno-industrial complex in which multiple countries play critical (sometimes irreplaceable) roles. There are widespread fears about the rapid technological ascendance of China and the looming prospect of Chinese firms commanding key segments of global value chains. Similar fears are now ascendant in Beijing, which has driven hard to win control over strategic imports and achieve a high degree of self-sufficiency.

In the high-tech realm, a schism is already evident between two blocs —one American-led and the other Chinese-led. Were a major war to break out in coming years, a central feature of the struggle would be an emergency restructuring of the Indo-Pacific economy between the two blocs. Understanding and being able to reorganize the complex supply networks to ensure continued delivery of priority goods and services would be critical to success. This would be especially the case were the conflict to be prolonged. Those nations and coalitions of nations that are best prepared and can best manage the dramatic changes required would have a substantial and potentially decisive advantage.[75]

Notes

1. "Joint Leaders' Statement on the Regional Comprehensive Economic Partnership (RCEP)", Australian Government Department of Foreign Affairs and Trade, https://www.dfat.gov.au/trade/agreements/not-yet-in-force/rcep/news/joint-leaders-statement-regional-comprehensive-economic-partnership-rcep.
2. Asian Development Bank, *Asian Economic Integration Report 2021*, https://www.adb.org/sites/default/files/publication/674421/asian-economic-integration-report-2021.pdf.
3. "Evolution of Trade Under the WTO: Handy Statistics," World Trade Organization, https://www.wto.org/english/res_e/statis_e/trade_evolution_e/evolution_trade_wto_e.htm.
4. Bruce Jones, "The Challenge of China's Rising Power on the Seas," *Wall Street Journal*, September 16, 2021, https://www.wsj.com/articles/the-challenge-of-chinas-rising-power-on-the-seas-11631808521.
5. Justin Sherman, "Beijing's Growing Influence on the Global Undersea Cable Network," Jamestown Foundation, *China Brief* 21, issue 18 (September 23, 2021), https://jamestown.org/program/beijings-growing-influence-on-the-global-undersea-cable-network/.
6. Jonathan Woetzel et al., *China and the World: Inside the Dynamics of a Changing Relationship* (McKinsey Global Institute, 2019), https://www.mckinsey.com/featured-insights/china/china-and-the-world-inside-the-dynamics-of-a-changing-relationship.
7. Emily de La Bruyère and Nathan Picarsic, *Two Markets, Two Resources: Documenting China's Engagement in Africa* (Washington, DC, and New York: Horizon Advisory, 2020), Prepared for the US-China Economic And Security Review Commission, https://www.uscc.gov/research/two-markets-two-resources-documenting-chinas-engagement-africa.
8. Greg Ip, "China Wants Manufacturing—Not the Internet—to Lead the Economy," *Wall Street Journal*, August 4, 2021, https://www.wsj.com/articles/china-wants-manufacturingnot-the-internetto-lead-the-economy-11628078155.
9. Credit Suisse Research Institute, *Global Wealth Report*, 2021, https://www.credit-suisse.com/about-us/en/reports-research/global-wealth-report.html.

10. Charles Cadestin et al., "Multinational enterprises and global value chains: New Insights on the trade-investment nexus," *OECD Science, Technology and Industry Working Papers*, no. 2018/05, 2018, https://www.oecd-ilibrary.org/industry-and-services/multinational-enterprises-and-global-value-chains_194ddb63-en.
11. UNCTAD, *World Investment Report 2020* (New York: United Nations Publications, 2020), https://unctad.org/system/files/official-document/wir2020_en.pdf.
12. "Foreign Direct Investment, Net Inflows (% of GDP)," *World Bank*, https://data.worldbank.org/indicator/BX.KLT.DINV.WD.GD.ZS.
13. Derek Scissors, *China's Overseas Investment Starts the Long Climb Back* (Washington, DC: American Enterprise Institute, 2021), https://www.aei.org/wp-content/uploads/2021/07/China%E2%80%99s-Overseas-Investment-Starts-the-Long-Climb-Back.pdf.
14. Nicholas R. Lardy, "Foreign Investments into China are Accelerating Despite Global Economic Tensions and Restrictions," *China Economic Watch*, Peterson Institute for International Economics, July 22, 2021, https://www.piie.com/blogs/china-economic-watch/foreign-investments-china-are-accelerating-despite-global-economic.
15. "Multinational Firms are Finding it Hard to Let Go of China," *The Economist*, November 24, 2022, https://www.economist.com/business/2022/11/24/multinational-firms-are-finding-it-hard-to-let-go-of-china.
16. Alexander Brown, Jacob Gunter, and Max J. Zenglein, "Course Correction: China's Shifting Approach to Economic Globalization," *Mercator Institute for China Studies: China Monitor*, October 19, 2021, https://merics.org/en/report/course-correction-chinas-shifting-approach-economic-globalization.
17. Chung-Ho Kim, "Red Supply Chain Versus Blue Supply Chain—What Will South Korea Choose?," *One Korea Network*, July 5, 2021, https://onekoreanetwork.com/2021/07/05/red-supply-chain-versus-blue-supply-chain-what-will-south-korea-choose.
18. "The Non-Zero Costs of Zero-Covid," *The Economist*, November 13, 2021, https://www.economist.com/business/2021/11/13/the-non-zero-costs-of-zero-covid.
19. David Barboza, "China's Shell Game," *The Wire China*, October 3, 2021, https://www.thewirechina.com/2021/10/03/chinas-shell-game/.
20. Jason Arterburn, *Party Capital: A Blueprint for National Security Due Diligence on China* (Washington, DC: Center for Advanced Defense Studies, 2021), https://c4ads.org/party-capital.

21. Thibault Serlet, "China's Tactics in Economic Zones," *Taipei Times*, October 30, 2021, https://www.taipeitimes.com/News/editorials/archives/2021/10/30/2003767000.
22. Sebastian Horn, Christoph Trebesch, and Carmen M. Reinhart, "China's Overseas Lending," *Kiel Working Papers*, No. 2132 (June 2019), https://www.ifw-kiel.de/publications/kiel-working-papers/chinas-overseas-lending-12820/.
23. Clark Gascoigne, "China's Illicit Outflows Were US$1.08 Trillion from 2002-2011," *Global Financial Integrity*, September 23, 2014, https://gfintegrity.org/chinas-illicit-outflows-2002-2011-us1-08-trillion/.
24. The 80% number can be seen in figure 1.2, page 12, of *Global Value Chain Development Report 2019*, by the World Trade Organization, https://www.worldbank.org/en/topic/trade/publication/global-value-chain-development-report-2019.
25. UNCTAD, *World Investment Report 2020* (New York: United Nations Publications, 2020), https://unctad.org/system/files/official-document/wir2020_en.pdf.
26. Reconnecting Asia Project, "Reconnecting Asia Project Database," *Center for Strategic and International Studies*, December 2020, https://reconasia.csis.org/reconnecting-asia-map/.
27. Steve Johnson, "Up to a Quarter of US Equity ETF Revenues Derived from China," *Financial Times*, October 4, 2021, https://www.ft.com/content/8b3e7e01-9a78-4e59-a289-a348dd0a5d3c.
28. All shipping data from UNCTAD, *Review of Maritime Transport 2020*, 2020, https://unctad.org/webflyer/review-maritime-transport-2020.
29. International Air Transport Association, *The Value of Air Cargo*, n.d., https://www.iata.org/contentassets/62bae061c05b429ea508cb0c49907c4c/air-cargo-brochure.pdf.
30. British Petroleum, *Statistical Review of World Energy 2021*, July 2021, https://www.bp.com/content/dam/bp/business-sites/en/global/corporate/pdfs/energy-economics/statistical-review/bp-stats-review-2021-full-report.pdf.
31. Ryan Woo and Liangping Gao, "Analysis: Fall in China's $1.3 trln Land Sales to Test Local Finances, Economy," Reuters, October 8, 2021, https://www.reuters.com/world/china/fall-chinas-13-trln-land-sales-test-local-finances-economy-2021-10-07/.
32. Kenneth S. Rogoff and Yuanchen Yang, "Peak China Housing," *NBER Working Paper*, no. 27697 (August 2020), https://www.nber.org/system/files/working_papers/w27697/w27697.pdf.

33. US Geological Survey, *Mineral Commodity Summaries 2021*, January 29, 2021, https://pubs.usgs.gov/periodicals/mcs2021/mcs2021.pdf.
34. UNESCAP, "Global Value Chains and Interconnectedness of Asia-Pacific Economies," in *Asia-Pacific Trade and Investment Report 2015* (Thailand: United Nations Publications, 2015), https://www.unescap.org/sites/default/files/Full%20Report%20-%20APTIR%202015.pdf.
35. Xin Li, Bo Meng, and Zhi Wang, "Recent Patterns of Global Production and GVC Participation," in *Global Value Chain Development Report 2019*, ed. World Trade Organization, 2019, 9–43, https://www.wto.org/english/res_e/booksp_e/gvc_dev_report_2019_e.pdf.
36. Ministry of Commerce of the People's Republic of China, *Statistical Bulletin of FDI in China*, 2021, http://images.mofcom.gov.cn/wzs/202111/20211125164038921.pdf, 38.
37. Li, Meng, and Wang, "Recent Patterns of Global Production and GVC Participation."
38. "Total Trade in Services," *UNCTAD Handbook of Statistics 2021*, UNCTAD, https://stats.unctad.org/handbook/Services/Total.html.
39. Susan Lund et al., *Globalization in Transition: The Future of Trade and Value Chains* (McKinsey Global Institute, 2019), https://www.mckinsey.com/featured-insights/innovation-and-growth/globalization-in-transition-the-future-of-trade-and-value-chains.
40. SWIFT, *Worldwide Currency Usage and Trends*, 2015, https://www.swift.com/swift-resource/19186/download?language=en.
41. Financial Crimes Enforcement Network (US), *Feasibility of a Cross-Border Electronic Funds Transfer Reporting System Under the Bank Secrecy Act* (Washington, DC: US Department of the Treasury, 2006), https://www.fincen.gov/sites/default/files/shared/Appendix_D.pdf.
42. Zongyuan Zoe Liu, "China Is Hardening Itself for Economic War," *Foreign Policy*, June 16, 2022, https://foreignpolicy.com/2022/06/16/china-economic-war-decoupling-united-states-containment.
43. He Xiaobei, "China's financial security in the face of geopolitical risks needs to be given high priority," Peking University National School of Development, November 24, 2022, https:// .aisixiang.com/data/138328.html.
44. "China is trying to protect its economy from western pressure,," *The Economist*, May 26, 2022, https://www.economist.com/briefing/2022/05/26/china-is-trying-to-protect-its-economy-from-western-pressure.
45. This data is from 2019, when Chinese citizens enjoyed travel abroad.

46. Michael Meyer et al., *How ASEAN Can Move Up the Manufacturing Value Chain* (Boston Consulting Group, 2021), https://www.bcg.com/publications/2021/asean-manufacturing.
47. Ben Blanchard and Yimou Lee, "TSMC Chairman Says Nobody Wants War Over Taiwan as Chip Supplies Too Valuable," Reuters, July 15, 2021, https://www.reuters.com/world/asia-pacific/tsmc-chairman-says-nobody-wants-war-over-taiwan-chip-supplies-too-valuable-2021-07-15/.
48. Daniel H. Rosen, *Eight Guardian Warriors: PRISM and Its Implications for US Businesses in China* (New York: Rhodium Group, 2013), https://rhg.com/research/eight-guardian-warriors-prism-and-its-implications-for-us-businesses-in-china/.
49. Kate O'Keeffe, Heather Somerville, and Yang Jie, "U.S. Companies Aid China's Bid for Chip Dominance Despite Security Concerns," *Wall Street Journal*, November 12, 2021, https://www.wsj.com/articles/u-s-firms-aid-chinas-bid-for-chip-dominance-despite-security-concerns-11636718400.
50. See, for example, Max J. Zenglein, *Mapping and Recalibrating Europe's Economic Interdependence with China* (Mercator Institute for China Studies, 2021), https://merics.org/en/report/mapping-and-recalibrating-europes-economic-interdependence-china; and James Rogers et al., *Breaking the China Supply Chain: How the 'Five Eyes' can Decouple from Strategic Dependency* (London: Henry Jackson Society, 2020), https://henryjacksonsociety.org/publications/breaking-the-china-supply-chain-how-the-five-eyes-can-decouple-from-strategic-dependency/.
51. Neil Hume, "China's Magnesium Shortage Threatens Global Car Industry," *Financial Times*, October 20, 2021, https://www.ft.com/content/1611e936-08a5-4654-987e-664f50133a4b.
52. Global Energy Monitor and CREA, *China Dominates 2020 Coal Plant Development*, 2021, https://globalenergymonitor.org/wp-content/uploads/2021/02/China-Dominates-2020-Coal-Development.pdf.
53. Nadia Schadlow, Arthur Herman, and Brayden Helwig, *Powering Innovation: A Strategic Approach to America's Advanced Battery Technology* (Washington, DC: Hudson Institute, 2021), https://www.hudson.org/research/17333-powering-innovation-a-strategic-approach-to-america-s-advanced-battery-technology.
54. The White House, *Building Resilient Supply Chains, Revitalizing American Manufacturing, and Fostering Broad-Based Growth.*
55. Frank Tang, "China Puts Supply Chain Security at Forefront to Avoid Being 'Strangled' by Sanctions, Analysts Say," *South China Morning Post*, November 10, 2020, https://www.scmp.com/economy/china-economy/

article/3109082/china-sacrificing-economic-growth-self-sufficiency-strategy.

56. "Next Japan PM Kishida to create economic security minister to counter China," *Kyodo News*, October 2, 2021, https://english.kyodonews.net/news/2021/10/cdf05f9ab761-breaking-news-kishida-to-create-new-ministerial-post-for-economic-security.html.
57. Chuin-Wei Yap, "Pandemic Lays Bare US Reliance on China for Drugs," *Wall Street Journal*, August 5, 2020, https://www.wsj.com/articles/how-the-u-s-ceded-control-of-drug-supplies-to-china-11596634936.
58. Amarnath K. Menon, "A Bitter Pill," *India Today*, July 4, 2020, https://www.indiatoday.in/magazine/cover-story/story/20200713-a-bitter-pill-pharmaceuticals-1696561-2020-07-04.
59. Shunsuke Tabeta, "'Made in China' chip drive falls far short of 70% self-sufficiency," *Nikkei Asia*, October 13, 2021, https://asia.nikkei.com/Business/Tech/Semiconductors/Made-in-China-chip-drive-falls-far-short-of-70-self-sufficiency.
60. Antonio Varas et al., *Strengthening the Global Semiconductor Supply Chain in an Uncertain Era* (Washington, DC: Boston Consulting Group; Semiconductor Industry Association, 2021), https://www.semiconductors.org/wp-content/uploads/2021/03/Strengthening-the-Global-Semiconductor-Supply-Chain_April-2021.pdf.
61. Kathrin Hille,, Qianer Liu, and Eleanor Olcot et.al., "China's Chip Industry Set for Deep Pain from US Export Controls," *Financial Times*, October 9, 2022, https://www.ft.com/content/e950f58c-0d8f-4121-b4f2-ece71d2cb267.
62. China Power Team, "How Much Trade Transits the South China Sea?," *China Power*, August 2, 2017, updated January 25, 2021, https://chinapower.csis.org/much-trade-transits-south-china-sea/.
63. By value, these figures for China and Japan are lower at 40% and 19%, respectively, reflecting the high proportion of lower value bulk cargos like crude oil through the sea.
64. China Power Team, "How Much Trade Transits the South China Sea," CSIS, https://chinapower.csis.org/much-trade-transits-south-china-sea/.
65. Michael McDevitt, *Becoming a Great "Maritime Power": A Chinese Dream* (Arlington: CNA, 2016), https://www.cna.org/cna_files/pdf/IRM-2016-U-013646.pdf.
66. Faisal Islam, "How the West Invited China to Eat Its Lunch," *BBC News*, December 10, 2021, https://www.bbc.com/news/business-59610019.

67. *LOGINK: Risks from China's Promotion of Global Logistics Platform*, U.S.-China Economic and Security Review Commission, September 20, 2022,https://www.uscc.gov/research/logink-risks-chinas-promotion-global-logistics-management-platform . See also Daniel Michaels, "Chinese Cargo-Data Network Poses Growing Risk, U.S. Analysis Says," *Wall Street Journal*, September 20, 2022, https://www.wsj.com/articles/chinese-cargo-data-network-poses-growing-risks-u-s-analysis-says-11663671601.
68. Emily de La Bruyère, *Acquisition Research: Creating Synergy for Informed Change* (Monterey: Naval Postgraduate School, 2020), 13.
69. "War (Insurance) – What Is It Good For?," *Allianz: News & Insights*, August 2019, https://www.agcs.allianz.com/news-and-insights/expert-risk-articles/war-insurance.html.
70. Ann Koh and Alaric Nightingale, "The Cost of Insuring Black Sea Shipping Is Out of Control," Bloomberg, April 9, 2022, https://www.bloomberg.com/news/articles/2022-04-08/ships-entering-the-black-sea-are-becoming-almost-uninsurable.
71. Euan Graham, *Japan's Sea Lane Security, 1940–2004: A matter of life and death?* (London: Psychology Press, 2006).
72. Anthony Cordesman, *South Korea's Civilian Vulnerabilities in War* (Washington, DC: Center for Strategic and International Studies, 2018), https://www.csis.org/analysis/south-koreas-civilian-vulnerabilities-war.
73. Evan A. Feigenbaum and Jen-Yi Hou, *Overcoming Taiwan's Energy Trilemma* (Washington, DC: Carnegie Endowment for International Peace, 2020), https://carnegieendowment.org/2020/04/27/overcoming-taiwan-s-energy-trilemma-pub-81645.
74. "Xi Says China Must Secure Energy Supply in 'Its Own Hands,'" Bloomberg, October 22, 2021, https://www.bloomberg.com/news/articles/2021-10-22/xi-says-china-must-secure-energy-supply-in-its-own-hands.
75. The better books dealing with aspects of international economics relevant to a major conflict in the Indo-Pacific include Dale C. Copeland, *Economic Interdependence and War* (Princeton: Princeton University Press, 2014); William A. Norris, *Chinese Economic Statecraft* (New York: Cornell University Press, 2016); and Stewart Paterson, *China, Trade and Power* (London: London Publishing Partnership, 2018).

Chapter 6

The Economic Impacts of Major War in the Indo-Pacific

A major war between China and the United States would result in the greatest macroeconomic dislocation seen in decades, and it would force the dismantling and restructuring of commercial networks across the world. The international economy would be divided into two primary blocs with highly restricted and markedly reconfigured interactions between them. Most of the trade and financial arrangements that characterize today's Indo-Pacific economy would be changed fundamentally and possibly permanently. This chapter describes the likely economic dynamics in each of the phases of a major Indo-Pacific war that are described in Chapter 4.

Economic Impacts of the Sustained Political Warfare in Phase 1A

The most dramatic changes would probably not be triggered in the opening phases of such a war. In phase 1A, most categories of trade such as resources, energy, food, consumer goods, and many types of manufactures and services would probably continue largely unchanged. Many of the Chinese political warfare operations envisaged in phase 1A are already being conducted against the United States, its allies, and Taiwan. In the face of these attacks, the allies and their partners have taken many steps to strengthen their defenses, and additional measures are in train.

Over time, as the effects of China's political warfare operations receive more public attention, other US and allied counteractions would follow. Mirroring the democratic world's response to Russia's invasion of Ukraine, foreign companies would reduce or close their operations in China and many international investors would slow or reverse their long-standing patterns of investment there. Governments and consumers in many countries would probably also become increasingly wary of Chinese-made products. China's economic decoupling from the major democracies would accelerate.

The type of large-scale political warfare envisaged in this phase of a major war would have a broad range of economic effects, whether intended or not. State-sponsored propaganda campaigns can mobilize publics against foreign commercial interests. Embargos, boycotts, protests, and closures impose direct costs on targeted companies. In recent years the Chinese state and nationalist citizens have taken politically motivated actions against companies from many countries, including the US, Japan, South Korea, Australia, Germany, and Sweden.[1] Large-scale and sometimes violent anti-Japan protests brought thousands of demonstrators into the streets in 2005 and again in 2012.

At various times both sides have been targeted in these campaigns. Indians have rallied to boycott Chinese goods whenever the giants clash in the Himalayas. Chinese-owned enterprises have been targeted during sporadic incidents in Vietnam, Myanmar, Tonga, and the Solomon Islands. Many international investments that have been made across the Indo-Pacific in recent decades would be at risk if geopolitical tensions rise.

Extended political warfare campaigns would also trigger both camps to tighten controls on the transfer of sensitive resources, technologies, and services. Extensive restrictions would probably be imposed on technologies and systems that have important military and security applications. Affected products would include many dual-use items such as commercial aircraft and drones, machine and optical tools, automotive and robotic systems, marine equipment, biological and pharmaceutical products, batteries, and telecommunication and media services.

Since 2017 the United States government has introduced new regulatory restraints on trade and investment with China. Entity lists have been published (requiring American institutions to stop all interactions with the targeted organizations) and foreign direct product rules (which prevent US-origin technologies being used to supply specific entities) have been introduced.[2] By early 2022, over one thousand Chinese entities were listed by US authorities.[3] The governments of Japan, South Korea, India, Australia, and the EU have also become more active in controlling Chinese access to key industries.

The Chinese regime has anticipated these types of restrictions and has worked for several decades to build stronger self-reliance. Initial priorities were national catchup programs in strategic military applications like nuclear weaponry, space systems, and supercomputing.[4] Next came active encouragement of an evolving portfolio of designated "strategic emerging industries," which included commercial aviation, machine tools, robotics, and pharmaceuticals.[5] Then in 2015, Beijing unveiled its Made in China 2025 program that strives to replace foreign suppliers with domestic alternatives and to drive Chinese market leadership in many advanced-technology sectors.[6] Accompanying these initiatives, China developed a national financial and information ecosystem that is mostly insulated from the rest of the world.

As a result of these tensions, flows of information and money between the sensitive strategic sectors of the US and China have been greatly reduced. Additional measures have been taken worldwide to secure "data sovereignty" and to prevent adversary states from interfering with national media (both formal and social).[7]

These developments are starting to weaken many of the producer specializations, sophisticated trading networks, and complex value chains that have generated so much prosperity in the Indo-Pacific. If present trends continue, foreign direct investment between the two emerging blocs will shrink further while financial flows within each bloc will expand.

In the developing world, Beijing will intensify its efforts to embrace a third grouping—a "Belt and Road bloc" within which Chinese investment and lending will be prioritized in return for political and strategic alignments.[8] Arrangements such as these would bypass US-established institutions such as the World Bank and International Monetary Fund.

The choices that countries make today about trade, investment, finance, communications systems, and information networks will have consequences in the event that tensions rise further and lead to a major conflict. As the US and China continue to develop separate regulatory architectures with different standards, some states may find themselves locked in to one bloc or another. A further escalation of tensions will make these political-economic blocs more distinct and entrenched.

Figure 19 displays the current pattern of trade between the ten largest economies in the Indo-Pacific and the routing of each country's ten largest export flows. The width of the individual lines reflects the relative value of that country's trade in 2019. This figure highlights the extent to which the economies of the Western Pacific are now highly integrated, the centrality of China to most of this activity and the density of trade movements, especially through the South China Sea and the Indonesian straits.

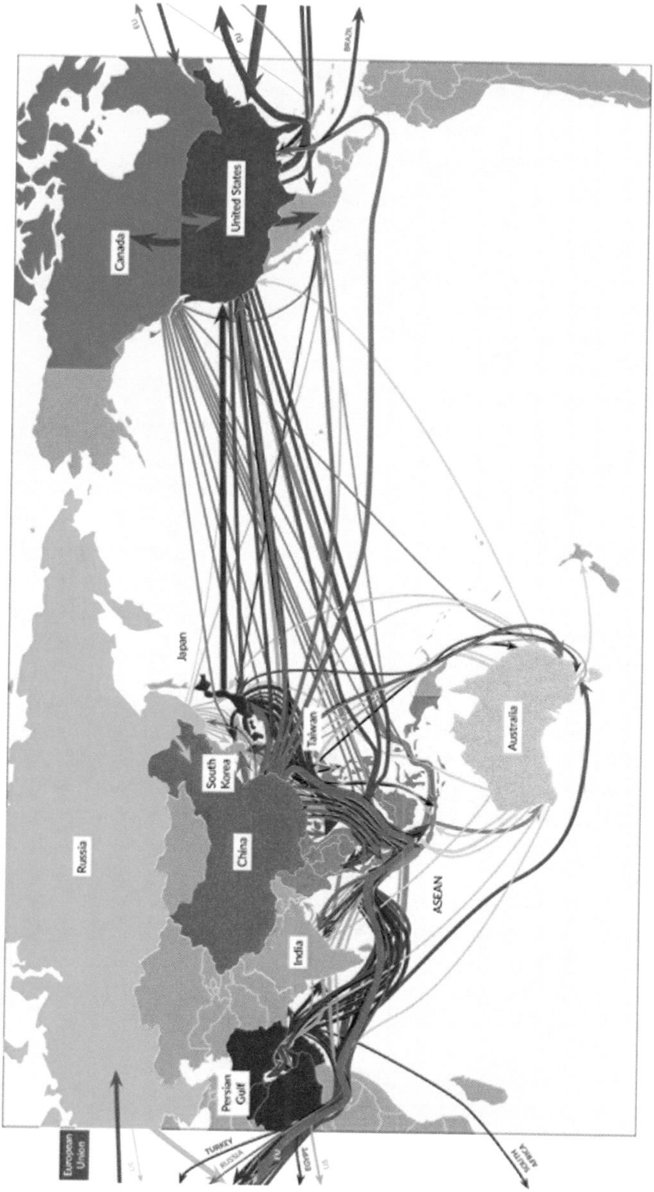

Figure 19. Approximate Pattern of Indo-Pacific Exports at War's Commencement .

Economic Impacts of the Greatly Increased Tensions in Phase 1B

Phase 1B of a major Indo-Pacific war would see a substantial escalation of tension and non-kinetic coercion between China (and probably Russia), on the one hand, and the United States and its allies on the other. China would be exploiting the relative openness and democratic freedoms of America and its allies to penetrate, manipulate, divide, dis-integrate, and cripple their societies in order to force major geostrategic concessions.

The US and its allies would be unable to respond in kind partly because they are not organized, trained, and equipped to do so. They would also have great difficulty penetrating the formidable layers of security that the Chinese regime has built to insulate its society from global pressures and to shield its population from the "corrupting" influences of Western values, opinions and beliefs.

In the circumstances of phase 1B, allied governments would feel compelled to respond strongly both to protect Beijing's local target (e.g., Taiwan) and to impose costs and escalatory risks on the Chinese leadership. Many measures could be considered, including:

- A new wave of tariffs, bans, or other import and export restrictions imposed on China and its partners.
- Tighter restrictions on some categories of allied investment and economic and scientific interaction with China, Russia, and other partners.
- Stronger economic, military, and political measures to strengthen the deterrence and defensive capabilities of locally targeted states, such as Taiwan.
- Tighter restrictions on Chinese immigration into the US and allied countries.
- Larger-scale operations to apprehend, charge, and try Chinese and other authoritarian state agents and operatives in the US and allied countries.

- Deep cuts in Chinese (and probably Russian) diplomatic staffing in allied countries.
- Greatly expanded security and economic cooperation between US allies and a much larger coalition of nonauthoritarian states.
- Ramping up US and allied political warfare (and especially information warfare) operations. A primary emphasis would likely be on exposing the character and motives of the authoritarian regimes, their subversive operations abroad, and the serious threats they pose.
- Coordinated campaigns to reduce China's influence in key international institutions.

In combination, these and related measures would reduce trade, finance, technology, and other economic flows to and from China. Beijing, for its part, would feel compelled to respond with new tariff, technology, immigration, and other restrictions of its own.

The overall impact of the actions of the two sides is likely to be a further contraction of economic interaction between China and the US and its allies, leading to China's detachment from important parts of the global economy. Foreign investment and business operations in China would contract markedly.

If phase 1B continued for an extended period, there would be a rebalancing of global economic activity not only towards the US, its allies and other democratic states but also to a range of developing countries in Southeast Asia, South America, and Africa that share a strong interest in resisting Chinese coercion and subversion.

Cyberattacks would feature prominently in China's political warfare operations, and they would deliver many strategic effects. The most damaging would be disruptions of essential functions such as communication, banking, transport, electricity, energy, food distribution, medical, and related services.

The potential for large-scale damage is substantial. From 2010 to 2019, 56% of electric utilities surveyed worldwide reported at least one shutdown or loss of operational data each year due to cybersecurity breaches.[9] The most notable case of a supply chain attack was the NotPetya virus operation in 2017 in which a state-sponsored attack on Ukrainian software infected millions of Windows servers globally. Maersk, the world's largest shipping company, suspended its electronic order dispatch system for three weeks and reportedly suffered losses of $300 million. The impact on global container logistics networks reverberated for several months.[10]

In 2018 the US government assessed that malicious cyber activity cost the country up to $100 billion annually.[11] Lloyds of London estimated that the ultimate cost of a major attack on the US electricity grid could be an order of magnitude higher.[12] A RAND report in 2016 asserted that both sides would suffer heavy direct losses from cyberattacks "in the event of a severe and protracted US-China conflict."[13]

There would also be the economic costs of societal disruptions caused by foreign manipulation of allied conventional and social media. Many state-sponsored attacks would likely be designed to foster political activism, protests, boycotts, panics over supplies, and community divisions.

Phase 1B would bring a further hardening of controls over strategic technologies, products, and services. The US could introduce a formal system of export controls covering all of its major allies and partners, analogous to the Coordinating Committee for Multilateral Export Controls (COCOM) arrangements that operated during the Cold War. A new COCOM-like system would rely on both the voluntary commitments of member states and enforcement through the use of tariffs, entity sanctions, quotas, export and import controls, ownership restrictions, and technology transfer rules.[14] China would reciprocate, most likely imposing embargoes on the export of strategic items such as processed rare earth metals.[15]

Taiwan would play a particularly important role. Because it is the global leader in the design, development, and manufacture of advanced semiconductors it would be at the heart of a new technology control regime. Semiconductor factories (or "fabs") are colossally expensive, and they are also very fragile. They depend on high levels of physical security and stability and a large number of inputs such as electronic files, optical masks, chemicals, and tools that are sourced from all over the world. Fabs are reliant on efficient transport, communications linkages, and highly skilled personnel, who might be influenced or intimidated by Chinese political warfare campaigns. Most Taiwanese senior managers and engineers have strong international linkages; they have family members abroad and they carry foreign passports. It is unclear how the global semiconductor industry would respond to the increasing danger of a kinetic conflict centered on Taiwan, but many key personnel and much of the intellectual property could move rapidly to safer locations overseas.[16]

As geopolitical tensions escalate, stronger controls would be introduced on international financial flows. Foreign direct investment between the antagonists would likely cease. Commercial banks might start to withdraw credit lines and demand repayment of cross-border claims. Short-term trade financing and shipping insurance rates would become more expensive as creditors demand higher returns to compensate for the elevated levels of risk. Prices of consumables and other short-term goods would probably soar, but the prices of long-term assets such as buildings and most equities would plunge. Mass sell-offs in share and other capital markets would be highly disruptive.

These financial tensions would have domestic consequences in all major economies. Although the United States and China have huge and largely independent financial systems, they are still vulnerable to shocks. The United States derives tremendous power from its position as the world's principal issuer of reserve currency, but this requires Washington to maintain an open financial system and to allow inflows and outflows of capital and frequent price instability. China, in contrast, has a financial system bulging with surplus savings but must maintain tight and inflexible control in order to preserve economic and political stability.

Much of the rest of the world is influenced by the ebb and flow of capital in these two giant systems and the price signals they transmit. If the US and China appear headed for conflict, global financial markets would be in turmoil.

Governments would not sit idly by. They would use monetary and fiscal measures in attempts to restore confidence and maintain a modicum of normality to import and export flows. They would probably also introduce capital controls to prevent the mass sale of assets and the transfer of the proceeds overseas.

The multiple instabilities anticipated in phase 1B would accelerate the division of the world trading system into blocs. Trade between the US and China would be greatly reduced and that which did continue would be "managed trade" with high levels of state control.

Industries which have a high degree of defense and security sensitivity would be restrained or banned from trade between the blocs. The United States Government has declared about 25 "critical and emerging technologies" that would be affected.[17] These are broadly defined (such as biotechnology and advanced manufacturing), and over time the list of controlled goods and services would grow. China has a similar list of sensitive industry sectors. Because many modern products and services embed these technologies, the list of items restricted or banned from trade between the rival blocs would expand, increasing the separation of industry ecosystems. Trade in common items such as consumer electronics (smartphones, TVs, etc.) and automobiles could be controlled because they incorporate extensive surveillance functionality. Financial protocols would also separate into blocs, making money transfer and payment transactions between them difficult. Internet applications such as social media which exploit artificial intelligence and mechanisms for personal information collection would divide further into a "splinternet" of competing but noncompatible ecosystems. If phase 1B is protracted, other sectors such as pharmaceuticals and medical supplies, civil aerospace, energy generation (conventional, renewable, and nuclear), automated machinery, and advanced materials could all be "securitized," and transactions between the adversary blocs would slow dramatically.

Industries such as electronics would be massively disrupted if further controls were placed on semiconductor exports to China. Multinational companies operating in China might find their factories there stranded and starved of high-technology supplies from international affiliates. Other companies might suddenly find their products on export control lists and lose their access to China's large market. China's export trade could suffer a series of major blows if Beijing also started to control technology flows. Enterprises in the respective blocs would have to find alternative customers and/or suppliers—something which today appears inconceivable for many industries. The bifurcation of the world into blocs could happen rapidly, but it would come at a very high cost for certain sectors.[18] The overall macroeconomic impact of decoupling in the high-technology sector alone would be serious, reducing GDPs by as much as 5% in some countries.[19]

Naturally, as trading conditions deteriorate, so would the availability of international trade finance. Foreign direct investment between the two blocs would be subjected to stringent controls and decline steeply. Other forms of investment and credit, such as bank lending, portfolio (share) equity, and debt, would also be cut heavily and international payment systems between the blocs would be crippled.

Both China and the United States and its allies could afford to conduct phase 1B operations indefinitely. Should phase 1B be prolonged, all parties would be effectively locked into a new cold war, with the ever-present potential for hostilities to escalate into full-scale conventional war at little or no notice. Alternatively, Chinese leaders may conclude that with the US and some of its allies struggling with deep domestic divisions and incoherent governments, the time was right to seize the initiative and escalate offensive operations into kinetic modes.

The Economic Impacts of Kinetic War Against a Regional State in Phase 2A

Phase 2A sees China crossing the kinetic threshold to use substantial military force against Taiwan or another regional state. Beijing would aim to defeat and occupy the regional state quickly and shock the United States, its allies, and most of the rest of the world into timidity and withdrawal.

However, such a major attack would likely drive the US and a large coalition of nonauthoritarian states to take substantial and sustained counteraction—including some steps towards wartime mobilization. Many countries would greatly reduce their political, military, and economic ties with China. Even if American forces avoided direct combat with the PLA, the US Congress would almost certainly call for the imposition of a wartime sanctions regime.[20] At a minimum, this would target specific entities and industries (particularly in the high-technology sector) with both export and import bans for trade with the US, allies and security partners. Existing international frameworks such as multilateral export control regimes would be used to restrict all designated trade with China.

In their more severe form, the US sanctions could be broadened and deepened to encompass all trade with China. Sanctions would be extended to other state entities such as airlines, shipping and logistics companies, and financial institutions. Washington would probably also invoke secondary sanctions to deter third parties from transacting indirectly in sensitive fields with Chinese and associated entities. This would prevent other countries dealing in an uninterrupted manner with China or face the risk of removal from the American financial system.

The outbreak of kinetic war in the Indo-Pacific would probably trigger a set of emergency controls over international financial transactions more severe than those imposed on Russia following its invasion of Ukraine. Markets could be shut, at least temporarily, positions locked and outflows restricted. Many countries would impose capital controls with immediate effect. Within days, governments could pass further legislation suspending or nationalizing the operations of adversary foreign enterprises within their borders. In some countries, Chinese businesses would be subjected to public boycotts and harassment. Within China, many foreign companies would fare even worse.

This crisis would quickly spill over into the domestic financial affairs of many countries. Much of the global financial system would be frozen, at least temporarily, and the chaos could be amplified by a barrage of Chinese and Russian cyberattacks launched against banks and other financial and business institutions.

Some third party states in Europe, South America, Africa, and elsewhere would find themselves economically entangled in a conflict in which they wanted no part. They would lobby the superpowers for exemptions from sanctions. However, if the US and China sustain heavy casualties, neither is likely to be in a mood to compromise. They would demand compliance.

The Chinese regime would feel compelled to respond strongly to what it would see as US and allied economic warfare. It would target selected US and allied industries and special interest groups in efforts to maximize the political cost of the conflict. The overall consequence would be to accelerate the decoupling of China and its close political associates not only from the US and its allies but also from much of the global economy.

The Chinese regime has been preparing to cope with extreme sanctions for some years. Beijing has squirreled substantial financial resources abroad and many of these assets are obscured from the view of US regulators. Beijing also has substantial credit swap lines with the central banks of several countries. Whether such measures would meaningfully help China to ride through a fierce Western sanctions regime is debatable.[21] What is more certain is that Beijing has assembled a very large and well-funded global commercial network on which it can draw. In these circumstances it would be a major challenge to institute an allied sanctions program that was fully effective.

Because of the scale, scope, and sophistication of China's industrial economy, the imposition of a severe sanctions regime would have massive consequences for global trade. Supplies of some categories of goods would be affected within days, and many supply chains would be thrown into chaos. An urgent restructuring of the global economy would be necessary.

A prominent example would be the serious disruption to the global value chain for electronics. Upsetting the air cargo timetables would have almost immediate effects on the delivery of end products. The greatest squeezes would, however, be on the production of discretionary consumer goods, such as smartphones, that are not immediately essential to the functioning of the global economy. A temporary buffer would be provided by the inventories of many essential components, such as memory and processor chips and passive electronic components (resistors, capacitors, and the like), that the industry holds.

Other supply chain stress points would emerge quickly. Materials and goods where Chinese producers hold a commanding market share would become scarce in Western markets within weeks, sending prices soaring as international customers scramble to procure alternative sources. These categories are likely to include exotic metals such as rare earth alloys that are critical for many high-technology industries.

Once the kinetic threshold has been crossed, shipping companies would immediately reassess their risk and many ships would be ordered to avoid the theater of conflict or vacate it as quickly as possible. If maritime transport links are disrupted, shortages of essential items such as fuels, food, and chemicals would become apparent in some countries within days.

All countries would need to rapidly assess their critical needs and the size of essential holdings. Most major countries in the Indo-Pacific hold strategic reserves of oil and other essential commodities such as coal, agricultural products and metals. However, there would be a scramble to secure on-going supplies. Widespread shortages would be inevitable and rationing systems would be introduced.

The United States and its allies, in contrast, would work to constrain or ban most, if not all, shipments to Chinese ports or to the ports of countries from which transshipment to China by rail, pipeline, or road would be possible. Government orders would soon stop most aircraft and shipping departures to enemy locations.

This would have profound ramifications for supply chains globally. Within days, ships and aircraft in the region would be corralled into safe ports, their crews and cargoes stranded indefinitely. Just-in-time production systems across many global industries (such as autos and electronics, which are dependent on components from the region) would shudder to a halt within weeks, and the disruption would quickly spillover into associated industries such as export, import, and retail trades.

The likely consequences of these intense kinetic operations for regional trade are portrayed in figure 20. This highlights the prospect that most regional trade would cease almost immediately with ships and aircraft fleeing to friendly countries. In the weeks that follow, commercial ship and aircraft movements within the first island chain would be rare and between the first and second island chains would be limited and tightly controlled. Those high-priority commercial movements that continued in and out of Japan, South Korea, and Taiwan would be routed to minimize transit and port time within 1,000 miles of the Chinese mainland. China, North Korea and possibly Iran, Pakistan, Myanmar, and Cambodia would be denied access to most maritime trade routes. Some restrictions are also likely to be applied to Russian trade.

This phase of the war would probably last 3–10 weeks[40] and would present a survival challenge for the trade-intensive economies of East Asia. Figure 20 depicts a situation in which trade flows in and out of Taiwan would be rare and Japan and South Korea might see 60–70% declines in their trade volumes. China could suffer even more. It would probably be subjected to an allied blockade bringing nearly all of its maritime trade to a standstill. In partial compensation, China would immediately expand import and export flows across its continental borders and airspace, especially with Russia. During this phase, China's trade with some neighboring ASEAN states (those on its land borders) might also continue, though perhaps at only 20–30% of prewar levels.

The end result would be a huge reduction in trade and financial flows from most of the world to and from China. However, not all international movements would cease. In the short span of phase 2B, shipments to and from most neutral Indo-Pacific countries—including the ASEAN states —would probably pause and then cautiously resume. Many shipments originally destined for China and some countries bordering China would be redirected to customers in other locations beyond the immediate war zone.

In phase 2B, China would probably attack and seriously damage US Japanese, South Korean, and other allied bases across the region. As casualties mount, official and public opinion on both sides would harden. There would be a "rally round the flag" effect in affected nations, leaving little room for early negotiation and compromise.

Within allied societies, governments would assume new powers of control over their economies and other aspects of civilian life. In most countries, mass media and communications would be more regulated, rationing would be introduced for at least some products, and the demands of wartime mobilization would dominate. Many people would be recruited or conscripted into the military. Others would be redeployed to completely different lines of work. In the past, most mobilized economies have experienced an acute shortage of labor. But until the processes of mobilization stabilize, short-term frictional unemployment would rise and special compensatory measures would be required. Most of the world's democracies would be confronted by challenges not seen for generations.

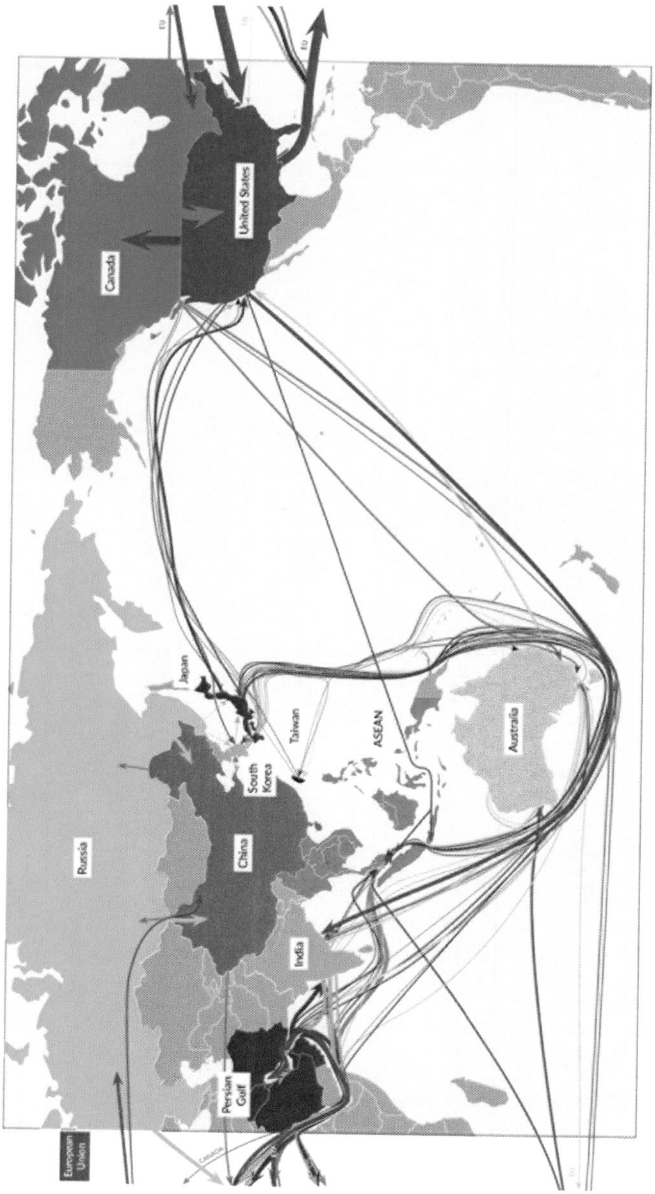

Figure 20. Estimated Pattern of Indo-Pacific Exports in the Initial Phase of a Major Kinetic War Between China and the United States in Phase 2B.

Maintaining economic and social stability during the transition to wartime economic operations would require careful management. Many governments would need to supply an emergency stimulus to their economies. In most countries this would be partly delivered via the funding of military mobilization, emergency infrastructure investments, and associated civilian support operations. But supplemental funds may need to be paid to households to ensure that people are fed and other essential services, like healthcare and basic retail are maintained. These would not be trivial tasks, especially if enemy operations seriously damage key infrastructure like the power, internet, and banking systems.

Particular challenges would arise for those companies and industries that are heavily involved in global supply chains—as a consumer, a producer, or both. If companies are closely linked to supply chains running through enemy states, many operations would slow markedly or stop completely. As long as the conflict continues, they would face the prospect of their business collapsing. They would need to scramble to find new suppliers and customers within the allied camp or in well-disposed and accessible neutral countries. But for companies with business models dependent on China, this may not be feasible.

While many companies would be in trouble, others would find offsetting opportunities in the military effort and the civilian economy. Additional opportunities would open up in the rapidly expanding manufacturing, infrastructure, food, logistics, and other sectors of allied countries. Some pressing needs would need to be met by "good enough" solutions. Innovation, flexibility, adaptability, and new market development would be the order of the day. For its part, Beijing would launch parallel programs to maintain China's most vital economic functions. Foremost would be to ensure that the population is adequately fed by releasing some of its strategic food reserves. China can normally rely on Russia and its central Asian neighbors for about 30% of its oil and gas needs, and these pipelines would be supplemented by rail and road shipment. To cut fuel use, nonessential travel by car and commercial aviation would be restricted and heavy reliance placed on China's public transportation system.

With its pervasive stability-maintenance infrastructure, Beijing would be prepared to enforce staff redeployments, rationing, and other economic controls in a far more draconian manner than in the West. China's labor dispatch system, which currently provides millions of factory workers to priority industries and companies, would redirect labor to meet wartime needs. But many rural migrant workers would probably be laid off in the first weeks of the war and ordered back to their home villages to help boost agricultural production.

Nearly all Indo-Pacific governments would activate emergency powers, giving them authority to requisition supplies and other resources from the private sector. Companies and individuals may be asked, or instructed, to give priority to supporting the national defense effort. Some businesses or their facilities could be nationalized, or their operations overseen and essentially directed, by government agencies.

Because the intense combat operations of phase 2B would probably only last a few weeks, most regional states would plan to operate in a temporary improvisation-economy mode. The initial kinetic combat phase would be fought mostly with forces in being drawing on existing stockpiles of munitions and material. There would be insufficient time to restructure economies to operate far beyond their normal modes. Emergency programs would be introduced for materials and parts recovery, recycling, and reuse in efforts to stretch self-reliance.

By the end of phase 2B, a massive reindustrialization program of strategic mobilization would be underway in many countries. Among the highest priority categories would be munitions and other military materiel, pharmaceutical chemicals, exotic metals, and basic electronic modules. Close coordination would be needed between the US and its partners to harmonize production and distribution priorities. They would also need to agree on a collective planning mechanism to build new production capacities.

The global financial system would gradually recover from the shock of phase 2B. Most nations have largely insular domestic financial systems. Provided these can be adequately protected from cyber interference, most domestic transaction systems should be restored within days. Certain functions might need to be controlled in order to ensure systematic stability. There may, for instance, be a need for limits to be placed on bank withdrawals, in addition to forbearance mechanisms introduced on loan repayments and accrued interest. Securities markets might be closed or restricted for extended periods.[41]

The impact on the international financial system would be more far-reaching. The freezes imposed on cross-border claims with states in the opposing bloc would remain. Capital and currency controls would continue between the adversary blocs. Sanctions would continue and be expanded. The sizeable currency reserves held by China which are mainly invested in dollar, euro, and yen bonds would be at serious risk. These holdings supposedly give Beijing leverage and a foreign exchange buffer in crises to pay for imports. But as the Western response to Russia's invasion of Ukraine demonstrates, the US and other Western governments control the trading of their own securities and they can, and likely would, refuse an adversary access to these markets in a war.

More drastically, the US could insist on the immediate and permanent removal of China from the Western payments system (including SWIFT and FedWire). China and Russia have been jointly building their own payments systems to prepare for this scenario.[42] They have made limited progress to date, but these systems would become extremely important to them in an emergency and might allow them to maintain payments to third parties that avoid Western sanctions. With the collapse of its trade, China's balance of payments surplus would evaporate and might be replaced by a deficit, requiring it to issue debt to those countries with which it still trades. Because these payments would not be in hard currency (easily convertible to other reserve currencies), they would effectively be barter transactions. Indeed, for a wartime China, barter might be an adequate mechanism for conducting most types of trade.

One possibility is that China might quickly and successfully expand its e-yuan, or digital renminbi, central bank digital currency (CBDC) as an alternative to the Western payments system. There would be some serious potential pitfalls to a CBDC strategy, such as the lack of a secure and reliable global internet infrastructure during the war. The e-yuan is a centralized, non-anonymous system entirely under the control of the Chinese authorities. This is nothing like the cryptocurrencies popular with some investors today. But the e-yuan could emerge as a payment medium adopted by authoritarian state corporates to clear their trade and bypass traditional Western-dominated payment systems.[43]

A key unknown factor is the extent of US wartime sanctions. Washington would certainly sanction all Chinese state entities and financial institutions directly. In a major war, secondary sanctions would probably be extended to other countries interacting with these entities. Russia would likely enable China to bypass the blockade in some sectors. If Russia is not sanctioned or not sanctioned fully, it might be able to intermediate some of China's trade with the rest of the world. This would open the prospect of Russia prospering as China's import and export hub. So, as with trade, Russia may be a significant source of financial leakage that undermines an allied economic blockade of China.[44]

Another important unknown is how effective US and allied sanctions would be against China's international commercial and financial networks. There are thousands, and probably millions, of China-connected entities abroad and it would be impossible to sanction most of them. Moreover, as discussed in chapter 5, most of these entities reside (legally speaking) in opaque offshore financial centers and it is difficult to predict what would happen in these jurisdictions in a major war. Many offshore financial centers might be unraveled with the stroke of a legislator's pen. Should that happen, chaos would follow but the US and its allies might be prepared to pay the price to further impede China's political economy.

Every country in the world would be affected directly or indirectly by a major war in the Indo-Pacific. But the exact nature and extent of the impact on each economy would depend on several geographical, political, and industrial factors.

The most general macroeconomic impact would be the sudden removal of much of China's productive capacity, almost 30% of the world's total manufacturing output.[45] This could not be replaced for many years, and indeed it could only be partially substituted. Therefore there would be a permanent loss of aggregate demand and supply in the world economy. China's own economy would suffer the heaviest losses, but the severing of economic ties with it would reverberate in all countries. The world would have to make do with much less stuff, there would be less variety, less innovation, more shortages, and much longer lead times for many products. The prices of most manufactured goods would rise, and many workers would need to move to new employment.

It is difficult to assess the full impact on the United States, its allies, and partners. In 2021 China shipped over 40% of containerized imports into the US, a figure that roughly aligns with retailer disclosures of origin.[46] However, American industry groups estimate that Chinese goods account for as much as 70–80% of non-grocery merchandise sold by some large US retailers.[47] Component imports from low-cost Asian countries (mostly China) contribute to 61% of the United Kingdom's gross manufactured output.[48] However, it is obvious that most of this activity is nonessential in nature. The world doesn't "need" to update consumer electronics, furniture, apparel, or cars with anything like today's frequency. And China doesn't need to build millions of new residential apartments every year, many of which are unoccupied.

What is clear is that sectors that currently trade heavily with China —consumer goods, electronics, construction, mining, retail, and many others—would greatly contract. The private sectors of many countries would experience permanent shocks to income and wealth. Long-term real interest rates would rise as China's $5 trillion annual savings pool is unable to participate directly or indirectly in world financial markets. The prices of major assets such as housing and international equity portfolios would probably fall.

The frontline states facing China—Taiwan, Japan, South Korea, India, and Vietnam—would have the greatest challenges. They would immediately lose their largest trading partner but, more importantly, they could also see their primary lines of supply (including for energy, food, and metals) substantially diminished for a while. Furthermore because of their potential direct involvement in the conflict, they face the prospect of huge damage to their economic infrastructures. Nevertheless, they will remain vital manufacturing bases for the allied countries, and their continuing physical access to the US-led bloc could be a major factor determining the progress of the war.

Countries outside the two blocs, particularly those that currently trade heavily with China, would also face serious disruptions. Due to their geographic distance from China and their reliance on long maritime supply routes to it, the commodity exporting states in the Middle East, Africa, and Latin America would see immediate reductions in their export incomes and the depression of their extractive and farming sectors. Because many of these countries rely heavily on affordable manufactures and credit from China, the loss of this trade would not be compensated by increased business with the US-led bloc or other economic partners.

Developing economies that are heavily dependent on trade with China may experience balance-of-payment and debt crises. Some countries in the Middle East (particularly Iran) might be able to continue exporting hydrocarbons to China via land routes, but the primary Persian Gulf energy exporters would almost certainly lose access to the Chinese market for the war's duration.

Outside China, the prices of oil and indeed many bulk commodities would fall, at least initially. Many national economies would face a double-whammy impact: the loss of primary export revenues on the income side and soaring prices of manufactured goods on the cost side.

This economic pain would have geopolitical consequences. The hardship experienced by the populations of some developing countries might generate civil unrest and sustained opposition to the allied economic blockade of China.

For those countries located in the combat zones, there would be the added complications of warfighting and the associated economic-industrial support effort. There would be huge demands on the industrial bases of the United States and its allies that have been allowed to wither in recent decades. They would need to convert or repurpose existing factories to supply essential items and simultaneously launch emergency programs to build substantial new infrastructure. They would also need to coordinate closely with the industrial allies in Asia and Europe to boost supplies of many types of capital goods and rapidly expand engineering and manufacturing capacities.

China would appear to have a decisive advantage in short-term mobilization. Beijing's leaders would have the support of a nationalistic populace that appears to be primed for conflict. China has a fully-fledged national security complex that would easily transition to a command system suitable for major warfighting. The Chinese authorities have immense financial and industrial resources at their disposal and the economic controls in place to ensure a degree of stability and some insulation from the initial shocks of war. However, the Chinese would soon be short of key material inputs to feed its major industries and nearly all of its export orders would evaporate. China's leaders appreciate that an allied economic and maritime blockade would pose an existential threat to their economy, to their war effort, and ultimately to the regime's survival.

As mentioned earlier, the intense warfighting anticipated in phase 2B could not be sustained indefinitely. While there is a possibility that one or both sides may call a halt and seek to negotiate a ceasefire and settlement, it is more likely that the war would continue at a less frenetic pace for several months and possibly for several years. This is the type of drawn-out exhausting struggle that is envisaged in phase 3A.

Economic Impacts of Phase 3A

From the start of phase 3A, there will be a much clearer economic separation of the two sides. China, Russia, North Korea, and probably Iran and Pakistan will likely be cooperating relatively closely. On the other side would be the United States, Japan, South Korea, Taiwan, India, Australia, New Zealand, Canada, the Philippines, and probably also the United Kingdom, France, Germany, most other members of NATO and the EU, and Israel.

Then there would be a large group of neutral or semi-neutral states. In the Indo-Pacific region Laos, Cambodia, Myanmar, Kazakhstan, Kyrgyzstan, Uzbekistan, Tajikistan, Turkmenistan, and Mongolia are likely to lean towards Beijing. Further afield, Belorussia, Syria, Cuba, and a number of South American and African countries would probably also tilt China's way. A larger number of neutral states might lean towards America's allies; these would probably include Indonesia, Singapore, Malaysia, Vietnam, and all of the remaining South Pacific island states. Further afield, neutral European countries and certain countries in the Middle East, South America, and Africa would probably also be sympathetic to the allied cause despite their lost trade with China.[49]

Trade, investment, technology, and other flows would likely restructure within the two main camps and in many cases increase in quantity and diversity. Some of the biggest shifts would be within the US-led coalition where there would be closer economic integration and, in some priority sectors, very rapid growth. This would be particularly notable not only in military system supply but also in energy, raw materials, food, and a diverse range of priority construction materials and manufactured goods. The US, its allies, and trusted partners would move to strengthen their individual self-reliance while simultaneously establishing new global value chains so as to rapidly grow their individual and collective capacities to supply priority military and civilian needs.

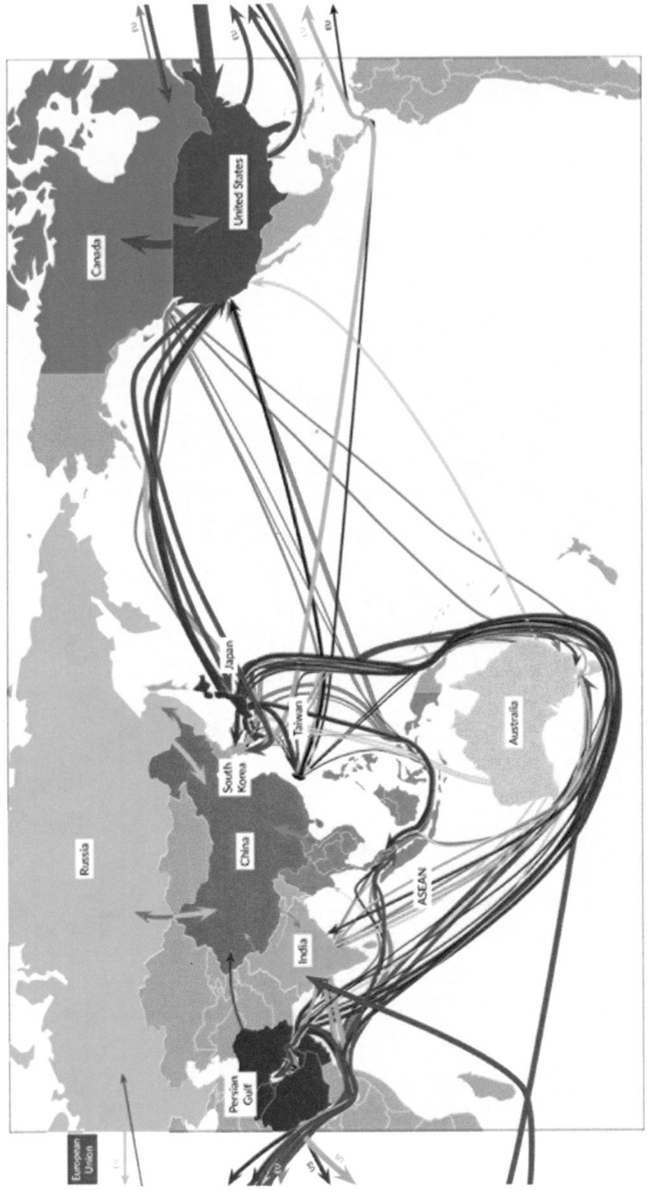

Figure 21. Estimated Pattern of Indo-Pacific Exports During a Major Kinetic War's Extended Phase 3A.

Similar but probably less dramatic shifts would occur in the economic relationship between China and Russia. Although Russia is a major resource supplier, China's economy dwarfs Russia's and China can already supply most of its needs from domestic sources.

In this phase of a major war, there would also be marked changes in the patterns of international trade and in the routing of international shipping and aircraft. A central assumption is that both sides would suffer significant losses following the first few weeks of a major kinetic conflict. Several American and allied bases in the Western Pacific would probably be heavily damaged. Both sides' navies and air forces would also suffer losses, with much of the Chinese navy lost or incapacitated. This would change the security outlook for allied shipping and aircraft in the theater and probably increase the security of allied shipments transiting outside the second island chain.

Nevertheless, for the US-led coalition, the further south and east in the Pacific and the further west in the Indian Ocean, (i.e., away from China), the safer the ships and aircraft would be. Travel to and within maritime Southeast Asia would be possible but would carry greater risk for at least the first few weeks of such a war. Air and sea travel within 1,000 miles of China's coasts or its offshore military bases in the South China Sea would still be risky. There would be major challenges in maintaining supply lines to US allies and partners in Central and Northeast Asia. Particularly difficult may be shipping movements to South Korea, Japan, Taiwan, and the Philippines.

Allied shipping routes would experience some of the largest changes. For instance, shipping travelling from the American West Coast to the Indian Ocean and vice versa would mostly passage south of Australia, rather than through the Indonesian archipelago and the South China Sea. And most allied ships heading to Japan, South Korea, Taiwan, and the Philippines would probably passage via designated, well-protected shipping tunnels from rendezvous areas in the Central Pacific. This rerouting would require longer travel times and increased costs but for much, if not most, of this phase, that will be the price for an acceptable level of security. The approximate pattern of trade and shipping movements across the Indo-Pacific in phase 3A is displayed in figure 21.

The Economic Impacts of Phase 3B

In the later stages of phase 3A, both sides would have options for what happens next. It is possible that one side is so exhausted that it decides to make significant concessions and sue for peace. It is also possible that neither side concedes and that the fighting extends phase 3A for a further period. Eventually however, one or both sides are likely to detect signs of wilting on the other side and choose to accelerate the enemy's collapse. There would be a number of options for attempting to bring the war to an end, most of which would require a period of intensified combat operations. This final drive for victory is the logic for phase 3B.

While this phase would see additional damage to the Chinese and allied economies and a further deepening of the separation between the two warring camps, the overall incremental impact on the global economy would probably be similar to that of phase 3A. Should the allies succeed in drawing some of the neutrals into the allied coalition, stronger trade, finance, and other economic connections with these countries would follow.

What, then, could be the ultimate impact of such a massive, protracted war on the world economy? RAND has estimated that in the first year alone the GDP of the US and China could be damaged by 5–10% and 25–35%, respectively.[50] More recent analyses have assessed the longer-term impact at over 50% of the output of affected countries, taking into account the catastrophic mortality costs, physical destruction and the permanent loss of trade (especially in high-tech goods).[51] In the First and Second World Wars, trade between the principal combatants dropped by 96–97%.[52] But the damage extended far beyond them. In 1944, for example, the Bank for International Settlements found that 43% of all prewar global trade had been "destroyed, suppressed, or blocked by state restrictions."[53] More recent studies show that a fracturing of US-China trade could cause a 12% decline in global GDP, with the burden falling most heavily on lower-income nations outside the two blocs.[54] A sustained Chinese quarantine of Taiwan could cost the world economy US$2.5 trillion annually, due to disruption of trade in semiconductors and other goods.[55]

Conclusions

The decisive determinants in a major war in the Indo-Pacific would include numerous economic factors spanning transport, energy, food, strategic materials, capital equipment, skilled workforces, trading partnerships, finance, healthcare, utilities, and information-communications infrastructures. The nations that can rapidly refocus and restructure these factors to build powerful war economies would be best positioned to prevail.

The United States enjoys a considerable advantage in international finance, but China has a far greater ability to generate internal financial resources through domestic savings. The US is likely to remain open financially, which means that its monetary economy will be subject to significant volatility, whereas China will keep its financial system largely closed, tightly controlled and very "stable." The US has the ability to cut China off from its own financial networks and this would hobble China's international economic operations. However, if Beijing enlists some major countries to its bloc they might collectively be able to create a basic payment system that bypasses the US and supports a Eurasian continental trade order.

On a more fundamental level, war is a contest of organizations. To examine only the techno-industrial and financial dimensions would overlook the intangible but equally important factors in the performance of the war economy. These include political, managerial, and social elements.

Among the most important qualitative factors are the standards of political and military leadership and industrial management.

Another key factor would be the level of preparation and planning that relevant agencies and industrial sectors put in place prior to the outbreak of kinetic conflict. The allies have an advantage to the extent that they already have trusted strategic partnerships and societal linkages. Their multinational companies and workforces are already well-adapted to operating complex high-tech value chains across multiple countries. However, in China's case, ties with partner states are strongest at the government level. China's advantage is in the deep vertical integration of its state enterprises and its presence in many basic but vital industries that have been mostly vacated by Western firms in recent decades.

Wartime is typically a period of intense innovative dynamism. By phase 3B, there is likely to be a race for game-changing and war-ending technologies and systems. The quality of the engineering and science complex in each of the warring blocs would have a significant impact on the course of the war. High levels of initiative, adaptability, and diligence in the workforces will be critical to success.

Indeed, it is the national, societal, and individual qualities of initiative, ruggedness, sacrifice and resilience that may matter the most in generating exceptional performance in the war economies. With its martial spirit of nationalism, and its formidable whole-of-nation response to recent challenges such as the COVID-19 pandemic, Beijing has signaled its understanding of this. A core challenge for the economic success of the allied democracies in such a war would be to develop and maintain the political, economic, and industrial unity and cohesion that would be essential for the task.

Notes

1. "Consumer boycotts warn of trouble ahead for Western firms in China," *The Economist,* March 31, 2021, https://www.economist.com/business/2021/03/31/consumer-boycotts-warn-of-trouble-ahead-for-western-firms-in-china.
2. Eliot Chen, "Making sense of sanctions," *The Wire China,* April 24, 2022, https://www.thewirechina.com/2022/04/24/making- sense-of-sanctions/.
3. James T. Areddy, "Fearful of Getting Cut Off, China Pushes for Self-Reliance," *Wall Street Journal,* May 3, 2022, https://www.wsj.com/articles/fearful-of-getting-cut-off-china-pushes-for-self-reliance-11651588187.
4. "High Tech Research And Development (863) Programme," Consulate General of the People's Republic of China in New York, October 21, 2003, http://newyork.china-consulate.gov.cn/eng/xbwz/kjsw/zgkj/200310/t20031021_5431224.htm.
5. Tristan Kenderdine, "China's Industrial Policy, Strategic Emerging Industries and Space Law," *Wiley Online Library,* May 12, 2017, https://onlinelibrary.wiley.com/doi/full/10.1002/app5.177.
6. Scott Kennedy, "Made in China 2025," *CSIS Critical Questions,* June 1, 2015, https://www.csis.org/analysis/made-china-2025.
7. Nigel Cory and Luke Dascoli, "How Barriers to Cross-Border Data Flows Are Spreading Globally, What They Cost, and How to Address Them," *Information Technology and Innovation Foundation,* June 19, 2021, https://itif.org/publications/2021/07/19/how-barriers-cross-border-data-flows-are-spreading-globally-what-they-cost.
8. Anders Sundell, "Visualizing Countries Grouped by Their Largest Trading Partner (1960–2020)," *Visual Capitalist,* February 11, 2022, https://www.visualcapitalist.com/cp/biggest-trade-partner-of-each-country-1960-2020/.
9. "Siemens and Ponemon Institute study finds utility industry vulnerable to cyberattacks," *Siemens,* October 4, 2019, https://press.siemens.com/global/en/pressrelease/siemens-and-ponemon-institute-study-finds-utility-industry-vulnerabilities.
10. Andy Greenberg, "The Untold Story of NotPetya, the Most Devastating Cyberattack in History," *Wired,* August 22, 2018, https://www.wired.com/story/notpetya-cyberattack-ukraine-russia-code-crashed-the-world/.

11. The White House, "CEA Report: The Cost of Malicious Cyber Activity to the U.S. Economy," *The White House,* February 16, 2018, https://trumpwhitehouse.archives.gov/articles/cea-report-cost-malicious-cyber-activity-u-s-economy/.
12. "Lloyd's Report: Cyberattack on US Power Grid Could Cost Over $1 Trillion Dollars," *Council of Insurance Agents and Brokers,* n.d., https://www.ciab.com/resources/lloyds-report-cyberattack-on-us-power-grid-could-cost-over-1-trillion-dollars/.
13. David C. Gompert, Astrid Stuth Cevallos, and Cristina L. Garafola, *War with China: Thinking Through the Unthinkable* (Santa Monica: RAND Corporation, 2016), https://www.rand.org/pubs/research_reports/RR1140.html.
14. In September 2022 there were reports that the United States, the European Union, and several American allies were considering possible packages of economic sanctions in an effort to deter a Chinese assault on Taiwan. See, for example, Ben Blanchard et al., "Exclusive: U.S. weighs China sanctions to deter Taiwan action, presses EU," Reuters, September 14, 2022, https://www.reuters.com/world/asia-pacific/exclusive-us-considers-china-sanctions-deter-taiwan-action-taiwan-presses-eu-2022-09-13/.
15. Scott Jones, "Think twice before bringing back the COCOM export control regime," *Defense News,* April 10, 2021, https://www.defensenews.com/opinion/commentary/2021/04/09/think-twice-before-bringing-back-the-cocom-export-control-regime/.
16. George Calhoun, "Why China (Probably) Won't Go To War Over Taiwan's Semiconductor Riches," Forbes, September 29, 2021, https://www.forbes.com/sites/georgecalhoun/2021/09/29/why-china-probably-wont-go-to-war-over-taiwans-semiconductor-riches/.
17. US National Science and Technology Council, *Critical And Emerging Technologies List Update* (Washington, DC: Executive Office of the President of the United States, February 2022), https://www.whitehouse.gov/wp-content/uploads/2022/02/02-2022-Critical-and-Emerging-Technologies-List-Update.pdf.
18. Daniel H. Rosen and Lauren Gloudeman, "Understanding US-China Decoupling: Macro Trends and Industry Impacts," Rhodium Group, February 17, 2021, https://rhg.com/research/us-china-decoupling/.
19. Diego A. Cerdeiro et al., *Sizing Up the Effects of Technological Decoupling:* IMF Working Papers WP/21/69 (Washington, DC: International Monetary Fund, March 12, 2021), https://www.imf.org/en/Publications/WP/Issues/2021/03/12/Sizing-Up-the-Effects-of-Technological-Decoupling-50125.

20. It is notable that even long-neutral Switzerland has stated that it would follow any EU sanctions imposed in the event of a Chinese invasion of Taiwan. "Swiss set to match EU sanctions if China invades Taiwan - agency chief," Reuters, July 30, 2022, https://www.reuters.com/world/asia-pacific/swiss-set-match-eu-sanctions-if-china-invades-taiwan-agency-chief-2022-07-30/.
21. Saleem Bahaj and Ricardo Reis, "Jumpstarting an international currency," VoxEU/CEPR, September 21, 2021, https://voxeu.org/article/jumpstarting-international-currency.
22. Tom Daly and Shivani Singh, "Explainer: What China keeps in its secretive commodity reserves," Reuters, August 5, 2021, https://www.reuters.com/world/china/what-china-keeps-its-secretive-commodity-reserves-2021-08-05/.
23. Mary Hui, "China is finally ready to test out its state crude oil reserves," *Quartz*, September 23, 2021, https://qz.com/2063870/china-is-finally-testing-out-its-state-crude-oil-reserves/.
24. Frank Tang, "Explainer: How big are China's crude oil reserves and how do they compare to the US' SPR?," *South China Morning Post*, November 23, 2021, https://www.scmp.com/economy/china-economy/article/3156952/how-big-are-chinas-crude-oil-reserves-and-how-do-they-compare.
25. International Energy Agency, "Oil Stocks of IEA Countries," International Energy Agency, May 12, 2022, https://www.iea.org/articles/oil-stocks-of-iea-countries.
26. Jeff Kucharski, "Taiwan's Greatest Vulnerability Is Its Energy Supply," *The Diplomat*, September 13, 2022, https://thediplomat.com/2022/09/taiwans-greatest-vulnerability-is-its-energy-supply/.
27. Ji-Kun Huang et al., "The prospects for China's food security and imports: Will China starve the world via imports?," *Journal of Integrative Agriculture* 16, issue 12, (December 2017): 2933–2944, https://www.sciencedirect.com/science/article/pii/S2095311917617568.
28. Holly Demaree-Saddler, "China achieves ample grain reserve," *World Grain*, May 4, 2021, https://www.world-grain.com/articles/15103-china-achieves-ample-grain-reserve.
29. Adam Minter, "One Reason for Rising Food Prices? Chinese Hoarding," Bloomberg, January 5, 2022, https://www.bloomberg.com/opinion/articles/2022-01-05/one-reason-for-rising-food-prices-chinese-hoarding.
30. "Japan's Food Self-Sufficiency Rate Matches Record Low," nippon.com, September 10, 2021, https://www.nippon.com/en/japan-data/h01101/.

31. US-China Economic And Security Review Commission, "Taiwan's ability to endure a PLA blockade," in *Annual Report to Congress 2021*, chapter 4: A Dangerous Period For Cross-Strait Deterrence: Chinese Military Capabilities And Decision-Making For A War Over Taiwan, November 2021, 410, https://www.uscc.gov/sites/default/files/2021-11/2021_Annual_Report_to_Congress.pdf.
32. Min Zhang and Mai Nguyen, "China's nonferrous group suggests commercial reserves for cobalt, nickel – media," Reuters, November 4, 2021, https://www.reuters.com/world/china/chinas-nonferrous-group-suggests-commercial-reserves-cobalt-nickel-media-2021-11-04/.
33. Jack Farchy and Mark Burton, "What Happens If the World's Key Metal Exchange Has No Metal?," Bloomberg, October 21, 2021, https://www.bloomberg.com/news/articles/2021-10-20/what-happens-when-the-world-s-key-metal-exchange-has-no-metal.
34. Kyounga Lee and Jongmun Cha, "Towards Improved Circular Economy and Resource Security in South Korea," *Sustainability* 13, issue 17 (December 22, 2020), https://www.mdpi.com/2071-1050/13/1/17/pdf.
35. Japan Agency for Natural Resources and Energy, "Japan's new international resource strategy to secure rare metals," *METI*, July 30, 2020, https://www.enecho.meti.go.jp/en/category/special/article/detail_158.html.
36. Damien Ma and Joshua Henderson, "The Impermanence of Permanent Magnets: A Case Study on Industry, Chinese Production, and Supply Constraints," *Macro Polo*, November 16, 2021, https://macropolo.org/analysis/permanent-magnets-case-study-industry-chinese-production-supply/.
37. Pete Pattisson and Febriana Firdaus, "'Battery arms race': how China has monopolised the electric vehicle industry," *The Guardian*, November 26, 2021, https://www.theguardian.com/global-development/2021/nov/25/battery-arms-race-how-china-has-monopolised-the-electric-vehicle-industry.
38. Song Jung-a, "South Korea's global battery dominance raises supply chain risks," *Financial Times*, October 7, 2021, https://www.ft.com/content/1be9bd48-28b7-4919-ae91-35e06ac926d7.
39. Victor Ferguson, Scott Waldron, and Darren J. Lim, "Market Adjustments To Import Sanctions: Lessons From Chinese Restrictions on Australian Trade, 2020–21," *SSRN*, April 14, 2022, revised May 9, 2022, https://papers.ssrn.com/sol3/papers.cfm?abstract_id=3945451.

40. As discussed earlier, the period of intense combat in phase 2B could not be sustained indefinitely by either side for two main reasons. Their stocks (especially China's) of theater-range missiles would soon run short, and both sides would also likely run out of worthwhile targets that are within range.
41. At the outbreak of the First World War, Wall Street was closed for four months—and the United States was not even a party to the war at that time. While such an extended intervention seems unlikely in the modern era, it is possible that certain markets like US Treasuries could be restricted.
42. Robert Greene, "How Sanctions on Russia Will Alter Global Payments Flows," Carnegie Endowment for International Peace, March 4, 2022, https://carnegieendowment.org/2022/03/04/how-sanctions-on-russia-will-alter-global-payments-flows-pub-86575.
43. Darrell Duffie, "Can China Conquer Crypto?: Beijing's Dangerous Quest to Control Digital Currencies," *Foreign Affairs*, April 22, 2022, https://www.foreignaffairs.com/articles/china/2022-04-22/can-china-conquer-crypto.
44. Zongyuan Zoe Liu and Mihaela Papa, "The Anti-Dollar Axis: Russia and China's Plans to Evade U.S. Economic Power," *Foreign Affairs*, March 7, 2022, https://www.foreignaffairs.com/articles/russian-federation/2022-03-07/anti-dollar-axis.
45. Felix Richter, "These are the top 10 manufacturing countries in the world," World Economic Forum, February 25, 2020, https://www.weforum.org/agenda/2020/02/countries-manufacturing-trade-exports-economics/.
46. Nathaniel Meyersohn, "The trade war comes to Walmart, Target and Macy's," CNN Business, May 23, 2019, https://www.cnn.com/2019/05/23/business/china-tariffs-trump-trade-walmart-retail/index.html.
47. "Fact Sheet: Walmart's Made in America Pledge," Alliance for American Manufacturing, 2020, https://www.americanmanufacturing.org/press-release/fact-sheet-walmarts-made-in-america-pledge/.
48. "UK falls behind on reshoring as reliance on Asian manufacturing imports grows," *The Manufacturer*, February 7, 2022, https://www.themanufacturer.com/articles/uk-falls-behind-on-reshoring-as-reliance-on-asian-manufacturing-imports-grows/.
49. Laura Silver, Kat Devlin, and Christine Huang, "China's Economic Growth Mostly Welcomed in Emerging Markets, but Neighbors Wary of Its Influence," Pew Research Center, December 5, 2019, https://www.

pewresearch.org/global/2019/12/05/chinas-economic-growth-mostly-welcomed-in-emerging-markets-but-neighbors-wary-of-its-influence/.

50. Gompert, Cevallos, and Garafola, *War with China*.
51. Jordan Schneider, "War Between the US and China," Effective Altruism Forum, August 12, 2022,https://forum.effectivealtruism.org/posts/E2BghQq9pwPgtHgiH/war-between-the-us-and-china-a-case-study-for-epistemic.
52. Reuven Glick and Alan M. Taylor, "Collateral Damage: Trade Disruption and the Economic Impact of War," *Review of Economics and Statistics* 92, no. 1 (February 2010): 109–110.
53. Nicholas Mulder, *The Economic Weapon: The Rise of Sanctions as a Tool of Modern War*, 284.
54. Carlos Goes and Eddy Bekkers, "The Impact of Geopolitical Conflicts on Trade, Growth, and Innovation," WTO, June 10, 2022, https://www.wto.org/english/res_e/reser_e/ersd202209_e.htm.
55. Kathrin Hille and Demetri Sevastopulo, "US warns Europe a conflict over Taiwan could cause global economic shock", *Financial Times*, November 10, 2022, https://www.ft.com/content/c0b815f3-fd3e-4807-8de7-6b5f72ea8ae5.

Chapter 7

Getting Fighting Fit

The central conclusion of this book is that the United States and its allies need to get ready for a much more serious challenge from China. The regime's extensive interference, coercion, mercantilist operations, intellectual property theft, and border intrusions have already led some countries to restrict Chinese involvement in their economies and societies.

But it is now clear that Xi Jinping is preparing to go much further. Xi has repeatedly threatened large-scale military operations to seize Taiwan, and he has restated claims to Japan's Senkaku Islands and additional swathes of Indian and Bhutanese territory. Xi's regime is now also asserting national sovereignty over the international waters in the Taiwan Strait and most of the South China Sea. The regime seems determined to keep its promises to the Chinese people to seize control of Taiwan, win undisputed dominance of the Indo-Pacific, and achieve the China Dream of national rejuvenation. Some allied officials and strategic thinkers are quietly discussing whether Beijing would stop if it succeeds in annexing Taiwan or move on quickly to seize other parts of the Indo-Pacific.[1]

So far the responses of the United States and its allies to the Chinese challenge have been cautious, reactive, and mostly incremental. There has been a modest uptick in defense spending in some countries and stronger expressions of support for the security of Taiwan, Japan, and the Philippines. The US Congress has passed the Taiwan Policy Act that authorizes several measures to boost Taiwanese security and help deter a Chinese attack.[2] Higher levels of security cooperation have been developed in the Quad, AUKUS, NATO and with a broader range of security partners. Some limited steps have also been taken to improve supply chain security and accelerate a few military development programs.

But the US and its allies are *not* racing to deter and, if necessary, to fight and win a prolonged multi-domain war against China and its associates. Members of the US Government have referred to China as the "pacing threat," and senior military officers have stressed the need for greater urgency and an acceleration of key programs. However, so far America's intensity of focus on the Indo-Pacific and the rate of strategic development there has been modest.

Is the US Alliance Heading for Defeat?

Given the slow and limited responses of the allies, a strong argument can be made that the United States and its Indo-Pacific partners are drifting towards a catastrophic defeat. No recent American administration has single-mindedly rallied the Congress, industry, and the nation to address the formidable challenge posed by the Chinese Communist Party. Until the late 2010s, most Western officials assumed that the forces of globalization would lead to a more moderate, less confrontational, and less dangerous China.[3] During the first two decades of the century, most politicians and officials were also distracted by the demands of counter-terrorism, Afghanistan and Iraq and, more recently, the defense of Ukraine. The result has been neither a determined multi-domain effort to deter Beijing nor an intense focus on preparing to fight and win a major war in the Western Pacific.

Some limited attempts have been made to inform the US and allied publics about the dangers posed by China, but these have mostly addressed tactical issues such as specific Chinese espionage operations, cyber threats, or military operations. While this reporting has been helpful, America's defense and broader security agencies are still structured for peacetime operations. They are not organizations driven by an urgent need to dramatically strengthen their capabilities to fight a major war.

In the armed forces of the US and its Indo-Pacific allies, there are many individuals and small groups who are deeply concerned about the immediacy of the China threat. A notable case is the US Indo-Pacific Command in Honolulu that has studied the challenges in depth and pressed hard for some modest additional force structure, facility, and other investments to improve the prospects of allied forces deterring an attack and surviving an initial Chinese onslaught.

However, this Pacific Deterrence Initiative and similar proposals have been poorly supported by political leaders.[4] Many congressional representatives have expressed verbal support but in practice have accorded a higher priority to social programs and to the employment and other benefits that might flow to their constituents from different types of government spending. The result is that most American military capabilities deployed to the Indo-Pacific are little changed from those of a decade ago.

The loss of American manufacturing and broader industrial supremacy is another strategic problem. It means that were a major war to break out in the period ahead, the US would be unable to mass produce many of the urgently needed munitions, missiles, and other consumables for at least 18 months. Large-scale production of most complex military systems would take longer—typically 4–8 years. Another consequence is that if a major war with China ran for an extended period, the US could probably not outproduce the China-Russia axis without drawing extensively on a network of allies and security partners across the globe.

The US and allied surrender of industrial dominance is a direct result of the sustained government and broader social discouragement of manufacturing investment. All levels of government and many broader parts of society have played roles: Taxation incentives have been removed, many new regulatory controls have been introduced, environmental and other approvals of major projects have been delayed for extended periods, electricity and other energy costs have increased markedly while simultaneously the reliability of supply has been reduced, and some governments have interfered with corporate procedures and operations. Hollywood and other parts of the Western media have contributed by often portraying corporate behaviors in unfair and unflattering ways. So when given an option to shift operations to more business-friendly environments—mostly in China—many corporations have not hesitated to move.

The result is that the US and most of its allies have effectively exported many of their manufacturing capabilities—from metals, chemicals, electronics, communications systems, and vehicles—to foreign countries, including the very authoritarian states that the allies might need to fight in a major war. The Indo-Pacific region now hosts a dense cluster of complex global value chains for strategically critical products in which China performs core functions. Key consequences of this are to seriously limit the production capacities that would be available to immediately support the allies in a major crisis and, in the event of a prolonged war, dramatically slow the speed and effectiveness of industrial mobilization.

A further challenge for the United States is the deep polarization of the American public, the mass media, and much of the country's social fabric. The relentless divisiveness that is so obvious in the United States raises serious questions about whether America could sustain its unity and resolve to fight a long war suffering heavy military and economic losses when the primary issues at stake on the other side of the world appear of marginal interest to the mass of the public. How long would it be before large "peace" demonstrations caused serious disruption to major American and allied cities and crippled some industrial centers?

Meanwhile, the regime in Beijing is well aware of all of these US and allied weaknesses and is conducting interference, media manipulation, cyber, and other political warfare operations to fan divisions, further weaken allied industry, delay defense funding, and foster societal incoherence, hesitation, and distraction.[5]

This is the environment within which a range of American and allied commentators have entered the fray to urge minimal change and caution against overreaction. Some do not believe that China poses a serious threat and that those arguing for urgent action are nationalist "hawks" simply trying to boost military budgets.[6] Others argue that, as with all of America's wars since Vietnam, the Chinese challenge is a matter for the military and those in uniform should simply get on with the job, without disturbing broader society.[7] Yet others believe that current tensions with Beijing have been caused by poor American and allied diplomacy. Negotiations with the Chinese regime should be broadened and intensified in order to cool the situation and dramatically reduce the prospects of war.[8]

There are still others who adopt a spirit of defeatism and suggest that the US and its allies should not attempt to stand in the way of China's inevitable economic, military, and political dominance.[9] The sooner the allies reach a compromise or accommodation with the Chinese regime on the future of the Indo-Pacific, the better. Some argue that the ceding of Taiwan and other disputed territories to Beijing would be a far better option for Washington than standing in China's way and fighting a long, costly war with an uncertain outcome.[10]

Then there are the bureaucratic realists who accept that the US and its allies should be better prepared to confront Xi Jinping, but refocusing and dramatically accelerating defense and security preparations are practically impossible. Getting government leaders, the huge defense, homeland security, and treasury bureaucracies, their associated congressional and parliamentary leaders, vital industries, and other key interest groups to suddenly spring from their current relaxed operating modes into a fast sprint is seen by some to be insurmountable and unrealistic.[11]

These issues are very serious. When the current level of American and allied preparedness is compared to the strong, determined, whole-of-nation progress being made by Beijing, it would appear that Xi Jinping is right to be confident. America and its allies continue to be heavily distracted by domestic and other international issues, and most are simply not addressing the realities of China's challenge with any urgency. So if a major war erupts in the Indo-Pacific in the period ahead, there is a real possibility that the United States and its allies will still be grossly unprepared, take huge losses, and suffer an ignominious defeat. This would be catastrophic for all democratic states—not just those located in the Indo-Pacific. The end result would be a radically different and more dangerous world: one dominated by authoritarian Marxist-Leninist-Maoist hegemony and the forced surrender of many elements of sovereignty to the Chinese Communist Party. This future would probably also prompt several countries to seek new ways of maintaining their independence, including the acquisition of nuclear and other weapons of mass destruction.

An Urgent Pathway to Fighting Fitness

Despite the problems and pessimism just summarized, this book argues that all is not lost for the United States and its allies. But the intensity of focus, the strategic determination, the energy, and the speed of allied defense and security preparations must rise markedly. If the allies and their security partners are to be readied to deter and, if necessary, to fight and win a major war over the future of the Indo-Pacific, much needs to be done to properly prepare. And it needs to be done quickly. The pathway to fighting fitness must address five key priorities.

Priority #1: Strategic Leadership

To address the challenges now confronting the US and its allies with urgency, committed national leaderships will be essential. Each nation's president or prime minister must appreciate the need, accord it a high priority, and insist on the energetic acceleration of preparations. Coalition nations must have their "A Teams" in charge.

All national leaders joining the coalition should be urged to demonstrate strong resolve to stand with their partners to actively support the foundations of a free and open Indo-Pacific. Beijing and the broader international community must be left in no doubt about the determination of the coalition to resist external challenges. A strong, consistent declaratory position will be an essential foundation for effective deterrence and for the acceleration of a broader range of security planning and preparations.

Another early task for national leaders should be to quietly encourage as many countries as possible to join the US-led coalition and take a stand against the coercion by and expansionism of authoritarian China.

Beyond the two primary camps, many countries would adopt neutral stances, with some leaning informally towards the US-led coalition and others leaning more towards China. The coalition could face the unpleasant possibility that many parts of the nonaligned community would be indifferent, resistant, and even hostile to the coalition campaign to thwart the Chinese regime.

In many allied countries, there will be sensitivities about how much is said publicly about the scale and speed of coalition preparations. Some governments will be concerned not to alarm their publics by highlighting activities that many would view as preparations for war. Some activities would likely be undertaken in secret in order to hide them from hostile powers. Other initiatives might be revealed as part of a campaign to strengthen deterrence and to boost coalition cohesion and morale. Many other initiatives may be portrayed as measures to protect the community from all-hazards threats such as extreme storms, floods, wildfires, and terrorist assaults.

Whatever approach coalition leaders choose to take, citizens must be kept informed about the deteriorating international situation and the general nature of the security challenges confronting their countries. Much of this should be done indirectly via congressional and parliamentary committee investigations and open conferences, media discussions, and debates. Government leaders can address some issues in public speeches and in discussion papers on key topics. The key point here is that by diverse means, allied publics need to be prepared psychologically for the possibility of serious security challenges and citizens given opportunities to contribute to debates and to prepare their households and neighborhoods. Many will wish to consider making personal contributions of skills, time, or other resources to assist. Some will volunteer to permanent or part-time military units. Others will self-organize to reinforce community security agencies, such as fire brigades, rescue teams, civil defense units, ambulance services, and hospital systems.

National leaderships would also have an important role in initiating and coordinating new fields of security cooperation with coalition partners. National leaders need to be personally involved in planning, coordinating, and overseeing the efforts of the international coalition so that preparations proceed at a rapid pace and that any obstacles encountered are swiftly overcome.

Priority #2: Powerful Combat-Ready Military Forces

The armed forces of the United States and its close Indo-Pacific allies are already of high quality; they possess relatively advanced levels of interoperability and are mostly well-trained and equipped. However, in order to meet the challenges of confronting the forces of an assertive China—and possibly Russia—important additional preparations will be required. These include:

- Agreement on campaign objectives.
- The raising of a combined headquarters to coordinate coalition strategy and campaign planning.
- Upgraded equipment and realistic combined training for priority categories of operation.

- Preparations for intense operational surges with very limited or zero warning time.
- Special programs to protect key military and other national assets from possible enemy preemptive strikes in the first hours of a war.
- Planning the rapid expansion of priority combat and civilian support units. These expansion initiatives would likely include the raising of new latent force (or reserve) military units as well as new investments in training systems and facilities.
- Resuscitating mobilization planning and preparations so as to markedly reduce the time required to bring to bear the full weight of national and allied resources in the event of war breaking out.
- An intensification of combined training with coalition partners to optimize joint operational performance and strengthen trust.
- Expansion of maintenance and repair capacities.
- Building appropriate stocks of fuels, munitions, high-usage spares, and other key consumables.

Publicizing a carefully selected range of these initiatives would signal the strength of allied resolve, increase doubts in Beijing about the viability of the regime's expansionist plans, and contribute substantially to allied efforts to deter China's initiation of war.

Priority #3: An Appropriate Geostrategic Posture

There is a need to urgently update US and coalition base and support systems in the Indo-Pacific. This is partly because the inherited basing system is both highly concentrated and poorly protected. Much of it is vulnerable to a preemptive barrage of Chinese missile and air attacks as well as to special force raids and sabotage strikes in the first hours of a war.

There is also a need to better align coalition basing locations and unit deployments to suit the types of operations likely to be conducted in the days leading up to war and in the first weeks of a major kinetic conflict. Coalition forces need base and support systems that are far more dispersed, duplicated, and much better protected than at present.[12]

Every effort should be made to complicate an enemy's targeting and ensure uninterrupted combat operations even when Chinese forces may be launching intense missile, cyber, space, and other strikes across the theater.

Special attention needs to be given to those forward locations likely to be struck by the full force of a Chinese assault in the first weeks of a major war. The prepared defenses in allied and partner territories located in the first and second island chains deserve especially high priority, including those in Taiwan.

Each coalition partner will need to decide how much effort it will devote to direct homeland defense, how much to support other coalition partners, and how much to conduct deep offensive operations. Much would depend on the priorities of the coalition campaign strategy, the levels and types of reinforcement received from geographically distant partners (especially those in North America and Europe), and the phase of war that was being waged at the time.

Another element of geostrategic posture concerns the degree to which local defense units and civil defense formations can manage homeland security and free up main-force military units for other operations. Well-trained local security and civil defense organizations could contribute substantially to the combat power that each country and the broader coalition is able to bring to bear.

A further important dimension of reconfigured geostrategic posture is the preparation of base facilities, exercise areas, and supply systems to host units arriving in the theater from distant coalition partners. In a major Indo-Pacific war, many thousands of coalition personnel and large numbers of complex military systems are likely to be deployed forward during the first weeks. Receiving countries must be prepared to welcome them, house them, feed them, and provide a full range of support facilities and services.

Priority #4: Preparations for Intense Economic Warfare

If the United States is to prevail in a major war it needs to deal with the consequences of losing its long-standing global manufacturing and industrial superiority. The solution is to organize a strong coalition of allied and partner countries to cooperate closely with the US in mobilizing and providing emergency manufacturing capacities in future crises and wars. If done well, this has the potential to overturn China's manufacturing dominance and return to a situation where the US-led coalition can bring to bear its combined manufacturing capacities, which in aggregate would be about double the size of China's ($7.3 trillion verses $3.9 trillion).[13]

Another essential step would be to establish coalition production priorities for at least the first two to three years of a major war. Exactly what would be needed by coalition military forces, civilian communities engaged in the war, and coalition forces that are forward deployed into other countries? Early decisions on these issues would be essential to guide coalition preparations for emergency production.

Coalition industrial planning for emergencies is likely to focus on three primary mechanisms to supply the required goods and services in a timely fashion:

- *Stockholding:* These are stocks of priority goods that are held precrisis by coalition partners. These holdings should be of a type and scale to supply all essential goods and services to support military operations and domestic livelihoods until the outputs of mobilized manufacturers can reach target levels. This would require stocks sufficiently large to support the intensive operations anticipated in phases 2A and 2B of a major war—probably for a minimum of three months.[14] Few, if any, coalition partners currently hold stocks of essential goods of this type and scale.
- *Domestic Manufacture, Service, and Repair Capabilities:* Coalition partners already possess industries able to produce, service, and repair most products and systems that would be needed by the US-led coalition in a war. However, many industries would need

to quickly change their product mixes and most would also need to markedly expand their production scale. This industry reconfiguration would not be simple or quick, although proper advanced planning and preparations could dramatically reduce production lead-times.

- *Reformed Supply Chains:* There is a need for the supply chains of all priority goods to be reviewed and, where appropriate, reformed. Supply chain design needs to shift from "just in time" to "just when trust." Enterprises that produce priority goods relying on component or other contributions from potentially hostile countries must remove those dependencies quickly. This may entail the replacement of some suppliers with partners located in coalition or other fully trusted countries. In many cases it would require production reshoring, near shoring, ally shoring, or friend shoring. Tentative steps are already being taken in some economic sectors, but national governments need to accelerate the pace by various means, including offering some key industries tailored incentives and transition assistance.

In the type of wartime crisis envisaged, the production of many nonessential items is likely to be reduced or halted, at least temporarily.

Because the circumstances of each coalition country will differ, the specific mechanisms used by national governments to facilitate emergency mobilization will differ. There are, however, some key features that would be adopted in most jurisdictions:

- A primary driver would be early planning and preparations to dramatically reduce emergency production lead-times for essential goods.
- An appreciation that governments cannot simply order or direct mobilization in their countries. Mobilization planning needs to be undertaken *in partnership with* their societies. While many mobilization activities would need to be launched by governments, most of the detailed industrial planning and preparations must be led and managed by corporate leaders. They are the people who

have intimate knowledge of their industries and command most of the production capacities.

- In most countries, detailed planning and preparations would be greatly facilitated by establishing industry-sector working groups. These would ideally comprise relevant corporate leaders, mostly serving in a part-time capacity. Such working groups would span all of the priority supply needs of serious emergencies, including energy and fuels, communications, munitions, electronics and optics, food, medical and pharmaceutical supplies, aviation, land transport, maritime transport, and so forth.
- Once optimal means and modes for the production of an essential product are determined, trial production should be funded to prove emergency production capabilities. Key production facilities and material supplies would need to be maintained, and relevant production staff accorded special reserve status to ensure their immediate availability in crises.

Some priority items would be manufactured using local facilities, and others would be supplied via trusted supply chains. Managing these complexities would be one of the drivers for establishing a coalition-wide mobilization council. Consultation and coordination would be needed on many issues such as the sorting of complementary and competing product needs, arrangements for the licensed use of intellectual property, the setting of production standards, and so forth. Precrisis decisions on these types of operational issues would be essential if the coalition is to possess the capability to mobilize rapidly and effectively.

The flip side of this largely defensive mobilization would be planning and preparations for offensive economic warfare.[15] This would entail the development of strategies and capabilities to constrain, undermine and, where possible, cripple an enemy's strategic industrial capabilities. These activities would properly be the preserve of national governments, preferably coordinated through a relevant coalition forum.

The organizational challenge facing the coalition is all the more stark when considering the nature of the adversary. The coalition would be a voluntary assembly of democratic states reliant on a complex network of mostly private industrial partners coordinating "horizontally." There are advantages to such an arrangement, such as flexibility, resilience, and innovativeness. But if not well planned, it has the potential to be a managerial nightmare. China, conversely, is a relatively monolithic, "vertically" integrated behemoth that can transition to a centralized command economy quickly. The authoritarian advantages are scale, secrecy, and speed. China has at times stunned the world with its sudden military-technological advances. Even in peacetime, it appears capable of completing development programs in timeframes that leave Western counterparts in the dust.[16]

The quality and pace of preparations for coalition-wide industrial mobilization would be a central determinant of who wins a major war in the Indo-Pacific. Absent such planning and preparations, the US-led coalition would be seriously handicapped and its defense and other capabilities would be starved of resources at a surprisingly early stage. In that event, Washington and allied capitals could face an invidious choice: either cede substantial territory and sovereignty in an unfavorable "peace" agreement or consider the early use of weapons of mass destruction to fend off the ascendant enemy. This book argues that quality mobilization-planning is not only an effective, inexpensive way of boosting national and collective deterrence but also an essential component of any serious defense preparations. It is sadly lacking in most coalition countries at present.[17]

Priority #5: Winning the Political Warfare Struggle

The resilience and unity of domestic populations are vital issues for both the US-led coalition and for China. This is part of the struggle that the US and its allies cannot afford to lose. Failure in the political warfare domain could quickly lead to the coalition's political collapse and defeat.

There are four primary factors in this struggle. First is the fragility of national unity in the United States as a result of the country's deep political and social polarization. Second is the ongoing Chinese and Russian campaign to exacerbate these internal divisions and foster incoherence, hesitancy, and eventual dis-integration. The third factor is the difficulty for coalition members of attempting to respond in kind by attempting to weaken domestic cohesion in China. This is largely because of the extensive defenses that Xi Jinping and his colleagues have built to shield the Chinese public from outside influences. And fourth is the contest for the support of the rest of the world. There are no simple or speedy solutions to these challenges, but each deserves serious attention.

The challenge of restoring American national unity is beyond the scope of this book. Suffice to say there is cause for both concern and hope. Chapter 3 highlighted the extent of American political and social polarization. A key consequence is that even initiatives that are patently in the national interest and agreed in principle by both major parties rarely have a smooth or speedy passage. Yet American history has often been characterized by a degree of domestic turmoil, and much of the country's dynamism springs from its competitive plurality. On one hand, wars fought by the US against major powers who possess the potential to be real threats have tended to galvanize the nation, but, on the other hand, lesser wars involving smaller countries and non-state actors fought in distant theaters have tended to generate bitter divisions, especially if the conflict is prolonged. At present, there appears to be widespread public appreciation of and bipartisan political agreement about the strategic importance of the Indo-Pacific and the challenges confronting American and allied interests there. Russia's invasion of Ukraine and NATO's strong response have further sharpened American concerns about the deteriorating international environment.

To effectively counter and defeat Chinese and Russian influence, deception, coercion, and manipulation in the US and other partner countries, there is a need, first, to expose these operations to the intense "sunlight" of public scrutiny.[18] An important lesson from the early phases of the Ukraine crisis was the positive impact of releasing classified details of Russian campaign planning at an early stage. This was pivotal to delegitimizing Putin's cause. Using a similar approach, the Federal Bureau of Investigation (FBI), National Security Agency (NSA), and other relevant US and partner agencies could release details of Chinese and Russian political warfare operations against US and coalition societies. A constant flow of these stories when combined with the arrest, trial and/or imprisonment, and deportation of foreign agents and "fellow travelers" could be expected not only to blunt the Chinese and Russian operations but encourage diverse elements of the US community to pull together against the common foe. An extension of this effort would be to conduct special briefing conferences and other events for coalition journalists and business and community leaders to strengthen their knowledge base and build a better informed foundation for public debates on security issues.

Chinese and Russian interference with American and allied electronic communications, including social media platforms, could also be subjected to much stronger coalition counters. Many types of operation could be shut down or seriously disrupted. In combination, these types of measures should markedly reduce the intensity of Chinese and Russian political warfare operations and weaken their potential to exacerbate domestic divisions in the US and elsewhere in the coalition.

Finally, there would be benefit in making efforts to break through, or outmaneuver, the great firewall of China and other regime defensive systems so that the US and its partners can communicate directly with the Chinese people, explain many of the economic, social, and political realities they face, expose leadership corruption, and undermine the CCP's legitimacy. None of this would be easy, but it certainly deserves serious consideration.

Can the US Alliance Prevail in a Major Indo-Pacific War?

It is time to address squarely the key question of this book. Can the US and its allies deter and, if necessary, fight and win a major war against China in the Indo-Pacific? This book concludes that if such a war breaks out before 2030, the American coalition would struggle to prevail and could suffer a devastating defeat. The type of war China plans would range over many more domains than just the military, and it would likely continue for a much longer period than is normally assumed. China's multi-domain campaign would need to be met and outflanked by similarly intensive multi-domain defensive and offensive capabilities. However, there are few signs that the US and its allies are making substantial progress in preparing for this kind of fight. Nor are they well advanced in establishing the type of coalition-wide planning, preparation, and coordination mechanisms that would be essential to sustain and ultimately win such a war.

America and its allies and partners are simply not match ready. Some members have acquired the right "uniforms" and pieces of equipment, but they have yet to sign up a full team. They have not seriously discussed their playbook, and they have not yet gotten around to building a reserve bench or buying additional equipment. Worst of all, they mostly continue to undertake day-to-day activities at a relaxed pace as though there is little prospect of having to "play the game." Their fitness to take to the field is patchy and they rarely stress themselves in training for the wide range of activities—especially the nonmilitary tasks—they would need to perform as soon as a "game" begins. Even if, despite the odds, they manage to gain the upper hand in the first couple of clashes, their prospects of winning the match quickly, decisively, and with minimal casualties appear low.

The solution is obvious. The US and its allies need to marshal a full team and get fighting fit; they need to coordinate their preparations and their logistic networks, and they need to exercise the coalition team in strenuous multi-domain practice sessions. They need to prepare for a contest of endurance that will test their entire societies. At a minimum, the US and its coalition partners need to progress the five priority areas discussed earlier.

If allied and partner governments decide to move quickly to do these things, they are capable of making substantial progress in 3–4 years. That is what is required if they wish to deter a major war and be certain of avoiding a disastrous defeat.

So *can* the United States and its partners prevail in a major Indo-Pacific war? Yes, but only if they launch a substantial program of preparations urgently. *Will* they do this? Will the US and its security partners dramatically lift their game and drive to effectively deter and be ready to fight and win a major war? As I write this in late 2022, there are few grounds for optimism.

Unfortunately, the United States and its allies have a long record of ignoring or underrating serious threats until the missiles start to fly and bombs start to fall. The lessons from the disasters at the Maginot Line, Pearl Harbor, and Singapore may be overlooked by current generations, but they remain very relevant today. If the US-led coalition continues on its present course and China launches a major war in the period ahead, the coalition would likely be shocked by heavy losses, lose major battles, and be forced to surrender substantial territory, possibly whole countries. The coalition would probably struggle to gain the upper hand for many months and maybe for several years.

The dangers of allied ignorance of the threat and shallow thinking about the risks now confronting the US and its allies are well understood by some British leaders.

When reflecting on the lessons from the first months of the Ukraine crisis for allied challenges in the Indo-Pacific, the former British foreign secretary, Liz Truss, observed:

> There's always a tendency—and we've seen this prior to the Ukraine war—there's always a tendency of wishful thinking, to hope that more bad things won't happen and to wait until it's too late...We should have done things earlier, we should have been

> supplying the defensive weapons into Ukraine earlier. We need to learn that lesson for Taiwan.[19]

The British prime minister, Rishi Sunak, built on these themes in November 2022 when he stated:

> Our adversaries and competitors plan for the long term...China is conspicuously competing for global influence using all the levers of state power. In the face of these challenges, short-termism or wishful thinking will not suffice.[20]

While American and allied leaders need to take those lessons to heart, there are few signs that many are doing so. They continue to tolerate inadequate strategy, poor cross-agency coordination, and frequent bureaucratic fumbling and delays. Unless the current trajectory is markedly changed, the US alliance will likely fail. It will be a case of doing too little too late. So it all depends on whether and when American and partner leaders are prepared to make fighting fitness a first-order priority.

The regime in Beijing knows this well. In the meantime it is watching closely, pushing ahead with its own preparations, and weighing its options.

NOTES

1. These matters have been raised in private by some senior officials and strategic analysts.
2. For details, see Demetri Sevastopulo, "US's Taiwan Security Bill Spurs Debate on Level of Support for Taipei," *Financial Times*, September 13, 2022, https://www.ft.com/content/a48ee082-a617-472f-bff2-83f8c6fb2dd9.
3. See a quality discussion of this in Aaron L. Friedberg, *Getting China Wrong* (Cambridge: Polity Press, 2022).
4. For details, see Dustin Walker, "Show me the Money: Boost the Pacific Deterrence Initiative," *War on the Rocks*, June 29, 2022, https://warontherocks.com/2022/06/show-me-the-money-boost-the-pacific-deterrence-initiative/.
5. For an insight into one category of Chinese operation, see Filip Jirouš , "Make the Green Serve China."
6. Michael D. Swaine, "China Doesn't Pose an Existential Threat for America: Concerns over China's rise are overblown," *Foreign Policy*, April 21, 2021, https://foreignpolicy.com/2021/04/21/china-existential-threat-america/.
7. Stephen Losey, "Americans' Trust and Confidence in the Military Is Decreasing, New Survey Finds," *Military.com*, March 10, 2021, https://www.military.com/daily-news/2021/03/10/americans-trust-and-confidence-military-decreasing-new-survey-finds.html.
8. Doug Bandow, "China and U.S. Should Keep Competition Peaceful," *China - US Focus*, April 17, 2021, https://www.chinausfocus.com/foreign-policy/china-and-us-should-keep-competition-peaceful.
9. Daniel Gros, "The US Must Accept China's Rise," *The ASEAN Post*, November 9, 2020, https://theaseanpost.com/article/us-must-accept-chinas-rise.
10. Hugh White, "Sleepwalk to War: Australia's Unthinking Alliance with America," *Quarterly Essay*, issue 86 (June 2022): 82–84.
11. Joel Gehrke, "National security adviser Jake Sullivan stunned by slow pace of federal bureaucracy," *Washington Examiner*, November 11, 2021, https://www.washingtonexaminer.com/policy/defense-national-security/national-security-adviser-jake-sullivan-stunned-by-slow-pace-of-federal-bureaucracy. See also US Department of Defense, *Summary of the Defense Strategy of the United States of America*, 10.

12. The US-Australia agreement reached in December 2022 to substantially expand the routine US army, navy, marine corps, and air force presence at facilities across the vastness of the Australian continent will make a substantial contribution to the achievement of this goal. For details, see Joint Statement on Australia-U.S. Ministerial Consultations (AUSMIN), December 6, 2022, https://www.state.gov/joint-statement-on-australia-u-s-ministerial-consultations-ausmin-2022/; and Ben Packham and Adam Creighton, "AUSMIN: Ties with US Army, Navy to Ramp Up," *The Australian*, December 8, 2022, https://www.theaustralian.com.au/nation/well-stand-by-you-antony-blinken-vows-to-plug-defence-capability-gap/news-story/7e5e0445e4ae53c2e83f16c50423269c.
13. UN Department of Economic and Social Affairs Statistics Division: National Accounts—Analysis of Main Aggregates 2020, https://unstats.un.org/unsd/snaama/.
14. See the discussion of the anticipated phases of a major war in the Indo-Pacific in chapter 4.
15. For a detailed examination of the planning and conduct of a major offensive economic warfare campaign, see Nicholas A. Lambert, *Planning Armageddon: British Economic Warfare and the First World War* (Cambridge, MA: Harvard University Press, 2012).
16. See examples in Newdick, "China Acquiring New Weapons Five Times Faster Than U.S. Warns Top Official."
17. Thomas A. Callaghan, Jr., "The Structural Disarmament of the West: Our Most Critical Defense Industrial Challenge," in *Industrial Capacity and Defense Planning*, eds. Lee D. Olvey, Henry A. Leonard, and Bruce E. Arlinghaus (Lexington: Lexington Books, 1983), 3–22. See also Cancian, *Industrial Mobilization*.
18. For an extended discussion of counter–political warfare options for the US and its allies, see Kerry K. Gershaneck, "Political Warfare: The People's Republic of China's Strategy 'to Win without Fighting,'" *Journal of Advanced Military Studies* 11, no. 1. (Spring 2020): 83–89, https://www.usmcu.edu/Portals/218/JAMS_11_1_Political%20Warfare_Kerry%20Gershaneck.pdf.
19. See Liz Truss quoted in Peter Walker, "UK Calls for Extra Vigilance on China Ahead of NATO Summit," *The Guardian*, June 29, 2022, https://www.theguardian.com/world/2022/jun/28/uk-calls-extra-vigilance-china-ahead-nato-summit.

20. Prime Minister's Office, "PM Speech to the Lord Mayor's Banquet," November 28, 2022, https://www.gov.uk/government/speeches/pm-speech-to-the-lord-mayors-banquet-28-november-2022.

Index

About the Author

Ross Babbage is a Non-resident Senior Fellow at the Center for Strategic and Budgetary Assessments in Washington, DC. He is also Chief Executive Officer of Strategic Forum and Managing Director of Strategy International (ACT) Pty Ltd. Dr. Babbage served as an Australian Government official for 16 years and has also held senior positions in business and at the Australian National University. His previous publications include *A Coast Too long, Which Way the Dragon? Sharpening Allied Perceptions of China's Strategic Trajectory* and *Winning Without Fighting: Chinese and Russian Political Warfare Campaigns and How the West Can Prevail.*

Praise for *The Next Major War*

"A timely, sobering, and essential read for anyone who wants to understand in detail how a major war in the Indo-Pacific would unfold, the strengths and weaknesses of the United States and China along with their partners, the likely economic and business impacts, and the measures that need to be taken now for the United States and its allies to deter China—and if necessary, to prevail. As concern grows that China will invade Taiwan before mid-century, the issues examined in this book are crucial for policymakers, militaries, academics, and business leaders to consider."

—**Bonnie Glaser**,
Director, Asia Program,
German Marshall Fund of the US

* * * * *

"In this prize jewel of a book, Babbage provides an eagle-eyed look ahead at the worst political, economic, and military crises in the near future—and, very importantly, a critical blueprint for averting these. Politicians, business leaders, journalists, and everyday citizens should read Babbage's urgent roadmap for deterring—or, as may be necessary, winning—the war Beijing is cooking up."

—**Matt Pottinger**,
former US Deputy National Security Adviser

* * * * *

"US officials now warn of a growing risk of war with China. But how might such a conflict begin? How long would it last? And what factors would be most important in determining its outcome? *The Next Major War* is an outstanding book that offers the deepest and most wide-ranging analysis to date of these questions, going far beyond the usual comparisons of weapons systems and operational concepts to explore the economic, political, and societal dimensions of a possible future clash between the Pacific superpowers."

—**Aaron L. Friedberg**,
Professor of Politics and International Affairs,
Princeton University

* * * * *

"In *The Next Major War*, Ross Babbage, one of Australia's foremost strategic thinkers, provides a timely, insightful, and much-needed net assessment of the threat posed by China to the Indo-Pacific liberal international order—and how to meet it. The insights derived from Babbage's study of the Indo-Pacific geopolitical chessboard and military balance exemplifies Clausewitz's coup d'oeil—the ability to see the interrelationships among all the major factors shaping the intensifying rivalry between China, and the United States and its allies. *The Next Major War* is a serious, important, and timely gem that is mandatory reading for all senior officials charged with deterring Chinese aggression and, should deterrence fail, defeating it."

—**Andrew Krepinevich, Jr.**,
President and CEO, Solarium LLC;
and Founder, former President, and CEO,
Center for Strategic and Budgetary Assessments

* * * * *

"Ross Babbage has produced a timely and clear-eyed study of the multitude of challenges posed by a resurgent China across the Indo-Pacific. His examination of alliance weaknesses—and the opportunities available to the US, Japan, Australia, and others in this dynamic environment—is highly relevant to government, military, national security, and scholarly communities across the globe."

—**Mick Ryan**,
Major General, Australian Army (ret.)

* * * * *

"*The Next Major War* is a sobering forewarning to the United States and its allies to take seriously the prospect of a major war with China. More than that, it is an urgent call to action to prepare for such an increasingly likely contingency. Babbage's book will be of intense interest to soldiers and statesmen alike."

—**Thomas G. Mahnken**,
President and CEO,
Center for Strategic and Budgetary Assessments; and
Senior Research Professor, Johns Hopkins SAIS

* * * * *

"*The Next Major War* is an absolute wake-up call for the national security/foreign policy/political 'ruling classes.' There's a lot more to taking on China than building a 500-ship US Navy and getting the military part right. Changed mindsets in all parts of society are required—this includes leadership in the business world. This book lays out the dangers and what's required to counter them. It offers perspectives that aren't readily found in existing literature on the China threat issue. The book synthesizes a wide range of existing information on the topic in a way not done before, including the author's original earlier research on Chinese and Russian political warfare, which is impressive on its own. This presents a new approach to analyzing and understanding the China threat, which is heavily covered by analysts and pundits, so producing a new or novel approach that stands out is no small feat. A strength of the book is its clarity; some of the topics—financial and economic, for example—can be hard to understand, yet these parts are clearly presented, which is also not easy to accomplish. The various conflict scenarios are easily laid out and flow well—another task that is not easy. As such, this book is a helpful tool for recognizing and understanding the range of issues and influences involved in national security matters—as well as the need for a broad perspective when assessing such topics."

—**Grant Newsham**,
Colonel, US Marines (ret.) and
former executive director, Morgan Stanley Japan

Cambria Rapid Communications in Conflict and Security (RCCS) Series

General Editor: Geoffrey R. H. Burn

The aim of the RCCS series is to provide policy makers, practitioners, analysts, and academics with in-depth analysis of fast-moving topics that require urgent yet informed debate. Since its launch in October 2015, the RCCS series has the following book publications:

- *A New Strategy for Complex Warfare: Combined Effects in East Asia* by Thomas A. Drohan
- *US National Security: New Threats, Old Realities* by Paul R. Viotti
- *Security Forces in African States: Cases and Assessment* edited by Paul Shemella and Nicholas Tomb
- *Trust and Distrust in Sino-American Relations: Challenge and Opportunity* by Steve Chan
- *The Gathering Pacific Storm: Emerging US-China Strategic Competition in Defense Technological and Industrial Development* edited by Tai Ming Cheung and Thomas G. Mahnken
- *Military Strategy for the 21st Century: People, Connectivity, and Competition* by Charles Cleveland, Benjamin Jensen, Susan Bryant, and Arnel David
- *Ensuring National Government Stability After US Counterinsurgency Operations: The Critical Measure of Success* by Dallas E. Shaw Jr.
- *Reassessing U.S. Nuclear Strategy* by David W. Kearn, Jr.
- *Deglobalization and International Security* by T. X. Hammes
- *American Foreign Policy and National Security* by Paul R. Viotti

- *Make America First Again: Grand Strategy Analysis and the Trump Administration* by Jacob Shively
- *Learning from Russia's Recent Wars: Why, Where, and When Russia Might Strike Next* by Neal G. Jesse
- *Restoring Thucydides: Testing Familiar Lessons and Deriving New Ones* by Andrew R. Novo and Jay M. Parker
- *Net Assessment and Military Strategy: Retrospective and Prospective Essays* edited by Thomas G. Mahnken, with an introduction by Andrew W. Marshall
- *Deterrence by Denial: Theory and Practice* edited by Alex S. Wilner and Andreas Wenger
- *Negotiating the New START Treaty* by Rose Gottemoeller
- *Party, Politics, and the Post-9/11 Army* by Heidi A. Urben
- *Resourcing the National Security Enterprise: Connecting the Ends and Means of US National Security* edited by Susan Bryant and Mark Troutman
- *Subcontinent Adrift: Strategic Futures of South Asia* by Feroz Hassan Khan
- *The Next Major War: Can the US and its Allies Win Against China?* by Ross Babbage
- *Warrior Diplomats: Civil Affairs Forces on the Front Lines* edited by Arnel David, Sean Acosta, and Nicholas Krohley
- *Russia and the Changing Character of Conflict* by Tracey German